AF553823

IRRIGATION DEVELOPMENT

ISSUES AND CHALLENGES

IRRIGATION DEVELOPMENT
ISSUES AND CHALLENGES

By

Dr. P. Narasimha Rao

Professor
Dept. of Economics
Acharya Nagarjuna University
Andhra Pradesh
(India)

DISCOVERY PUBLISHING HOUSE
NEW DELHI-110002

First Published – 2007

Reprinted – 2026

ISBN: 978-81-8356-207-2

Irrigation Development
Issues and Challenges

Published by:
DISCOVERY PUBLISHING HOUSE
4383/4B, Ansari Road, Darya Ganj
New Delhi-110 002 (India)
Phone: +91-11-23279245; 23253475; 43596065
Mobile: +91 9811179893 / +91 9871656464
E-mail: discoverybooksindia@gmail.com
orderdphbooks@gmail.com
namitwasan9@gmail.com
web: www.discoverypublishinggroup.com

Printed at:
Infinity Imaging Systems
Delhi

Preface

Development of irrigation infrastructure has been chosen as the main strategy in recent period to address the present agrarian crisis both at central and state level. In the state of Andhra Pradesh too there is a policy shift in favour of creating large scale canal irrigation. It would be a critical factor influencing the agriculture scenario as it actually unfolds in the decade to come. There is a considerable anxiety about the likely changes in agricultural scenario in the state. The thrust of the irrigation policy is to create irrigation facilities to an additional 65 lakh hectares at a cost of Rs. 1 lakh crore or more. This is expected to solve the agrarian distress that prevailed in Andhra Pradesh.

However, experience has thrown up a number of problems, irrigation progress and policies has attracted criticism on several grounds. Delays in completion of projects, under-utilization of their potential low quality of irrigation, adverse ecological and social consequences are principal issues. Without addressing the above issues, giving priority to new projects is to be examined.

The strategy for irrigation development should be based on the ultimate irrigation potential of the State. Varying estimates of the ultimate irrigation potential has been provided by different organizations. The present irrigation programme needs critical assessment considering the water resources available, present levels of utilization, problems faced by the sector for the past two decades. In the light of this, several questions concerning to the scale and priority of water resources development need to be answered. Further, there is a need to answer questions like priorities giving to different sources of irrigation and taking up the new projects against the optimum use of existing facilities.

While the cost of creating additional potential is increasing, a major problem in this sector has been the under-utilized irrigation potential created. The gap between potential created and utilized is a matter of serious concern in view of the magnitude of funds spent on this sector. The implications of present policy on these important issues have to be examined. The relative cost of activities, the objective of increasing agricultural production, by solving the drainage problem has to be examined and needs policy attention.

Another criticism is that irrigation policies attracted more importance to major and medium projects and neglected minor irrigation sources. The linkage between tank water and groundwater has not been recognized properly. The tanks are the only source which ensures ecological balance and better groundwater-table. This has not been given enough attention that needed. The present groundwater exploitation in state indicates an alarming situation. Falling water-tables and depletion of ecological accessible groundwater resources will have far reaching economic and social consequence. The effects of these consequences are to be analyzed. Watershed development is advocated as much cheaper and more effective method of water resource development. The merits of watershed development are established. While 56 per cent of the net irrigated area depends upon groundwater source, conservation of groundwater resources and their proper utilization through watershed development programme assumes significance. The seminar should focus its discussion on these issues.

Many problems of irrigation sector are contributed to the lack of institutional structure and local initiatives. Efficient use of water is possible by strengthening of WUAs. The irrigation reforms on participatory irrigation management need policy evaluation. When the main objective of the government is to increase agricultural production, the relative cost be alternative means of achieving this objective is to be taken into consideration in determining the resources devoted to provide irrigation facilities. The irrigation facilities are to be developed within the limit set by economic feasibility.

There is a criticism that short sited competitive policies currently shaping investment decision. The policy measures for new projects are very strong and the propensity to commit the government to new projects without necessary technical preparation and unmindful economic viability of investments is being widely debated. Another criticism is that starting more projects than that can be accommodated within the available resources. Implications of these tendencies have to be assessed. This book made an attempt to identify the gaps in approaches to irrigation development and would help the government in strengthening the policy making process, so that policies gain relevance.

Editor

Contents

Contributors

T. Hanumantha Rao, United Nations (OPS) Consultant on Land and Water, Former Engineer-in-Chief, Irrigation, Government of Andhra Pradesh (Tel : +91 – 40 – 23402048)

Ch. Veeraiah, Former Irrigation Consultant, Govt. of Andhra Pradesh

Kolli. Nageshwara Rao, General Secretary, Integrated Irrigation Development Committee of A.P. Vice President, All India Kisan Sabha

Dr. N.B. Reedy, Associate Professor, Dept. of Applied Economics, Andhra University

Dr. D. Pulla Rao, Associate Professor in Dept. of Applied Economics, Andhra University

Dr. P.N. Rao, Professor, Department of Economics and Applied Economics, Acharya Nagarjuna University.

MG Chandrakanth, University of Agricultural Sciences, GKVK, Bangalore-560065

M. Shamaladevi, University of Agricultural Sciences, GKVK, Bangalore-560065

P. Srinivas, Research Scholar, Department of Economics and Applied Economics, Acharya Nagarjuna University.

Dr. R. Venkata Rao, Faculty Member, Department of Economics and Applied Economics, Acharya Nagarjuna University.

Dr. K. Dasaratharamaiah, Head and Associate Professor, Department of Economics and Applied Economics, S.K. University, Anantapur, A.P.

D. Sreenivasa Rao, Research Scholar, Department of Economics and Applied Economic, S.K. University, Anantapur, A.P.

Dr. A. Ranga Reddy, Professor, Department of Economics, Sri Venkateswara University, Tirupati-517 502

Dr. B. Nagaraja, Assistant Professor of Economics, Sri Venkateswara University P.G. Centre, Kavali.

C. Sailaja, Reader in Economics, D.K.W. College, Nellore.

Dr. K. Adiseshu, Agro-Economic Research Centre, Andhra University, Waltair–530 003.

K. Madhu Babu, Agro-Economic Research Centre, Andhra University, Waltair–530 003.

M. Sankara Reddi, Secretary, CHETANA, Srikakulam.

Prof. M. Sundara Rao, Special Officer, Department of Rural Development, AUPG Centre, Etcherla, Srikakulam

K. Kishore Babu, Research Scholar, Department of Economics, Acharya Nagarjuna University, Guntur.

A. Balakrishna, Research Scholar, Department of Economics, Acharya Nagarjuna University, Guntur.

G. Sreedhar, Professor, Department of Economics, Sri Kirshna Devaraya University, Anantapur.

B. Chinna Rao, Agro-Economic Research Centre, Andhra University, Waltair–530 003.

1

Integrated Water Resources Development in Andhra Pradesh and Problems faced in "Jalayagnam"

T. HANUMANTHA RAO

Introduction

Construction of irrigation projects is taken up on a massive scale in Andhra Pradesh. In the history of irrigation development, there is no such precedent in the State and this activity, is going to boost the irrigation sector, in a significant manner benefiting irrigated agriculture throughout the State. Twenty-six major and medium irrigation projects costing Rs. 46,000 crores (Revised to Rs. 67, 823 crores) are taken up for execution. Out of this, eight projects are programmed to be completed within two years and the balance 18 projects within five years. The increase in cost, though happened within one year of taking up execution of works, is mainly due to increase in scope of the projects as well as the realistic costs of land acquisition, relief and rehabilitation. In addition to these 26 projects, it is proposed to construct several other major irrigation projects like Polavaram, Pranahitha-Chevala and it is estimated that about Rs. 1.00 lakh crore would be needed to complete all these projects. When such a massive programme of execution of works is taken up, it is bound to cause several problems mostly in the shape of displacing habitats and effecting people living in the submersion areas. In this context, an in depth analysis of all aspects relating to water resources development as well as the possible problems that would arise in the process of execution of works, would be needed. This is with a view to see that serious problems may not arise during the course of execution of works and also work out a methodology to solve various issues technically, as well as sociologically to the satisfaction of the people affected.

The purpose of this paper is to analyse the problems faced in the water sector and suggest possible solutions for consideration. Though it may not be possible to find ready answers for various issues, yet a study and analysis would lead to working suitable solutions.

Allocation of Water within the Three Regions of Andhra Pradesh

Nine major irrigation projects on Krishna river are taken up for utilizing the surplus flows available in the river, according to the conditions stipulated in the Bachavath award. In addition to this, 3 more projects on Krishna river, based on assured water at 75% dependability, have also been taken up for execution. The requirements of water in these 12 projects will have to stand as designed since financial commitments are already made. There is no scope for taking up any more schemes based on surplus water on Krishna river. With regard to Godavari river, the allocated water of 1480 TMC is not fully utilized. It is estimated that only 680 TMC of this, is under-utilization now, and the balance 800 TMC will have to be fully utilized. In addition to this, there will be surplus flows in most of the years due to non-utilization of the allocated waters to the upper riparian states. Considering this as 300 TMC, it is possible to plan utilization of 1100 TMC, in addition to the water presently being utilized in Godavari. Projects like Polavaram Pranahitha-Chevella, Yellampally, Devadula, Dummagudem, Tadipudi, Pushkaram, Alisagar, Gutpa, Sriram Sagar 2nd stage, SRSP flood flow canal, Itchampalli and several other medium projects are proposed for utilization of Godavari water. Some of these are yet to be started, where as many of them have been grounded. With regard to allocation of water, these projects can be considered for all purposes as committed and further use of balance quantity can be planned. While planning in such a manner certain guidelines may have to be followed in order to have equitable distribution of water to the needy areas of the State and also to set right the regional imbalances. For example, 1100 TMC quantity of water can be utilized for irrigating upland areas in Telangana, as well as diversion of water to Krishna river to take care of drought prone areas of Rayalaseema. The apportionment of water and the manner in which this has to be done cannot be spelt in detail at this stage in a paper like this. It is suggested that a Committee of Technical persons of all the 3 regions may be constituted to go into the details of the same and work out the best alternatives to satisfy the above guiding principle. This can be later reviewed by a committee of party leaders of the 3 regions and draft proposals finalized. As this is a rigorous exercise, it may be take 3-6 months time to complete such a task. State Government can then take a view on these proposals of allocation of water and start formulating proposals for implementation after due completion of the projects now taken up for execution. The guiding principle is that when a project on Godavari is taken up for execution, it should be taken up with a firm commitment on water usage and finances.

Number of Flood Days in Krishna River and Utilization of Surplus Flows

Nine projects on Krishna river are contemporized to utilize surplus flows in the river. According to the Bachawath award, such flows going to the sea can be utilized by the Andhra Pradesh state. It is, therefore, needed to work out the number of days when such flows would occur. When once the upper riparian states start utilizing the allocated shares of water, there will be reduction of flow in the river at the state border and Andhra Pradesh has to accept this situation. Also when Andhra Pradesh fully utilizes, its allocated share of its 811 TMC of water, there will also be a certain reduction in flow of the river on the downstream side. As such, a simulation exercise of long-term hydrological data considering these factors will have to be made and the number of days in which the water would go to the sea and the quantity of the same will have to be estimated. Such simulation exercise was roughly done by me about 15 years back, and it worked out to 25 days. When Telugu Ganga project was contemplated in 1983, it was then estimated that the number of such days would be 60 and then to be on the safe side it was reduced to 45 days while working out the project details. In the case of designing the

Pothireddypadu Head Regulator, it is taken as 30 days. This appears to be fairly correct, but however there is a need to do a long-term simulation exercise, considering the later period flows in the river from 1976–2006. Viewed from this context, the provision of 44,000 cusecs discharge for Pothireddypadu Head Regulator and the main canal up to Banakacherla cross regulator appears to be in order. Though this may appear to be a sudden increase from the earlier 15000 cusecs, yet the same is inevitable for technical reasons. When it is contemplated to utilize 112 TMC for the requirements of Telugu Ganga project, Madras Water Supply, Galeru Nagari, SRBC, PABR and when it is required to draw these quantities of water in a period of 30 days, such a discharge becomes a technical necessity. When once these 5 projects are sanctioned and works are under execution, the quantity of supply for the requirements of these projects through the Head Regulator and the Main Canal is only a Technical issue. However, objections are being raised for this increased regulator capacity and no objections were raised for the 5 projects which have already been started and presently under execution. If at all, an objection is to be raised, it should have been for the utilization proposed under the 5 projects but not for the Head Regulator capacity. However, the main reason of apprehension of Head Regulator capacity is that, at a later date, assured flows also may be drawn through this regulator, effecting the interests of the Nagarjuna Sagar project, Krishna delta and Hyderabad water supply. The Government have rightly given clarifications on this to clear such apprehensions. Though the intentions are good, applying the principles in practice would be a major issue in this case. There is a need to constitute an empowered authority representing the interests of the three regions of the State to regulate the flows in Pothireddypadu Head Regulator on a day to day basis complying with the principles already laid down by the Government through various G.O's issued in this regard.

The principle of availability of flood flows in 30 days adopted for Pothireddypadu Head Regulator will have to be followed for all other schemes drawing surplus water from Krishna river. For example, in the case of Handri Neva project, it is presently designed for drawing water for 120 days. This has to be reduced to 30 days and greater pumping and canal capacities will have to be provided to facilitate drawing the surplus flows available in 30 days. Similarly Srisailam left bank canal (Alimineti Madhava Reddy Canal) will have to be designed for drawing water for 30 days as against the present 90 days contemplated. When water is to be supplied for 120 days during the crop period and, it has to be drawn in 30 days, there is no possibility to supply water to the crops in the balance 90 days unless storages are built up in the shape of balancing reservoirs. In the case of Telugu Ganga project, storages of 32 TMC balancing reservoirs were built at Veligallu and Brahmamgarimattam. However, there are no such balancing reservoirs on SLBC. It is, therefore, necessary to construct suitable balancing reservoirs across Gudipallivagu, Saslervagu, Halia etc. and investigation for the same will have to be done in detail to work out exact locations and capacities. Also the tunnel of SLBC will have to be designed to draw water in 30 days. The same principle will have to be applied in the case of Kalvakurti lift irrigation scheme, Nettempadu lift irrigation scheme and Koyalsagar lift irrigation scheme, all based on drawing surplus flows from Krishna river. Any different type of technological treatment between Pothireddypadu Head Regulator and other similar schemes drawing surplus water from Krishna river, would lead to inter regional and even inter district conflicts. Also doubting and suspecting the intentions of Government, from any quarter should be avoided. Apart from these issues, it will be technically necessary to design all the schemes on the same principle if the same have to function successfully. In addition to drawing or pumping the required higher discharges, construction of balancing reservoirs would also become necessary, for all the schemes based on surplus water.

There is an impression in some quarters, that because off-take levels of some schemes are kept much lower than the sill level (841 ft.) of Pothireddypadu Head Regulator, water can be drawn in more than 30 days and hence there is no need to increase the discharges. This is not correct. If any water is drawn from a level below 841 ft, it would amount to utilizing the assured 75% dependable flows or depleting the stored water in Srisailam. Since it is contemplated to draw only surplus flows, such a method shouldn't be resorted to. For example it is reported that the pumping level for Kalwakurthi lift scheme is 811 ft. In such a case, irrigation water shouldn't pumped when the water level in the reservoir drops below 841 ft. However, drinking water requirements can be pumped even when the water level goes down, similar to the case of Hyderabad city water supply from Nagarjunasagar reservoir. In the case of SLBC tunnel, though the sill level is provided at 825 ft. level, it requires an FSL of 850 ft. in the canal to draw 4000 cusecs, and hence this is in order for the purpose of drawing surplus flows.

Preparation of Detailed Project Reports (DPR) and Execution of Works

Most of the irrigation projects taken up by the Government are of the type of excavation of canals. Head works (Dam) are involved only in the case of some medium irrigation projects and Polavaram dam. The State has got technical skills to prepare the detailed reports for all these works. It would not be prudent to call for technical bids following EPC (Engineering, Procurement and Construction), since there is no need to procure engineering from any bidder. The Central Designs Organisation of the State as well as the Investigation wing are having skills to prepare estimates for tunnels also. However, the State had chosen EPC system for the reasons stated by them as timely completion of work without any extra costs for any reason of change in design, as the responsibility of designing is also with the tenderer. The disadvantage of the system as presently being flowed would become evident and clearer during the later period of execution, since the EPC system is not followed in toto. The case in point is that the tenderers are not giving the designs and drawings at the time of evaluation of the technical and financial bids. They were given a time of 1 week to 3 weeks time to submit their technical bids involving investigation, designs and drawings whereas it requires 3 to 6 months for the same. However, the tenderers were made to agree for any changes in design that the Government would make later on, while approving the designs of the contractors. In order to ensure this, Government is safeguarding its interests by taking an agreement from the contractor that he will abide by the changed designs made by the Government given later on, and that he will not claim any extra towards the same even though it may cost more amount, than the design given by the contractor. When such a compliance, would entail in losses to the contractor, he would not be encouraged to complete the works and would prefer taking up this case for redressal through a Court of Law. As per Law of Contract, any agreement on unknown factors would be null and void and even if the contractor signs for complying with an unknown factor, it would not stand before Law, as valid. On the other hand, if there is a design suggested by the Contractor, that would meet the technological requirements and if such a design costs significantly less, the benefit of the same would go to the contractor and not to the Government. There are several instances recently reported in the media, that when a contractor suggested replacement of 30% of cement by fly-ash and submitted the designs fully complying with the various technical requirements, the entire benefit would go to the contractor, if the same is approved by the Central Designs Organisation of the Government. Another example is regarding different grades of cement concrete. A dense design concrete mix would reduce the use of cement and yet meet the design requirements of strength. The contractor would then stand to gain by using less cement then originally contemplated. Also such savings running to several hundreds of crores of rupees would not be available to the Government. Thus, a situation may develop later on where a contractor is likely to be benefited by an economical design and when a costlier design is given by the Government, he would seek a remedy through a Court of Law. All these problems would not be felt in the earlier stages of construction, but will be faced during the middle and later stages only. FIDIC System of procurement of works (tendering) adopted by World Bank and other international organisations is a well tested method throughout the world. It would be prudent to adopt this method for the future contracts duly safeguarding the aspects regarding timely execution of works and no claims for extra compensation or payments for whatever reason it may be.

Certain procedural irregularities have occurred while prequalifying category 1 contractors. This has resulted in court cases, mudslinging, occusations and counter-occusations, between political parties. An irregularity committed to save time and quickly start execution of works, had actually resulted in a delay of several months. All this could have been avoided by issuing a fresh short notice (1 week) notification for prequalification bids, incorporating the relaxations of qualifications. A procedural error was committed in relaxing the norms only to the 9 bidders who tendered, shutting off the others who would satisfy the relaxed qualifications and yet have not tendered earlier (as they felt that they are not eligible). It is a recognized fact that errors are possible only when something is being done and not otherwise. In all such cases in future the Government can take full advantage of the skills and expertise available in its Law and Finance Departments, in order to avoid errors and complications later on.

Lift Irrigation Schemes

Most of the lift irrigation projects contemplate pumping to high heads ranging from 100–300 metres. Power consumption charges at Rs. 2 per unit for I.D crops would work out to Rs. 2000–6000 per acre, depending upon the season of the crop (Kharif or Rabi) and the actual head of pumping. Since all the projects are designed to irrigate one crop and that too by supplementation during Kharif season, it can be estimated that the power charges may be about Rs. 3,000 per acre on an average. However, the farmer would not be able to bear this burden if past experience in the case of lift irrigation schemes where the head of pumping is not more than 30m (functioning in the Irrigation Development Corporation), is any guide. It is, therefore, necessary to supply free power to the lift irrigation schemes through specially dedicated hydro-electric power stations constructed under the irrigation budget. The farmers can however bear the expenditure of operation and maintenance of canals of the pumping schemes (excluding power charges). In the case of lift schemes, operation of the same will have to be done by the Government, and water delivered into the canals. The canal distribution system can be maintained, in the same manner as the surface water distribution system and the farmers associations can be made responsible for operation and maintenance of the same. However, the Government will have to bear the burden of ordinary repairs, special repairs and renewal of pumpsets and also maintain the pumping mains.

It is estimated that 2800 MW of hydropower will have to be generated for meeting the power requirements of all the lift irrigation projects taken up by the Government. Most of these, will have to be met through the future hydro-electric projects on Godavary river. It is therefore necessary to plan and construct these hydro-power projects and complete the same along with the irrigation projects. Also HT lines along with transformer yards will have to be built, to supply power over long distances to the lift schemes on Krishna (Handri Neeva, Kalwakurthy, Nettempadu, Koilsagar) and stage pump houses for lift schemes on Godavari river. These activities are very much lagging behind and hence they have to be speeded up. This is a formidable task, but this would turn out to be a key factor in achieving results under the whole "Jalayagnam" programme, and hence this should not be relegated to the back burner.

Design, Discharges for Kharif Season, I.D Crops

Irrigation for Kharif season I.D crops would be mostly of the type of supplemental irrigation to rainfed crops. This can also be called as life irrigation. Depending upon the agro-climatic conditions of the area, incidence of rainfall and duration of droughts, the need for such irrigations would arise. This can vary from 2 to 6 wettings during a crop period. It is not the total rainfall that is important in calculating the number of irrigations. The number of drought spells are periods when the rainfall does not occur will have to be evaluated statistically. Such a methodology for 75% dependability, was worked out by me and was given in the case of minor irrigation. Since the number of irrigations vary from year to year depending upon the distribution of rainfall in a given year, the statistical method to work out 75% dependability would be needed. It is reported in the media that the quantity of water required from project to project is varying drastically from 14,000 acres per TMC to 25,000 acres per TMC. Though this may appear as a contradiction in irrigating ID crops, it need not be so. It has to be actually worked out based on the above principles. More important than this, is the design of canals to provide such supplemental irrigation or life irrigation. These design principles are given by me in the guidelines published by the Government for minor irrigation schemes and lift irrigation schemes. In essence, the design discharge of irrigating Kharif ID crops would be significantly more than that of the Rabi ID crops. This is because Rabi season crops can be irrigated for an irrigation depth of 50 mm in a rotation period of 8–10 days, where as the same amount of water will have to be supplied to the crops during drought periods in Kharif season, in a rotation period of 3–4 days. When there are no rains for nearly 8–10 days, all the farmers would need water at the same time, and a shorter rotation period will have to be selected. This is because no farmer will be prepared to wait for rotation period of 10 days, when once there is need for water to the crop and the crop is already showing signs of wilting. It may sound paradoxical that the design discharge of Kharif ID would be almost double than that of Rabi ID though the total quantity of irrigation water for Kharif season crop may be ½ to 1/3 of that of Rabi season crop. This aspect was not properly understood and the canals which were designed based on "duty norms" in the earlier days have failed to supply water for the full command area. The reasons for such non supply of water were wrongly attributed to wastage and excess usage of water by farmers, non cooperation by the farmers, absentee landlordism, in-appropriate selection of crops etc. However, there were years when the full command area would be irrigated, even though the design discharges are based on 'duty concept'. This is because in such years, there were timely rains and the need for irrigation was very less and was almost nil. I had the occasion to hear from farmers that water comes to their fields through canals, only when it rains! Realistic design of distribution system, is therefore needed in the case of Kharif ID crops. Similarly the discharge capacity of pumps would be more. However, this design can be streamlined and moderated by introducing balancing reservoirs and pumping for the entire period of flood days.

Realistic designs of canals and pumpsets should be done though the same would increase the cost of the project. This is needed to meet the requirements of command areas.

Inland Water Navigation

World Water Forum (WWF) in its meeting held at Kyoto during March 2003 (Attended by 82 Nations, including India) has made an important recommendation that all future water resources development projects in the world, should have inland water navigation facilities built in as a component of the project. When such facilities are provided, it is possible for flat bottom sea going vessels up to 2000 tonnes capacity, requiring a draft (depth of water) of 1½ metre to ply in the rivers up to the sea mouth. The same vessels can also travel in the sea and transport goods to any port. Such facilities were already achieved in developed countries during the 19th and 20th centuries (e.g. Saint Lawrence Seaway connecting the Great lakes to Atlantic ocean in USA, Mississippi, Misouri, Ohio rivers in USA, Rhine Danube linkage and Rhone, Volga systems in Europe). The same is now being developed in the projects now under construction in China (e.g. 3 Gorges dam). Inland water navigation would not only provide cheap transport of bulk goods, but also provides employment throughout the year for rural, non-land holding population. Also this as an eco-friendly transport when compared to the high levels of pollution in road and rail transport systems. When cheap transport and water is available, mineral based bulk industries would come up in the hinterland of the river basin. All these activities would lead to economic growth of the area and also livelihood support of the landless rural population. It is, therefore, suggested that all the future projects like storage reservoirs at Polavaram, Ichampalli, Pulichintala, and barrages at Yellampalli, Dommagudam etc., should have navigation facilities and locks to enable plying of flat bottom sea going vessels.

Projects on Godavari

In order to utilize flood flows of about 800 TMC (ultimate 1100 TMC) in Godavari river, it would be necessary to construct 3 reservoirs across Godavari – one near Suraram in between the confluence of Pranahita and confluence of Indravati river, the second one near Kantalapali upstream of Yeturunagaram and the third at Polavaram (as originally agreed between the 3 States). It would be necessary to construct two reservoirs instead of one at Ichampalli in order to generate the required hydro power as well as fully store the flood flows of the order of 10–15 lakhs cusecs flowing for about 10–15 days in a year. The earlier contemplated Ichampalli project has some basic disadvantages to Andhra Pradesh, since only 27% of the power can be utilized by the State though 78.1% of expenditure of the project has to be borne by Andhra Pradesh. Also only 85 TMC of water can be utilized for irrigation. It would be preferable to construct two reservoirs (instead of Ichampalli), one near Suraram and another near Kantalapalli to generate about 1500 MW power and utilize 500 TMC excusively for Andhra Pradesh. In addition to the three reservoirs, four barrages can be constructed one each near Yellampally, Chennur, Edira and Dommagudam. Investigation for these barrages as well as the two reservoirs will have to be done to exactly locate the same, and work out the details. It is possible to develop 3600 MWs of power from the three reservoirs and four barrages. This power can be utilized to pump water from Godavari river to irrigate uplands in Telangana as well as divert water to Krishna basin. It is also possible to supply this power to the four major lift projects proposed on Krishna river.

Alternatives for Polavaram Dam

The present proposals of the Government to retain the Full Reservoir Level (FRL) of the Polavaram project at 150 ft level was already agreed to by the three Sates and also the same was mentioned in the Bachavath award. The design for this proposal is quite sound and hydraulic model studies conducted have confirmed the suitability of the spillway and the changed river course on right flank. This is a terminal reservoir on the river and should therefore have as much bigger capacity as possible. However, in order to reduce the submersion area, the FRL was already reduced about 3 decades back from 185 ft. to 150 ft. and hence any further reduction in FRL would not be in the interest of the project. This was clearly mentioned by me earlier in various meetings and relevant publications. However, I have examined the technical issues if the height is reduced from FRL 150 to 130 ft. (the minimum draw down level of earlier design) and concluded that it is preferable to keep the original design without reducing the height. This was not properly understood in some quarters though correctly reported in the media, and they thought that my proposal was to reduce the FRL to 135 ft. This alternative of FRL 135 ft. would become a solution only when the Government is not in a position to construct the dam for FRL 150 ft. and it wants to reduce the submersion area (villages, lands and forests). When the canals are already under construction it becomes a waste when the dam is not constructed. There were certain alternatives suggested by others for avoiding Polavaram dam altogether by constructing barrages across Sabari river and diverting the flows through a tunnel to Polavaram Left bank canal. It was also proposed to utilize the barrage at Dommagudam to feed the Polavaram Right bank canal. Though the proposals may appear to be sound and attractive, it requires a detailed hydrological study, in order to examine whether the required quantity of water can be supplied during the non flood period for various uses contemplated under the Polavaram project. *Prima facie* it appears that there is a need to store the flood water occurring in Sabari river and Godavari river. A few lakh cusecs would be flowing in Sabari river during the floods. The same will have to be either stored in Sabari or Godavari after its confluence. Even if it has to be diverted through a barrage and stored elsewhere it is not possible to utilize the full flood flows in the river. Similarly the storage at Dommagudam would be nominal and will not be able to impound any flood flow. The crux of the problem is how to store the flood flow of 10 lakhs cusecs to 15 lakhs cusecs flowing for 10–15 days and supply the same during the non-flood period for the requirements of Polavaram project. Even with storage at Polavaram dam, there is a shortage of nearly 72 TMC for meeting the requirements of the project during the period from November to May. It is, therefore, necessary to examine the hydrological feasibility and work out with daily working tables of inflow, outflow and storage in order to evaluate the feasibility of the alternatives.

There is a criticism that construction of Polavaram canal works were started much earlier and the works on dam are not yet started (Feb 2006), and that the construction of dam ought to have been taken up first, and canals later on. But there is another argument that canals would take longer time to construct than the dam, and the example of Nagarjunasagar project is cited, for taking up canal construction in the first instance. The ground reality and technical aspect is that construction of dam will take not less than 5 years and the canals would take only 3 years if the needed funds are kept at disposal. This is because the entire length of canal can be tackled simultaneously, where as in the case of dam, it involves distinct stages, one after the other, such as excavation of foundations, foundation treatment, construction of dam lift by lift, gates erection, head sluices, power house equipment etc. Nagarjunasagar canals took more time than the dam because of inadequate flow of funds. Projects like High Aswan Dam, Egypt (almost same size as Polavaram) took 8 years for construction of dam and 4 years for canals. It is, therefore, necessary to obtain all clearances and consent of submersion people and commence construction of dam as early as possible.

Pulichintala Project

In the case of this project, on the request of the then Minister, (for utilizing the flows in Krishna river), I have sent during September 2003 proposals for five barrages to be investigated, in lieu of the dam proposal. If found feasible and attractive, this can be taken up instead of a dam proposal, which involved submersion of villages, forest lands, lime quarries, Nagarjunasagar ayacut etc. The then Government has not investigated the barrage proposals and the successive Government, as reported in the media had examined the same, and opted for construction of the dam. In the wisdom of Government when it decided to opt for the dam and started executing the same, the issue of alternatives or examination of the same may not be relevant. All the alternatives are appropriate, up to a point of time, and that is before execution of any proposal, and they may not be relevant after the works are started and are in various stages of progress.

Designs to be approved by Central Water Commission

In the Bachavath award, it was mentioned that the designs of the Polavaram project will have to be approved by the Central Water Commission. It is contended by the Andhra Pradesh State Government that Central Water Commission had already taken a view with regard to various major and medium irrigation projects, that there is no need to send the designs of the same, for their approval, since the State Government is having a fully competent Central Designs Organisation capable of doing this work. Though such a contention would be relevant in the case of other projects, this has to be examined in the context of the Bachavath award on Polavaram Dam and the spirit behind the award. Apart form meeting the specific requirements of the award, for several reasons it will be necessary for the Andhra Pradesh State Government to send the designs to Central Water Commission for their approval. This is required since submersion is involved in upstream States of Chhattisgarh and Orissa. Calculations pertaining to back water curve, and the extent of submersion occurring when the reservoir is under FRL conditions with peak flood occurring in Sabari river, will have to be examined in detail by the Central Water Commission as well as by the upstream States. In these computations, certain technical assumptions are made, while 'routing' the peak flood when the reservoir level is at 150 ft at the dam site. These assumptions mainly relate to field conditions such as values of coefficients of rougosity, vegetative cover along the flanks of the stream, topographic conditions including the types of soils of the river and its margins. The assumptions made in the calculations by one State, need not necessarily be agreed to by the other State, where submersion is involved, and also an organization like Central Water Commission will have a fair and neutral role to play on all such matters. It would be therefore in the interests of Andhra Pradesh, that these designs of the project are sent to Central Water Commission as well as to the upstream States for their perusal as well as confirmation on submersion areas in other States. Recently it is reported in the media that though Andhra Pradesh Government is contending that there is no submersion in other

States, Orissa Government had submitted to the Central Water Commission that 588 hectares of land in Malkangiri Taluk in that State will get submerged, effecting 6316 families. Also Chhattisgarh has contested that 2398 hectares of land (17 villages in Kunta block) will get submerged in their State. Transparency in designs will therefore facilitate thrashing out certain initial minor issues which may pose bottlenecks later on. If experience is any guide, such issues have become bottlenecks and delayed construction of projects like Janjhavathi and Vamsadhara stage II for nearly two decades. Another example is that during heavy floods in 2005, Maharashtra Government had contested against Karnataka Government, regarding the excess submersion caused in their State by keeping water level at Almatti dam at FRL conditions. They blamed the Karnataka Government for the havoc caused in their State on account of back waters of the Almatti dam, and demanded depletion of water level in the dam for which Karnataka Government did not agree. Such problems can be sorted out during the beginning stage of the project, than when they become major issues, later on.

Quality Control

The departmental staff will have to do the Quality Control of works, executed in the irrigation projects. In the present system of execution of works, the contractors are doing the work of investigation, design and execution and as such the departmental staff is not having any role either to mark out the works, organize the material, labour and machinery for execution of works or stepping up the tempo of works. Even for preparation of bills the contractor has to take measurements and submit the bills. Also the contractor will have to ensure good quality on works. Thus the Department staff has no other work except to make some checks of the bills of quantities and satisfy regarding quality of works and arrange payments for the same. The only technical work that they have to perform would be Quality Control. There is no point in allocating this work also to a private agency by inviting bids for the same. In the case of execution of major works in the Department like Nagarjunasagar dam. Srisaialm dam, Pochampadu dam, the Quality Control and laboratory tests were entirely done by the department with exclusive staff allocated for this, in addition to the usual field staff incharge of works. The same concept was adopted for all the irrigation projects in India. In the case of industries also (public sector as well as private sector) quality control is very much within the domain of the particular industry. Only when certain quality control tests had to be conducted outside the country like U.S., U.K., etc., private reputed agencies like M/s Lyods were engaged for this purpose. This is more of the type of a cost effective reliable method and resorted to, only when it would become cumbersome and too costly for the staff of the industry to make frequent visits abroad for such Quality Control inspections and tests. When the works are executed within the State and the departmental staff are available at site, there is no reason why the quality control has to be delegated to any private agency. Payments made to such agencies would be an additional burden on the State. Apart from this, somebody has to take the responsibility and be accountable for the quality. It has to be appreciated that in the long run it would turn out to be disastrous to entrust such important functions of safety and stability of structures to a private agency. Quality control is always best done through departmental officials rather than by contracted private individuals. The concept of privatizing quality control and making payments for the same will have to be viewed from the above context and it is worthwhile for the Government to reexamine this issue and take proper decisions.

Krishna Water Disputes 2nd Tribunal

There are several issues to be raised before the 2nd Krishna Water Dispute Tribunal. The State Government is already having a list of these issues and they are very much in order. In addition to the points, already raised by the State Government a few more aspects can be considered. In the catchment area of river Krishna, there is an extensive drought prone area. Groundwater is being pumped to such an extent that it resulted lowering of water-table levels significantly. Data (1969-70 to 1999-2000) in the three States show lowering of water-table below bed of rivers by 20m in some places. On account of this the river is now recharging water-table during the dry periods instead of groundwater draining into the river, as happened earlier to 1970s. The loss in flow of the river due to this is estimated as 1.85 BCM (65 TMC) at Karnataka-Andhra Pradesh border. The base flows occurring through groundwater draining into the river and its tributaries also got reduced drastically. As per figures quoted in the 5th International R&D Conference on Water Resources (Feb 2005), the reduction in base (groundwater) flows in Bhima river at Andhra Pradesh-Karnataka border is 250 MCM (9 TMC) and that of Tungabhadra river at Andhra Pradesh border is 700 MCM (25 TMC) during the period 1970 to 2000 (between January & May). Thus the total reduction of base flows to Andhra Pradesh is 34 TMC (9+25). The first tribunal considered that there will be re-generated flow in Krishna River due to irrigated commands, to an extent of 70 TMC. There is also no regeneration of flows in the river (due to irrigation), in view of the improved water management practices and I.D. Cropping pattern now being followed in the command areas of Krishna Basin. Thus, the entire assumption of availability of 70 TMC regenerated flows in the river has got to be reassessed. It is felt that there will be no contribution of regenerated flows in the future also, due to efforts being taken by the 3 State Governments to improve irrigation efficiency. In view of the above the 75% dependable yield of Krishna river will have to be reduced by 169 TMC (65+34+70) due to losses in river bed, reduced base flows and absence of regenerated flows. An estimation of reduction in surface flows in 20 years from 1976 to 1996 was indicated as 7 BCM (247 TMC) during the same R&D Conference. Thus, the total reduction in flow in the river is 416 TMC (169 + 247). However, the aspect of reduction on surface flow (247 TMC) in 20 years needs hydrological statistical refinement and therefore may get altered. The reduction of 169 TMC of base flows etc. is actually felt and hence is realistic. One important argument to be advocated by Andhra Pradesh would be to insist that 2060TMC, 75% dependable flow is no more available in the river and that this has to be reduced by 416 TMC. This would result in not sanctioning any more new projects in all the 3 states based on 75% dependable yield. Andhra Pradesh is having a provision for utilizing surplus water of the river during good rain fall years and hence this reduction of 75% dependable yield will have no impact on the new projects, taken up by the A.P. Government, which are all based on utilisation of surplus flows. Though Andhra Pradesh has no right on this water, yet it can utilize the same, going to the sea. In order to utilize this surplus flows, the State Government will have to organize construction of structures like dams, canals storage reservoirs etc. Though such a measure is not an economically attractive one, since the utilisation of the same will only be in "surplus years", yet the State Government has to resort to this method in order to meet the requirement of drought prone areas of Rayalaseema and Telangana Regions. In an earlier judgment the Supreme Court has viewed that though this is permissible, the State Government should not construct permanent structures for using surplus water. It has to be convincingly argued that it is not technically feasible to utilize surplus water without the construction of structures like dam, canals etc. If necessary the Tribunal and Courts may be requested to take technical opinion on this, through a committee appointed by them and make the award. It has to be impressed that mearly giving a facility for utilizing surplus water in the shape of writing (award) on paper, it can not be practically implemented, unless structures to utilize the same are constructed on the field.

Continuing Education for Engineers

It is a recognized fact that Science and Technology is doubling in a very short period in recent times. It is estimated that the doubling period of knowledge in this area got reduced from 1000 years during the 18th century to a few decades now. This means to say that knowledge in Science and Technology has more than doubled from 1970 till date. When this is the situation, continuing education and training on specialized disciplines would be very much needed for engineering personal in the State. Though to some extent, this is being done for bureaucrats, management personal etc, this is totally absent in the case of engineers. As a result, it has become a routine to hear that our engineers are not knowledgeable and experienced and therefore we have to obtain skills from outside. It has to be remembered that the strength of the engineering department would be entirely resting with the staff of the department and not by temporarily borrowing or depending from other sources. It is, therefore, necessary to formulate a programme of continuing education and practical training for the engineers engaged on irrigation projects as well as other works. This should be a continuous phase and should not end abruptly. It is seen that several retired engineers are re-employed are taken on contract in order to meet the technical requirements. This is not a desirable method since the strength of the dept. should not be the strength of retired persons. Though as a rule, retired employees should not be reemployed, it is still happing in practice. Another anomaly is that the same retired persons when they were working while in service were not considered as experts, but yet were termed as experts after their retirement. If a committee has to be constituted to examine specific issues it is advisable to constitute the same by inviting working persons from Central Water Commission rather than constituting the same with retired persons. The State Government working Chief Engineer could be the convener of the Committee. This is necessary to get suitable technical expertise, in the interest of works. One more aspect to be considered in this context, is that skills and talents are not available in the private sector, for irrigation projects, since, this activity was totally a governmental monopoly right from the beginning. The so-called experts from private sector are either not really experts in project design and execution, or the very same retired persons joining the private sector. The situation in structural engineering is totally different from major irrigation projects, since there are several structural works in the private sector where adequate skills and talent are available. The difference between these two disciplines of engineering is not properly noticed while taking policy decisions.

Ensuring Technical Questions in Meetings

During several discussions organized by the State Government on irrigation projects, various technical questions raised by the participants are being answered by other than Chief Engineers. Replies by concerned Chief Engineers' are conspicuously absent in the meetings. This is not a good development, and does not lead to strengthening the technical institutions. Also wrong technical information is being given. For example, when there was a question regarding the discharge through SLBC, replies were given, that with a sill level of the tunnel at 825 ft (FSL 850 ft.) by increasing the head of flow (when the water level in the reservoir is above FSL and up to FRL 885 ft.), It is possible to increase the velocity from 2 mts. per second to 6 mts. per second, thus increasing the discharge from 4,000 Cusecs to 12000 Cusecs. It was also further explained that velocity is equal to "2GH" (a well-known hydraulics formula applicable for orifices and sluices) and hence higher discharge of 12000 Cusecs is possible. A technical scrutiny would suggest that both these replies are totally wrong. The tunnel of 43.5 km long with a diameter of 9.2 mts. would technically function as a gravity pressure pipe line when subjected to hydraulic heads up to 885 ft. level. Adopting a co-efficient of rougocity of 0.018 for the tunnel and applying hydraulic gradient' method, the velocity of flow in tunnel works out to 2.37 mps. when water level is at FRL 885 ft. as against 1.951 mps. without such a pressure head. Thus, the increase in discharge would be only from 4,000 Cusecs to 5,566 Cusecs and not 12,000 cusecs as replied in the meeting. The orifice formula of velocity equal to "2GH" is not applicable to this situation (when worked out in this manner it gives an absurd velocity of 22 mts. per second). It has to be recognized that any wrong replies given by Government would also lead to doubts in the minds of others and complicate the situation which can be totally avoided.

Political leaders in the Government will have to take the best advantage of the personal available in the Government in the form of administrators and technical personnel. This aspect has also been considered while formulating the "business" rules and Secretariat instructions, with regard to leaving the option to the Chief Engineer to discuss the matter with the minister and (or) Chief Minister, when his proposal is being negatived. The objective is that Government/objective may get the best advantage of skills and expertise of Chief Engineer as well as the Secretariat.

Kolleru Lake

The State Government is taking commendable steps for restoring Kolleru Lake to its original condition obtained about 40 years back. Measures are being taken up by Government to protect the lake up to 5 feet contour level and also construct 2 regulators (one at the entrance to Upputeru and another at the end of Upputeru). The aspect of compensating the private lands up to 14,407 acres lying within 5 feet contour will have to be done speedily in order that an extent of 75,613 acres of fish tank is available through out the year. This would be several fold more than the huge number of small fish tanks extending to a total year of about 15,000 acres. The entire 75,613 acres of a huge fish tank can be exploited, as intensively as that of a small fish tank and economic gains can be obtained. The procedures and management methods adopted in the case of Lake Laguna, Philippines would be of interest in this regard. Some problems have arisen in this lake, and the same were solved technically and managerially about 1½ decades back. A visit to this area by a multi-disciplinary team would be of some advantage for planning activities in Kolleru Lake. In addition to this, I suggest that the following measures are taken up in order to get best results:

a) All roads within the 5 feet contour constructed earlier will have to be removed and in their place cart track stilt bridges erected. These bridges will be similar to those constructed for jetties with column supports through piles driven in the soil in the bed of the Lake. Decking for the bridge would be of a light type to facilitate movement of carts, lightweight vehicles, motor cycles etc. These roads were constructed early under the presumption that the villages will have to be connected to each other. Such connection and communications in an environment of a lake should be through the medium of water and should never be a conventional road, since such a construction has to be technically prohibited within a lake area. Even though a bridge is provided for passage of water from one side to the other, such a passage would be limited in length and this causes afflux, i.e. rise of water level on the upstream side of the lake when compared to the down stream side of the lake. Such a phenomenon was noticed at Peda Yedlagadi when the road was constructed between Eluru and Kaikaluru. There was a water level difference of 2.5 feet between one side of the road and the other side of the road. Such affluxes (rise I water level) would create heavy submersion in agricultural lands surroundings the Lake, during the monsoon periods. This is due to prevention of sheet flow of water within the lake. Providing one more bridge would still be not a solution for the existing Peda Yedlagadi bridges.

b) During the monsoon rains in 2005, it is seen that a water level of 13.5 ft. is obtained as against the earlier ever maximum of 9.5 ft. in the lake. This is due to obstruction of sheet flow of water in the Lake as well as reduced area of the lake due to encroachment of fish tanks in levels higher than 5 ft. contour. It is, therefore, necessary to remove all the fish tanks encroaching into Lake and lying below 9.5 ft. contour. The hydraulic features of the lake will have to be recognized to appreciate the need for this. When the peak flood inflow into the lake is 1,20,000 cusecs and the maximum outflow possible through Upputeru, is 15,000 Cusecs, it would result in inundation and storage would be build up within the lake. If the lake area is reduced, higher water levels (higher than 9.5 ft. up to 13.5 ft.) would result, inundating villages and agricultural lands surroundings the lake. Thus, the absence of sufficient area for the lake would create havoc in the neighbouring villages, as happened in the year 2005. It is, therefore, essential that all the fish tanks existing up to 9.5. ft. contour will have to be removed and the lands used for agricultural purposes as done earlier. In order to facilitate this, the land owners of such lands can be made to share the benefits of pisciculture in the big lake of 75,613 acres.

) **Channelisation**: Crores of rupees were spent earlier for channelisation within the Lake to facilitate the water flow through Upputeru during the times of floods. Such a step is not technically necessary. It has been proved through 3D model studies, that channelisation is not technically required. It has to be appreciated that the Lake hydraulics is different from channel hydraulics. Sheet flows occurs in a Lake, whereas channel flows occur in a drainage system. Applying principles of channel hydraulics to Lake hydraulics is totally wrong. As such this activity of channelisation can be totally avoided. The important aspect to be understood here is that sheet flow of water in the lake, should not be obstructed for any reason. It is reported recently in the media that some peoples representatives have requested to take up channelisation works within the lake and requested funds to be allotted for this purpose. Sensitising and educating the public on these technical aspects will therefore become a necessity.

d) All along the 5 ft. contour, a shelter belt 200 to 300 mts. wide with man grove tree species will have to be developed. These trees growing up to 20 to 30 feet height will survive inundation as well as dry conditions and support bird life. Migrating birds require trees for them to nest, thrive and breed. The food requirement for these birds would be met through the fish in the Lake. When these birds arrive in huge numbers, tourism can be developed through out the year. Apart from bird watching, water sports activities would create a boom in tourism as is happing now in the back waters of Alleppy in Kerala.

e) **Navigation:** Locks will have to be constructed at the two regulators to facilitate flat bottom sea going Vessels up to 500 tonnes capacity (50 lorry loads of fish) to ply within the lake as well as in the Upputeru channel. These flat bottom vessels need a draft (depth of water) of 1m and would be capable of plying in Inland waters as well as in the sea. Thus, a ship load of fish can be taken from the lake to Kolkata or any other port in a period of 4 to 6 days directly, without any trans-shipment enroute. Such Inland water navigation would result in fetching higher prices for the fish catch in the Lake and establish good commercial contacts for the fishermen to the attractive outlets all along the coast up to Calcutta. This will not only result in higher income but would also provide livelihoods for the local people through out the year(through navigation).

Cropping Pattern

The choice of crops will have to be left to the farmers. Under the new projects, now under construction, it is expected that 15 lakh acres would be given irrigation facility during the Kharif season of 2006. This is a significant area and cropping pattern will have to be planned appropriately to suit the types of soils and the agro climatic zones. For example, when supplementation to rainfed crops is planned during the Kharif season, farmers choice will have to be preferred especially in the black soil areas. Though project design may specify that ID Crops will have to be grown during Kharif season, the farmers of black clayey soil areas would not favour it. They feel that any irrigation activity in black soils would result in damage to the ID crops during the times of heavy rains and they would therefore like to raise wet crops (paddy). This is the experience of black soil area farmers in the various projects which were already completed. Project design in such cases will have to be modified for supplying irrigation water to raise wet crops in Kharif season. In order to minimize the water requirements for paddy crop SRI method will have to be insisted since this requires only 50% of the conventional water supplies. However, in the case of red soils, supplementary irrigation (life irrigation) can be followed and Kharif ID crops can be raised.

Farmers Wells

Technology pertaining to electrical and mechanical engineering aspects are not properly disseminated in the private sector of pumping groundwater for irrigation purposes. There is a lack of technical understanding among the village mechanics, electricians, dealers and the farmers in this regard. Replacement of existing foot valves with frictionless foot valves (ISI marks) is a recommendation suggested several decade back and it required a lot of pressure from the Government side to implement the same. Again for better power (voltage) regulation, higher power factor has to be achieved through installation of capacitors, and this aspect also is not appreciated in the villages. Often high head pumps are being utilized for low head pumping applications. This results in lower efficiency of the pump and thus there would be greater consumption of power. Selection of pump has to be done on Q-H curve basis and not on HP basis. This means that the head of pumping has to be correctly assessed with regard to lowest water level conditions in the well, fiction losses through pipes and pump selected should have capability to pump to this maximum head. However, the maximum efficiency of the pump will have to be achieved during the most probable water level conditions in the well. This has to be estimated based on average depth of water-table level in the well (dug well or bore well). The discharge can match the yield in the case of bore well and the number of hours of pumping required in the case of dug well. The HP requirement of motor has to be calculated based on discharge and head and next higher size motor can be selected for coupling with the pump. For example, if 3 HP is required as per the pump requirement, a 5 HP motor can be used and the increased power consumption in such a case will be about 1 or 2% and not 66% as commonly understood in the villages. There is an advantage of using a higher rated HP motor, since the same will not get burnt under low voltage conditions. The diameter of windings for a high rated motor will be more and any increase in amperage flows of current due to low voltage can safely pass through the windings without getting heated up. Thus, a slightly higher HP motor would be working satisfactorily even under low voltage conditions prevailing in the rural areas. In order to compensate for the resulting low power factor, an appropriate capacitor can be installed.

Power for Pumping Irrigation Water

The farmer in the surface water irrigation project gets water to his field without paying any contribution towards cost of the project. Also he gets water to his land, without making any effort. The farmer having irrigation through groundwater source, will have to incur the capital expenditure as well as maintenance expenditure to get water to his field. This maintenance expenditure, not only includes ordinary repairs and special repairs for the equipment but also periodical replacement of equipment due to various causes. In order to maintain equity between the farmer using surface water and the other using groundwater, it may be necessary that some relief is provided to the farmer using groundwater in some shape or another. One method is to provide free supply of power to the farmer since he had already incurred expenditure on the capital cost. However, this becomes economically untenable, to maintain good quality power and it also results in wasteful usage of power as well as excessive pumping of groundwater. Hence such free power will have to be restricted for the really needed low income economic groups. One method is to supply power for the weaker sections who are classified as small and marginal farmers. This would not be a simple technical process, but involves several other issues like socio-economic, policies of different political parties, quality of power (voltage) supplied, including number of hours of supply. Since it is not possible to give a simple and straight line recommendation on this, it is usual to decide such matters on administrative and economic grounds.

It was recently announced by the Government that in order to make farmers eligible for free supply of power, they should install capacitors and frictionless foot valves for their pump sets. With regard to foot valve, it is necessary that the farmers should comply with this, in order to reduce, the power consumed. When a frictionless foot valve is introduced in place of the existing high friction foot valve, the head of pumping gets reduced (due to reduction in frictional head). When a kilowatt hour meter (energy meter) is fixed in the switch board, it would record lesser power consumption. It is therefore justifiable that the farmer should contribute his bit of effort to reduce the burden on the State TRANSCO (Electricity), when he is utilizing free power given to him. However, in the case of capacitor, the picture is somewhat different. On account of introducing a capacitor, the power factor gets improved which in turn would reduce the "wattless current" (pulsating current). In other words, if the energy meter is fixed in the switch board, the number of units consumed would be the same for a given installation whether the capacitor is installed or not. When the "wattless current" component reduces, the benefit entirely goes to the TRANSCO (Electricity) and the benefit to the farmer is only indirect in the shape of better regulation of power due to higher voltages being obtained. This is because voltage drop due to "wattless current" is significantly reduced. Thus introducing a capacitor would help the Electricity Authorities directly, but not the farmer. It is suggested that this component may be done by the Electricity Department as the benefit is entirely derived by them, though indirectly, the farmers would be happy to have better voltage than earlier. Again from operational and technical reasons it is easy for the concerned electricity wing to install this as a part of the item of the switch board. Apart from first time installation, it is equally important to maintain and replace the capacitor when needed. It is somewhat similar to the energy meter being fixed by the Electricity wing and maintained by them. It would be therefore appropriate that frictionless foot valve is taken care of by the farmers and installation of capacitor taken care by the TRANSCO (Electricity Wing). This would be appropriate from technical, logical, administrative and maintenance points of view.

Minor Irrigation Tanks

There are nearly 84,000 minor irrigation tanks in the State. About 85% of these tanks need restoration and rehabilitation. During good rainfall conditions thousands of these tanks are getting breached every year. Some of the breached tanks also cause havoc in damaging railway tracks leading to disruption of traffic and railway accidents resulting in loss of life. It is necessary to restore these tanks to the design standards and provide spillway (surplus) capacity following the hydrological guidelines given by the Chief Engineer, Minor Irrigation in 1986. All tanks designed and executed according to these guidelines have not breached at any time even under heavy rainfall conditions. This is because, the earthen dams were built according to standards and the surplus arrangements are made to suit the maximum daily rainfall occurring in the given area in a return period of 25 years (as per norms of India Meteorological Deptt.). When all the tanks are restored and function satisfactorily, it would be possible to bring an additional area of about 20 lakh acres under irrigation. This activity is, therefore, of great importance in obtaining irrigation benefits within a short time and also such benefits are distributed through out the State. Though the exact cost of such restoration works cannot be estimated without investigation, yet it is likely to be around Rs. 5000 crores. It would be pertinent to observe that major and medium projects head works are not breaching during the times of heavy rainfall (e.g. year 2005), whereas thousands of Minor Irrigation Tanks are breaching is such years. This is due to substandard design in the first instance. This has to be set right as early as possible in order to safeguard the existing tanks in the State, and add irrigation potential of 20 lakh acres, which was lost all these years.

Watershed Management

Technology required for watershed development will have to be of low cost type and mostly obtained through vegetative activities. Earlier technology implemented during the past two decades did not result in drought proofing, according to the studies conducted by several international and national organisations. A new technology under the name "Four Water Concept" was developed and implemented in some states of India including Andhra Pradesh since a few years. This technology has an advantage of 100% participation of beneficiary, equity of benefits between the ridge area farmers and valley area farmers. When this technology was implemented it resulted in base flows (springs) occurring in the main stream and drought proofing the area with enough of groundwater being available during successive drought years. All the dug wells in the watershed would get additional recharge making them functional even during the summer periods. Also there is no need to drill bore wells for irrigation purposes since adequate groundwater would be available through dug wells. The recharge measures comprise of 11 structural activities (no work costing more than Rs. 6,000) and eight vegetative activities. It is found that modified PERON principle is applicable in this case. Thirty per cent of increase in recharge will be happening though structural works costing

70% of the programme, whereas 70% of increase in recharge will be happening with 30% cost of the programme. Cement based check dams across 3rd and 4th order streams are totally avoided in this concept. Mini-Percolation Tanks are proposed near ridge and sub-ridge valleys. A technology for raising successful rainfed crops even during drought years is contemplated. This is made possible by improving the soils structure within the root zone of crop to hold 35% moisture content (field capacity) as against the 10% in red soils existing now. This is achieved by raising green manure crop, before main Kharif season crop and raising cover crops during the post Kharif period and summer periods. The green manure and mulch will be ploughed into the soil at the appropriate times. This will not only improve the moisture holding capacity of soil, but also the fertility status, through organic manure. The increased moisture storage can support the crop during a drought spell of 30-35 days in Kharif season. Thus a successful rainfed crop can be grown even during long spells of drought. It is observed that in several districts, the rainfall was about 600 mm. even during the drought years. With such a rainfall, it is possible to raise successfully rainfed crops even during drought years, if the enhanced soil moisture can support the crop during the drought spells.

Water Management under Minor Irrigation Tanks

A majority of irrigation tanks were constructed in red soil areas. The ayacut under these tanks, though they may appear black in colour, are actually red soils, turned black, over a period of intensive paddy cultivation with green manure and farm yard manure added to the soils. In most of these tanks, soils in the ayacut will be of light textured type amenable for cultivation, with dry land implements. When these soils are not puddled, cultivation can be done using ordinary ploughs and other rainfed crop implements like seed drill, harrow etc. In the present practice, irrigation under the tanks would be commencing from the middle or end of August by which time some storage will get accumulated in the tank. Thus there may be no crop in the tank ayacut during the rainy months of June and July. It is a paradox that in the surrounding rainfed areas, crops would be growing in a lush manner, where as there will be no crops in the ayacut area though there is enough soil moisture available, to support a crop. The farmers will have to wait till some in-flow occurs in the tank, and a sizeable storage is built up. One method to make use of the soil moisture for raising paddy, will be to sow the seed into the soil through a seed drill like any other rained crop. With the soil moisture available, paddy comes up like any other rainfed crop and this crop can be irrigated from August onwards. Since there is no standing depth of water, the weed growth that occurs, will have to be removed by operating a four tyne or six tyne cultivator (called *Guntaka*) and by manually removing the weeds growing along the row of crops. In this practice of water management, tank water is conserved and it is possible to irrigate a second crop for the entire area. Usually groundnut crop will be grown during the period November to end of February, when crop water requirements during this period would be minimum in a year. It is found that when such practice were adopted in Kurnool district, there was no reductions in crop yield for paddy when weedicides are applied and there was a reduction of 10% yield when weedicides are not applied. The farmers would get double the income than what they were getting earlier, (when the lands were puddled in the month of August). I suggest that this water management practices may be adopted for all minor irrigation tanks in red soil areas. It may be possible to adopt this practice in about 50% of the existing 84,000 nos. minor irrigation tanks in the State (42 lakh Ac). This would create an additional irrigation potential of about 21 lakh acres (2nd crop) with negligible costs. The only cost to Government would be in the shape of extension and demonstration trials. Video tapes (in Telugu and English) and relevant literature (where it is extensively practiced in 18,000 Ac under tanks) are also available.

Relief and Rehabilitation of Project Displaced People

The State Government had stated that the package of relief and rehabilitation now being implemented in projects is most liberal when compared to the existing package elsewhere in the country. However, it was contended by some social activists, that in certain respects the relief measures of other State Governments are more liberal. For example displaced persons who were residing in the villages for a minimum of one year period before notification (is issued for acquisition), are eligible for compensation in other States, where as in Andhra Pradesh it is fixed as 3 years (instead of one year). Further it was contended that in States like Gujarat and Rajasthan, widows and handicapped without any age limit, were treated as separate families whereas there is no such mention in the package of Andhra Pradesh. It was also contended that a higher compensation of lands for house sites up to 502 sq mts is being given in other States (Gujarat, Maharashtra and Madhya Pradesh), whereas it is only 150 sq mts in rural areas and 75 sq.m in urban areas in A.P. Several other issues like money required for building a house, land required for allotment under cultivation etc., are stated to be much better in other States than in A.P. I suggest that these aspects may be reviewed and appropriate decisions taken in order to translate the commitment of the Government into action. Though these are relatively minor in nature, yet they are vital and important for the displaced persons.

World Water Forum (attended by 82 countries including India) in its meeting held at Kyoto-Japan during March 2003 had resolved that the displaced persons should be the 'first beneficiary' of any water resources project. The terminology of 'first beneficiary' amounts to that benefits due to the project for the displaced persons should be more than the economic gain of the command area farmer on an average. So far, relief and rehabilitation packages are oriented towards liberal compensation of assets and creation of amenities including giving the economic benefit, which are all of the type of one time activities. In order to operationalise the recommendations of World Water Forum (WWF), it requires a far more effort on the rehabilitation side. This amounts to creating new livelihood opportunities, training in these new livelihoods, including retraining in the same field or a different one. Monitoring the economic growth of the displaced persons, will have to be done every year and corrective steps will have to be taken, in order to achieve the economic growth programmed. Thus these activities would continue even after the project is completed till such time the displaced persons achieve the economic growth programmed earlier. Wherever such economic growths were achieved in the rehabilitated areas of the 3 Gorges dam, China, the responses from displaced persons were interesting. The young generation up to age group of 35 years were totally positive for the Water Resources Project. The middle age group of 35 to 60 years were happy that they were able to earn better economic returns, than earlier, and were highly hopeful of the future of their children. The age group above 60 years, were however not happy with the project, since they are displaced from their traditional homes and thrown out 500 km away. Thus the general situation is that majority of the displaced persons are favourably inclined to this project. It is also mentioned in the World Water Forum that the displaced persons should also "request for the project", and in order to facilitate this, economic growth package will have to be implemented. Also free education for the children of displaced people, in professional colleges like medical and engineering will have to be provided, when they get seats for the same. It was also recommended by WWF that the R & R packages should be started 2 years before the commencement of construction of the project.

Modernization of Irrigation Systems

The State Government has formulated proposals for modernizing several irrigation projects in the State. It was reported in the media that in addition to the Nagarjunasagar Canals and distribution system (costing Rs. 3000 crores), Krishna delta, Rajolibanda ayacut, Ghanapur ayacut, Nizamabad ayacut, Kadam ayacut are all included in these modernization proposals. It is a good management principle to maintain the irrigation systems out of income earned to supply water to the ayacut. If the income is very low, it will hardly be sufficient to operate the system. If the income is moderate, it can take care of ordinary annual repairs and special repairs, needed once in a few years. If the water rate structures is adequate enough to undertake major repairs, then there would be no need to spend capital funds for such maintenance. A sound management principle is therefore to utilize capital funds only for creating new irrigation potential and not for maintenance. As such it has to be ensured that repairs to damaged structures and proper upkeep of the system should all be done through the water rates collected. It is preferable that the modernization proposals of any existing project is not done unless there is a need for saving water or for increasing the command area under the project through water thus saved. The ordinary repairs and special repairs should not be carried out, as a principle under the modernization proposals but should be done only through income earned from the ayacut. It would be in the interest of funding new projects, that the expenditure on modernization of existing projects should be limited only to saving water and bringing additional area under irrigation. It is also sensible that capital expenditure should not be incurred unless new irrigation potential is created, through water saved.

Riverine Riparian Rights

After the construction of Godavari and Krishna anicuts, about 150 years back, flows in the river downstream of the structures got very much reduced especially during the summer months. In certain months, the entire flows of the rivers were exclusively utilized in the delta ayacuts and hence there was no flow into the sea. When this happened, consecutively for over a century, it resulted in environmental damage. This damage got intensified during the past three decades, after the construction of barrages in place of anicuts. There was no possibility of allowing any water into the sea during summer months, since the available flows in the river are hardly sufficient to meet the rising demand, in the delta. When new dams are proposed across Godavari river, it has to be ensured that certain minimum flows go to the sea even during summer months. This is necessary for preserving the mangroves along the coast line, fisheries activities related to special species which live in the sea and breed in fresh water. Also such a flow would prevent salt water intrusion in the groundwater aquifers of coastal areas. Presently several villages in the coast line had to be supplied with drinking water from elsewhere, since the groundwater in their areas had become saline. This trend has to be arrested and by such continuous release of water into the sea, the groundwater in the coastal areas can be made potable over a period of time. In any new irrigation project taken up on Godavari, it is usual to consider the riparian rights of existing ayacut on the downstream side. Similarly the riparian rights of the river itself will have to be considered for utilization of water in future dams across the Godavari. This can be termed as the "riverine riparian right" and the quantity of water that has to be allowed to flow to the sea, will have to be calculated in each river system. As a rough guide (thumb rule) 10% of flow diverted to canals should be allowed to flow to the downstream of the structure into the river. This amounts to utilizing 90% of the yield for the ayacut area, and 10% of the yield for riverine riparian rights to flow into the sea.

Irrigation Efficiency

Considerable effort is being exercised on the financial monitoring of irrigation projects. Also in the modernization (rehabilitation) of existing projects financial monitoring is being done. It is equally important to monitor the irrigation efficiency of any project taken up for modernization. It is stated that the irrigation efficiency is about 30% in the existing projects in the State. In the process of modernization, this irrigation efficiency will have to be improved to 45%. When this is done, it is possible to irrigate 50% more area than now, by utilizing the same quantity of water. However, it is not possible to achieve such increase in efficiency all of a sudden even though money may be spent on modernization aspects. This requires continuous activity and intense monitoring every year. The increase in efficiency can be achieved gradually in small steps every year, over a period of 5 years. For example, if the irrigation efficiency increased to 35% in one year, it has to be increased to 40% during the next year. Periodic measurements of flow of water, implementation of better water management practices (e.g. SRI cultivation), prevention of deep percolation losses as well as seepage losses etc. and improved agronomic practices will have to be introduced in the fields, in order to achieve results. These measures include improving the structure of the soil through green manure and farm yard manure, intermittent irrigation as against inundation irrigation, keeping mulch on the field during summer months etc. Though this activity would increase the irrigated area by

50% no separate funding is required. The funds available under modernization of projects would be adequate for this purpose.

In the case of paddy crops 'SRI' method of water management practices may be introduced in all the privately owned wells, minor irrigation tanks and selected pockets of major and medium projects where there will be no water logging. It was reported that in various 'SRI' trials conducted on the farmers lands, the usage of water got reduced to less than half than the earlier practice. Hence this method can be adopted and water saved wherever the farmer has control on water application to his field. In the case of I.D crops (irrigated dry) sprinkler and drip irrigation may be followed in all places where groundwater is being pumped. This will improve the irrigation efficiency to 75% and 95% respectively.

Gaps in Irrigation Sector

There are four major gaps in irrigation sector which require bridging. The first gap is between irrigation potential created and actually utilized. This aspect is sufficiently taken care, through the existing monitoring system of interdepartmental type in the districts. As this is a well identified gap talked about in various meetings and discussed in detail, there is no further need to reemphasize this. The second gap is fertility status of soils, as it should be according to the project report versus the actual in the field. There is lot of improvement needed to build the fertility status of soils in the command areas, in order to comply with those recommended in the Project Report before sanction to the same is given. For example, when the Project Report would stipulate that the organic carbon content will have to be built up to a level of 0.9% from the existing 0.15%, the soils would still have only 0.2% even after irrigating the land for over a decade. This fertility gap in the soils will have to be bridged and brought to the levels specified in the Project Report in order that higher production levels as envisaged in the Report are achieved. The third gap is with regard to productivity aimed in the Project Report while calculating the benefit cost ratio (justifying the project) and the actual productivity. It is seen that in the case of paddy crop productivity remains at 2.5 tonnes of rice per hectare, even though the project is completed about 10 years back, as against the productivity of 4 tonnes rice per hectare envisaged in the Report. This gap will have to be bridged as early as possible, in order to achieve the results of the project. The fourth gap is pertaining to irrigation efficiency. When irrigation efficiency of 40% is planned and in practice it is only 25% then it amounts to certain areas in the project not getting water. This irrigation efficiency gap will have to be bridged by better agronomic practices as already mentioned and when this is achieved, it is possible to supply water to the tail end areas also. In some cases improper maintenance and inadequate designs may be responsible for not getting water to the tail end. However, in most cases, it is seen that more utilization of water in the upper reaches is responsible for making the tail end ayacut suffer.

Finances for Projects

Finance is a major constraint in achieving Jala Yagnam and this is well recognised. In fact lack of adequate finances was the main reason for the limping progress on irrigation projects during the past two decades. However, the present Government had taken certain bold steps to launch a massive programme requiring nearly one lakh crores. This may be quite formidable at the outset and may perhaps result in despair at a later date when things do not develop in the desired manner. Though there are limitations for expenditure on the irrigation projects, from the State resources, it is not incorrect to depend heavily on grants from Central and other sources. The financial experts had already cautioned regarding the extent to which loans can be taken to avoid debt trap. However, this appears to be the only easy way to bridge the gap since there is also a limitation to the extent of grants that can be obtained from the Central Government. Special financial plans with a mixline of raising bonds, deferred payment of loans, peoples contributions, introduction of water cess will have to be thought of. In other words, persons already getting benefited through irrigation water would form an important source for gathering funds. This would be a rightful choice, since it is not equitable to unduly charge the non-landholding population any more to benefit the land holding population. Though the people who are not directly benefited by irrigation activities will have to be charged to some extent to contribution to the finances (State funds, Central Government funds etc.), there is a limit to which such contributions can be made. It is necessary to formulate new methods for gathering the finances. One method is collections from the beneficiaries as a periodical levy spread over the period of construction of the project. In other words, this amounts to the beneficiaries contributing to the capital cost of the project. There is also limitation to this since about 50% of the land holding population may be small and marginal farmers. In such cases a special device will have to be worked out to see that they get bank loans on the surety of their lands and contribute to this capital participation. This is similar to a farmer getting his capital for digging well and installation of a pump through the bank loan mortgaging his landed property. This method was adopted for financing the Mahatma Gandhi Lift Irrigation Scheme on N.S left canal, about 3 decades back. All innovative measures with regard to mobilizing finances for the projects will have to be thought of. One such method is to tap the share market, as recently done in the case of the 3 Gorges Dam, China. I suggest that a team of experts may be constituted representing bankers, SEBI, share market and recognized economists to suggest innovative ideas to mobilize finances. If adequate steps are not taken, there is a risk of stopping the projects in the midstream, as happened elsewhere in the developing countries (e.g., Africa and Latin America).

2

"Blue Revolution" for Conservation and Optimal Use of Water

CH. VEERAIAH

"WATER" is a prime natural resource and a precious gift of nature to human kind. It hardly needs emphasis to explain that water plays an important role for sustenance of life, development of civilization and culture and uplift of economy in the country. It is a scarce resource, which with Judicious planning of conservation and utilization can provide long lasting benefits on a sustainable basis. The available water, therefore, must inevitably be harnessed for optimal use and must be released after generating maximum benefits with a minimum possible environmental effect. Self-sufficiency in food and energy is an important national goal. India, facing the population explosion, has a critical role to play in increasing food and other agricultural production, promoting rural development and sustaining economic and social gains. The available water resources will, therefore, have to satisfy the increasing demand for irrigated agriculture, which plays on important role in increasing the food and fibre supplies. Irrigation is, therefore, of utmost importance.

India has 2.45 per cent of the world's land resources and 4 per cent of its fresh water resources. Twelve per cent areas of the country receive an average rainfall of less than 610 mm annually and only 8 per cent areas receive more than 2500 mm. Cherrapunji in the eastern part of Meghalaya receives annual rainfall of 11,000 mm while western Rajasthan receives only 100 mm. The variability of the rainfall from month to month and year to year for the same place is very high.

More than 90 % of the annual run-off in peninsular rivers and over 80 per cent of the annual run-off in the Himalayan rivers occurs between June and September. Many of the small rivers totally dry up during the summer. The Indians numbered 1088 millions account for about 17% of the world's population of 6.45 billions in A.D. 2003. India, with 4% of the world's fresh water resources has to support 17% of the total world population. It is evident that a large number of Indians are facing acute water shortage. The number of those with no access to safe water supply and sanitation is unacceptably high. So every one of us has to develop a proper civic sense to do nothing that would spoil the element so vital for our survival.

Utilizable Water Resources in India

National Commission for Integrated Water Resources Development Plan (NCIW RDP) in its report indicated that the total annual water resources of the country as 1953 billion cubic metres (BCM). Out of the availability of 1953 BCM, the Commission has assessed that utilizable water resources will be 1086 BCM, comprising 690 BCM from surface flow and 396 BCM, out of the total replenishable groundwater resources of 432 BCM.

Per Capita Availability

Although, the average water availability in the country remains more or less fixed according to the National Hydrologic cycle, the per capita availability is reducing progressively owing to increase in population. In AD 1991, when the population of the country was about 846 millions, the national average per capita was around 2308 cubic metre per year which has gone down to 1900 cubic metre by 2001, when the population rose to 1027 million. By AD 2050, when the population is expected to rise to 1640 million, per capita availability per year may further go down to about 1190 cubic metre. According to the International Agencies, any situation where per capita availability is less than 1700 cubic metre, is considered as water-stressed and less than 1000 cubic metre is water-scarce. Even though it appears that the National average per capita availability of water by AD 2050 is above the limit of 1000 cubic metre, i.e., water scarce, some of the river basins, namely Cauvery, Pennar, Sabarmati and Mahitapi etc., are already under water-scarce condition and some more will reach the scarcity condition in due course with the rise of population. This shows how scarce the water resources in the country are.

Irrigation Development in India

In the past five decades, tremendous progress has been made in the country in water resource development. Particularly since the beginning of planned era of development from 1951, a number of major and medium projects were taken-up and completed which helped in developing large irrigation potential. The irrigation potential has been increased from 22.6 million hectares (mha) in pre-plan period (1951) to mha by the end of the 9th Five-year Plan (2002) consequently, food grain production has been raised from 51 million tonnes in 1951 to about 208 m tonnes at present. This made the country not only self-reliant in food production but also helped exporting surplus food. The population of India which was 361 millions in 1951, has raised to about 1027 millions by AD 2001. In the past five decades, the food production has been increased to 4 times, while the population increased to about 3 times. The irrigation development compounded with green revolution in the agricultural sector has enabled India to become marginally surplus country from a deficit one in food grains.

Future Water Needs

The United Nations Agencies have estimated that the population of India would reach to about 1640 millions by AD 2050 and stabilize at that mark due to various reasons. At present, the average consumption of food grains per capita per day is about 550 grams. At the International Standard of 750 grams per capita per day, the total requirement of food grains for the growing population of 1640 millions by AD 2050, will be about 450 millions tons. To achieve this target, many more dams will have to be constructed to create additional irrigation potential to use the remaining water resources.

The present utilization of water (AD 2000) for various sectors and the future demand by AD 2050 are shown in the following statement.

Utilization of Water in AD 2000 and AD 2050

Sl. No.		Utilization in AD 2000		Demand by AD 2050	
		Quality (BCM)	Percentage	Quality (BCM)	Percentage
1	Domestic	33	4.4	90	7.8
2	Irrigated	630	84	807	70.2
3	Industrial	30	4	80	7
4	Power Generation	27	3.6	90	7.8
5	Others including Navigation Pisci culture Environment etc	30	4	83	7.2
	TOTAL	750	100	1150	100

Irrigation has traditionally been the largest consumer of water. At present, 84% of the total quality of water is used for irrigation. However, with the growing population, improved economy, increased urbanization, high degree of industrialization and most importantly the need for sustainable environmental and ecological management, there is multiple and serious competition for water from high-value non-agricultural sectors. It is seen from the above table that due to competitive extra demand of water by other sectors, the percentage utilization of water for irrigation sector will be reduced from the present 84% to 70.2% by AD 2050. So our aim should be to increase the agricultural productivity per unit volume of water, per unit of cropping area, per unit time.

Lag in Utilization of Irrigation Potential

One of the major criticism of irrigation sector is about the large gap between the irrigation potential created and its utilization. Out of the irrigation potential of 100 mha created so far, about 87 mha is being utilized which corresponds to 87% utilization of the created assets. With the high cost of construction of projects of about Rs.80,000 to Rs.1,00,000 per acre of irrigated land, such a huge gap of 13% is undesirable and every effort should be made to reduce it to the extent possible.

Andhra Pradesh – Land Potential

- Geographical area - 678 lakh acres
- Cultivable Land - 414 lakh acres
- Percentage of cultivable land - 61per cent

Because of increasing pressure on land for urbanization, industrialization and other development works, there will be no possibility of extension of cultivable area any further.

Water Resources

Sl. No.	River Basin	Yield at 75% Dependability (TMC)	Yield utilized so far (TMC)	Balance yet to be utilized (TMC)
1	**Surface Water Sources**			
a.	GODAVARI	1495	790	705
b.	KRISHNA	811	728	83
c.	PENNAR	98	98	Nil
d.	OTHER 37 BASINS	342	233	109
	TOTAL	2746	1849	897
2	**Groundwater**	1074	458	616
Grand Total		**3820**	**2307**	**1513**

Irrigation Development in Andhra Pradesh

Over the past 5 decades, many major irrigation schemes such as Tungabhadra, Nagarjunasagar, Srisailam, Sriramsagar, Jurala, Somasila etc and many more medium and minor schemes have been compeleted during the plan period. As a consequence, the irrigation potential in the state has been increased considerably as shown in the table on next page.

The irrigation potential which was about 67.60 lakh acres up to the pre-plan period (1951) has been increased to 194.0 lakh acre by the end of the 9th Plan (2002). The ultimate irrigation potential that can be created with all the available surface and groundwater sources, is about 278.30 lakh acres. Further irrigation potential of 84.30 lakh acres is yet to be created by constructing the remaining projects, on-going and under contemplation.

Irrigation Potential in the State

(In Lakh Acres)

Sl No.	Details	Major & Medium Schemes	Minor Schemes		Total
			Surface	Ground-water	
1.	IP created in pre-plan period (1951)	41.40	18.50	7.70	67.60
2.	IP created to the end of 9th plan (2002)	80.00	48.00	66.00	194.00
3.	Ultimate IP with available water sources	123.60	56.80	97.90	278.30

Performance of the Existing Irrigation Systems

Despite major achievements in expanding the irrigated area and in increasing and stabilizing the agricultural production, many major and medium irrigation schemes are performing far below their potential. The utilization of irrigation potential did not keep pace with its creation and there is a sizable gap with regard to the area irrigated, the yields produced and the farm income generated. There is considerable wastage of water due to over-application in top ends of the distribution system resulting in water shortage in the tail-end reaches. The water-use efficiency is estimated to be in the order of 30-35% in the case of traditional surface irrigation systems, against 50-60% in some developed countries. Even a marginal improvement in the efficiency of water-use to about 40-45% will result in saving about 30% volume of water which can be utilized for extending the area by about 30%. At present, about 80 lakh acres of land is being irrigated under the major and medium schemes in the state. By improving the water-use efficiency to 40-45%, an additional area of about 24 lakh acres can be brought under irrigation with the same water that is being utilized at present which otherwise costs about Rs.20,000 crores for construction of new infrastructure.

"Blue Revolution" for Conservation and Optimum Utilization of Water

In the mid-sixties of 20th century, green revolution in the agricultural sector has been introduced in the country. A component in Green Revolution technologies based on fertilizer application and the use of high yield varieties, improved water management, helped boost productivity of crops. Recently, in one of his speeches, the Prime Minister, Dr Manmohan Singh has called upon scientists to bring about a second Green Revolution which would have a special focus on dry land agriculture and would address the needs of small and marginal farmers as the first revolution has no much effect on them. It is well and good. Any number of green revolutions are needed to improve the agricultural productivity to cope up with the future demand of food and fibre of the growing population. But the most unfortunate thing is that nobody talks of "Blue Revolution" that is essential for conservation and optimum utilization of water which is the most important input for agriculture and is becoming scarcer and scarcer day by day. So, it is high time to start "Blue Revolution" in order to conserve water and increase the agricultural productivity to cope up with the future demands of the ever-growing population.

Major part of the poor performance of the irrigation system is attributable to the management deficiencies in inefficient and inequitable delivery of water to the agricultural farms and sub-normal farm development. Some important aspects concerning improved water management, are dealt with in the following paragraphs. Management interventions to improve water productivity in Agricultural Sector.

i) Operational Planning

Timely and equitable distribution of water to the field and adoption of proper application methods have great bearing on water-use efficiency and productivity of crops. Generally, farmers in the head reach having better accessibility, not knowing the implications of excessive water application to their fields, are tempted to draw excess water. They not only suffer by way of low production and damage to their lands but also deprive the farmers in the lower and tail-end reaches of their legitimate share of irrigation supplies. Therefore, it is necessary to ensure equitable, timely and efficient water utilization in the system by organizing irrigation scheduling and coordinated water delivery plan.

An operation plan together with irrigation scheduling is an effective tool to put constraint on the top-end farmers from drawing excessive water and thus ensuring equitable distribution of water among all the farmers. So there is an imperative need to implement operation plans for all the projects in the state in the interest of conservation of scarce water.

ii) Conjunctive Use of Surface and Groundwaters

Development of surface (canal water) irrigation, which has been under practice for centuries in India, has resulted in degradation of land in some of the commands. Gradual rise in water table and related problems of water-logging and soil salinity/alkalinity have surfaced mainly because of lack of effective drainage system, improper water management, inadequate maintenance of distributary system etc. Integrated and coordinated development of surface and groundwater is the most suitable strategy for irrigation development in alluvial soils. Conjunctive use of surface and groundwater will not only increase the irrigation potential but also mitigate the problem of water-logging by keeping down the groundwater level to a safe limit.

As the farmers in the command areas are habituated to get irrigation supplies by inexpensive gravity flow at their fields, they may not be enthusiastic to drill bore-wells and tap groundwater at their expense. So in the interest of conserving surface water and controlling the underground water table without causing damage to the crops, it is advisable that the Government may provide financial assistance to the command area farmers in this regard. This should be made mandatory in all command areas in the interest of conserving canal water to a considerable extent.

iii) Re-use of Irrigation Water

Not the entire water applied on the agricultural farms is consumed by evapo-transpiration or percolation into the soil.

About 15-20% of water applied, flows out of the farms either as surface water or sub-surface flow into the neighbouring drains and from there it reaches a river. The water reaching drains from agricultural farms may be diverted by gravity, wherever feasible, or pumped back and re-used for irrigation. This water diverted for re-use is a boon to the tail-end reaches of the distributory system, which do not receive the designed flows normally.

iv) Improved Methods of Irrigation – Sprinkler and Drip Systems

Improved methods of Irrigation like sprinkler and drip are being recommended for achieving higher irrigation efficiencies.

In sprinkler system, water is conveyed through a network of pipes under pressure and sprinkled on crops as drops forced through nozzles of smaller diameter. Sprinklers tend to irrigate more uniformly than gravity systems and therefore, efficiencies typically average about 70%. As there is negligible percolation into the soil, lot of water is saved in sprinkler system of irrigation. Sprinkler system is particularly effective in sandy and undulating terrain.

In drip irrigation system, a network of porous or perforated piping installed on or below the soil surface, delivers water directly to the Crop roots. This keeps the evaporation and seepage losses extremely low. To sufficiently irrigate the same crop, drip systems may apply 20 to 25% less water to the field than conventional sprinklers and 40 to 60% less than the simple gravity systems. For fruits, vegetables and orchard crops, drip irrigation is found to be more suitable.

These sprinkler and drip systems are more suitable especially in the regions of low rainfall.

v) System of Rice Intensification (SRI)

"Less can produce more" is the motto of the system of rice intensification. It means, with usage of about half the quantity of water that is normally used in the conventional gravity flow system, productivity of Crop of 2 to 3 times can be achieved. As rice crop in the country consumes major share of Irrigation supplies, adoption of SRI can save huge quantities of water to increase the crop yield by 2 to 3 times of the normal system in vogue. A comparative statement of the various items in the SRI system is given below:

Items in the SRI System

Sl. No.	Item	As per the traditional system	As per the SRI
1.	Seedbed area per acre of cropped field	5–10 cents	1 cent
2.	Seeds per acre of cropped field	20 kgs 2 kgs	
3.	Nursery period	25–30 days	8-12 days
4.	Fertilizers	More chemical fertilizers	Minimum or no chemical fertilizers and more organic manure
5.	Watering	Field always under inundation	Soil moisture is maintained, hence saving of water about 50%
6.	Average productivity per acre	2250 kgs	4000 to 7000 kgs.

In the interest of achieving higher yields and conservation of water, the State Government should encourage farmers to adopt System of Rice Intensification in all the project commands. It may also be considered to make this SRI practice to paddy crop mandatory in all the commands in the State.

vi) Volumetric Measurement and Rational Pricing of Water

Water, no doubt, is a gift of nature. But for it to reach a consumer there is a value addition. It is, therefore, very necessary to run water supply systems on commercial principles treating water as an economic good and not a free commodity. Unless the water is metered and a rational price is attached to the protected water supply similar on the lines of power supply, be it for drinking purpose, irrigation or industrial use, it will continue to be looked up on as a more or less free commodity and used wastefully to a great extent. The water rates should meet at least the operation and maintenance charges. Hence, water is to be billed on volumetric basis and collected strictly, to foster the motivation for economy in water use by the consumers. While fixing water rates for irrigation, the support price for the produce should also be taken into consideration.

vii) Renovation of Tanks

Tanks have been traditionally been an important source of irrigation in South India. Proper maintenance has always been the key of reaping the full benefits of this inexpensive source of water for irrigation as well as domestic purposes. But due to deterioration in the status of tank bunds, most of the tanks are frequently breaching even due to normal rains and getting emptied. Hence, the renovation and modernization of tanks by strengthening of bunds, improving of surplussing arrangements, restoring its original capacity and integrating the tanks with major canal systems, wherever feasible, should form one of the strategies of water conservation.

viii) Participatory Irrigation Management (PIM)

The present mindset of a majority of the population is that 'Water is Government's Business'. Unless human conduct towards water changes drastically, technological solutions will be of no much use. It has already been recognized that unless farmer community is involved in an organized way in the operation, management and maintenance of irrigation systems, the objective of increased utilization and production from irrigation commands cannot be realized; and even if realized cannot be sustained in the long run.

Many shortcomings of present irrigation management could be reduced by effectively involving farmers in the irrigation management. Formation of farmers' associations at minor, distributary and project levels offers considerable scope to improve the present situation. In the PIM system, the department is responsible for supply of water at the head of the distributary or minor and below the head. Water Users' Associations (WUAs) would be responsible for distribution, operation, maintenance and management of the secondary and tertiary portions of the distribution network. Within the area of operation of WUAs, the role of the Government would be advisory and limited to the technical assistance to WUAs.

The State of Andhra Pradesh already passed legislation in this regard in 1997 and has been implementing the Act with partial success due to various deficiencies. These deficiencies are to be rectified to achieve full advantage of the participation irrigation management.

ix) Recharging of Groundwater

Groundwater has played a significant role in India's economy. The source has gained importance as a source of drinking water and food security. It is contributing at present about 50% of irrigation water and 80% of water for domestic use in rural areas and 50% of water for urban and industrial areas. Because of the groundwater abstraction structure being under the direct control of the users, groundwater has become the preferred source of water users. Hence, utmost care should be taken to maintain balance between the recharge through rainwater source and exploitation by pumping for various purposes. If properly recharged through the traditional system of watershed management, percolation tanks, etc., the groundwater source will be a boon for the drought-prone areas.

x) Accountability for Irrigation Water

An Irrigation Officer is responsible for rendering accounts for the money he spends on works and other items. Also, there is check on him through pay and accounts system. But the officer is not made accountable for the water, worth hundreds of lakhs of rupees, he draws from the reservoir and supplies to the crop fields. In absence of such accountability, it is not known hwo much water is lost as conveyance loss and operation loss. In the canals, deep percolation loss in the field, surface and sub-surface flow into drains and finally how much water is actually utilized for the crop. If an irrigation officer is made accountable for the receipts of water drawn from a reservoir and the issues he makes to the crop field, including all losses, he pays much attention to regulate canal drawals as per the actual needs of the crop and reduce the losses. Thus, there is much scope to conserve considerable quantities of water which is being wasted now.

Hence, suitable action may have to be taken by the Government in making irrigation officers accountable for the water drawn and supplied by them to the fields during every crop season. This goes a long way in minimizing the losses and improving irrigation efficiency.

By adopting all the above physical, administrative and the managerial interventions, the water productivity in agricultural sector can be improved to a considerable extent in the existing irrigation systems.

Hence, it is opportune time to start **"Blue Revolution"** in the State for conservation and optimal use of Irrigation Supplies.

> "Vision Without Action, is a Day Dream"
> "Action Without Vision, is a Nightmare"
>
> —*Japanese Proverb*

3

Integrated Irrigation Development: Andhra Pradesh

KOLLI NAGESHWARA RAO

On 13-9-2005 G.O. No. 170 has been released by the A.P. State Government to issue administrative permission to extend the Pothireddypadu head regulator and the canals from Srisailam Reserviour to Owk Reserviour. The purpose of this extention is to draw 40,000 cusecs of water from Srisailam Reserviour to supply

15 T.M.C. to Chennai drinking water

29 T.M.C to Telugu Ganga

38 T.M.C. to Galeru-Nagari

19 T.M.C. to S.R.B.C.

101 T.M.C. Total

It created a big hevoic between Rayalaseema, Telangana and Coastal Andhra leaders and in between the command area's farmers of Srisailam, Nagarjunasagar and Krishna Delta. Finally this G.O. has been amended and released as G.O. No.3 to implement in co-ordination with G.O.No.69 and to extend the drawl of water from Pothireddypadu regulator from 40,000 csusecs to 44,000 cusecs. So that 10 T.M.C. water could be supplied to PABR also in drought-prone Ananthapur District. In practice 10 T.M.C. of water will be supplied from Pothireddypadu to K.C. Canal and that 10 T.M.C. which used to be released from Tungabarda Dam to K.C. Canal as per the direction of Bachawat Award will be diverted to PABR.

In deed even in this emended G.O. the water to be drawn from the foreshore of Srisailam Reserviour, such as

40 T.M.C to Handri-Neeva

43.50 T.M.C. to Veligonda

25 T.M.C to Kalvakurthy

30 T.M.C. to SLBC (Madhava Reddy)

5.5 T.M.C. to Hyderabad drinking water

144.00 T.M.C Total

Not included

May not be from Srisailam Reserviour but above Nagarjunasagar from Krishna River

20 T.M.C to Nettampadu

20 T.M.C. to Bhima

40.00 T.M.C Total

All togather 295 T.M.C have to be utilized besides allotted water 17.84 T.M.C. to Jurala and 39.90 T.M.C. to K.C. Canal, from the upstream of Nagarjunasagar from Krishna River.

Out of this

15 T.M.C. to Chennai drinking water

19 T.M.C.to S.R.B.C.

11 T.M.C to Veligonda (Out of 43.5 T.M.C. to Veligonda 11 T.M.C has been allotted from the evaporation water 33 T.M.C of Srisailam Dam)

20 T.M.C to Bhima (This 20 T.M.C. is allotted in 1996 from Krisha Delta to Bhima by A,P, Government presuming to save from Krishna Delta Modernization).

12.50 T.M.C. to S.L.B.C. (which is allotted from Tailend Canals of NSP out of 30 T.M.C. necessary to this project.) 5.5 T.M.C. to Hyderabad Drinking Water

83 T.M.C. Total

This dependable water and the remaining surplus water have to be drawn from the upstream of Nagarjunasagar. To utilize this much water all together 117000 cusecs of water have to be drawn from Krishna River from the upstream of NSP.

When it became difficult to get allotted water also to K.C. Canal, Nagarjunasagar and Krishna Delta after Allmatty and such other projects have.been constructed by the upper states on river Krishna which are being supplied through allotted water how to safeguard the crops under the projects which are being constructed depending on the surplus water of Krishna River is a problem. On the one side some more water to be supplemented to safeguard the crops under these projects and on the other side to compensate the scarcity of water to Nagarjunasagar and Krishna Delta also some other arrangement should be done. To arrange the water to coverup the scarcity to these projects which were allotted dependable water and to supplement water to the projects which are being constructed depending on the surplus water, to both the categories of projects also only way out is to divert the water from Godavari to Krishna where the water is sufficient.

In Krishna basin the water is less and the cultivating lands are more. Where as in Godavari basin the cultivating lands are less and water is more. Hence in 1951 Khosla Committee recommended to transfer approximately 350 T.M.C. of water from Godavari basin to Krishna basin. In 1961 Gulhati Commission also recommended in the same manner. In 1973 and finally in 1980 Bachawat Tribunal recommended to construct Polavaram Project on river Godavari and to transfer 80 T.M.C. water from Polavaram to Krishna Delta.

Dummagudam Project which has been brought out as one among the demands of A.P. Ryotu Sangam at the time of indefinite hunger strike organized before the Assembly from 1999 March 22 demanding to utilize Godavari Water for the irrigation development of mainly Telangana and A.P.

The previous government accepted to construct Dummagudam to supply water for irrigation in Khammam District. The present state government announced to extend it to compensate the scarcity of water in Nagarjunasagar project through supplementing Godavari Flood Water by transferring

135 to 198 T.M.C. Out of this some water may be supplied directly to command area under left canal and some water directly to Nagarjunasagar.

To supplement 36 T.M.C. more to Krishna Delta the State Government started to construct Pulichintala on river Krishna. Pothireddypadu, Polavaram, Pulichintala and Dummagudam these four projects are the four main wheels of the integrated irrigation development cheriot of Andhra Pradesh. If any wheel among these four is punchered or neglected, integrated irrigation development in A.P. will be put in to trouble and there is every chance to erupt animosities between the three regions and in-between the command area's farmers under these projects. Hence it is a must to construct these four projects.

Polavaram

Polavaram Project is being constructed on river Godavari at the village Ramaiahpeta in Polavaram Mandal of West Godavari District

To be created irrigation facility under Polavaram

In Viazg District	1.5 lakh acres
In East Godavari	2.49 lakh acres
In West Godavar	2.58 lakh acres
In Krishna	0.61 Lakh acres
Total	7.18 lakh acres

To Vizag Steel Plant to other Industries and on the way to 540 villages, 25 Lakh population drinking water will be supplied. 960 M.W. Electricity will be produced. 84.70 T.M.C. Water will be transferred to Krishna Delta (out of this 4.70 T.M.C. will be evaporation loss). The live capacity of this project is 75.20 T.M.C. and 305.50 T.M.C. of water could be utilized.

To construct this project there was an agreement between the states, Andhra Pradesh, Chhattishgarh (old M.P) and Orissa at the time of Bachawat Tribunal. Basing on that agreement Bachawat recommended to construct this project. In deed at present these neighbouring states are opposing this project. But because the recommendation of the Bachawat tribunal is supreme these objections may not stop the construction of this project.

The necessity of this project first advanced by Sri Sonti Rama Murthy from 1942 when he was the Chief Secretary of Madras State. Not only Dr. K.L. Rao upheld the necessity of this project but also he was the designer of this project by staying in America for 3 months and taking the Assistance of the Expert Engineers in America. At that time it was called as Ramapadasagar, because it was proposed to construct at the height of 200 feet to utilize approximately 1000 T.M.C. water and at that level the water touches the feet of Sri Rama's idol at Bhadrachalam. At that level the expected submergence was very high and unbearable. Hence finally it was decided to construct this project at the height of 150 feet because it is the level of natural submergence when 36.00 lakhs Cusecs of water flows in the river, may be with long gab.

Out of 80 T.M.C. which will be transferred to Krishna Delta from Polavaram, 45 T.M.C. dependable water could be utilized to stabilize to some extent under the projects in often drought-prone districts like Nalgonda, Mahaboobnagar, Rayalaseema, Prakasam and Nellore Districts. The remaining 35 T.M.C. will be utilized by the upper states in river Krishna as per the agreement.

An other 36 T.M.C. which will be utilized to Krishna Delta through Pulichintala also could be utilized in the above-mentioned drought-prone districts of A.P. The water which will be transferred from Dummagudam to Nagarjunasagar command area and project also could be used in the drought-prone districts as mentioned above. And already 20 T.M.C. has been allotted from Krishna Delta to Bhima. All together from 236 T.M.C. to 299 T.M.C. could be used in drought-prone areas and could be stabilized under all these projects.

960 M.W Electricity which will be produced at Polavaram could be used to most of the lift irrigation projects which will be constructed in Telangana and Rayalaseema. Approximately 2500 M.W. of electricity is necessary to all these projects. It need not be reiterated here again that the Hydro Electricity costs only 0.25 paise per unit, where as Thermal Power costs Rs.2.00 per unit. If Polavaram is not constructed not only the

cheap electricity is not possible to other projects, but to Polavaram lift also we have to seek up to 500 M.W. of costly electricity.

Through these projects when it is going to be stabilized and balanced in most of the drought-prone areas in A.P. some are opposing to all these four projects on some plea. All must know what are those objections? Are they factual or fake? And how to over come these objections and construct these projects?

Objections against Polavaram

1. World Bank

World bank is opposing all major and medium irrigation projects. And gave directions to all the State Governments and the Central Government also in 1997, that the construction of any new major and medium projects will be the last one in priority. First the existing projects should be privatized. Next the on going projects may be completed. And new minor schemes may be taken up.

In deed the A.P. State Government without caring this direction is resorted to construct these projects. Some individuals are arguing that Polavaram is being constructed to develop navigation in the state, because development of navigation is the policy of the World Bank. That is why the state governrment is constructing Polavaram.

Not only in the construction of Polavaram but also in the construction of any other project in A.P. the main direction is not at all navigation, but only irrigation and drinking water. At present whoever is opposing this project on some plea is nothing but supporting World Bank on this issue. The merits and demerits of this statement that when some opposing polavaram by saying that the construction of Polavaram is implementation of the World Bank Direction of navigation it is better to leave it to their integrity or self consciousness.

2. Triabal Issue

Tribal organizations and some others also are saying that the tribals should not be moved from their native places such as hills and vallies. Such tribal areas will be submerged in Polavaram and it should not be constructed.

The Submergible areas and people in Polavaram

In Polavaram Reserviour	110567 Acres
In Canals	24328 Acres
Villages	276 Nos.
Families	44574
Papulation	177275
Submergable Families	
In East Godavari	3472
In West Godavari	6959
In Khamma Dist.	34143
Tribal Families Total	21109
In East Godavari	1853
In West Godavari	2223
In Khammam District	17033

It need not be reiterated here again that most of the tribal societies are being organized with the financial assistance of Multi National Companies which are under the influence of World Bank.

But some of the intellectuals are saying that by keeping the tribals in the hills and vallies it is impossible to develop them. Because the funds allotted to the development of the backward people even in plain areas is reaching the real beneficiaries only 16 paise, out of every one rupee. This has been stated by Rajiv Gandhi in the Parliament. Under these circumstances the funds that are being allotted to tribals also may reach the real beneficiaries very meagerly.

The Supreme Court judge also commented in the Sardar Sarover Project case that if any body says to keep the tribals in the hills means is nothing but obstructing their development. They should be given share in the scientific and social development.

Hence, they should be brought out. They should be paid proper compensation and the Polavaram Project should be constructed.

As per the R & R scheme of the State Government, land to land will be given. To tribals it is compulsory. And to others if the land is available it will be given.

R & R Scheme

Land to Land: To Tribal's Compulsory	
To others if the land is available	
House site	150 meters
To construct the house	Rs. 40,000
To Tribals for shifting	Rs. 15,360
To those who lost the land completely	
750 days wages	Rs. 40,000
To who could save 2.5 acres	
500 days wages	Rs.32,000
To who could save 5 acres	
375 days wages	Rs. 24,000
For shifting of tribals	extra Rs. 32,000
On all items extra to tribals	25 per cent
For the transportation	Rs. 5,000
To cattle shead	Rs. 3,000
Total to a poor tribal family	Rs. 1,43,360

Government announced that this R & R Scheme is liberal, better than central scheme and also better than the R & R schemes of any other state in India.

Some political parties and individuals who are in favour of the construction of all these projects as well Polavaram are demanding that the R & R scheme should be discussed in every village which are submergible. And after taking the opinions of those villagers it should be implemented in co-ordination with their opinions.

They are suggesting

To pay extra to a poor tribal family	Rs. 1,00,000
To others	Rs. 50,000
To construct a house	Rs. 1,00,000

To Tribal in all items	extra 50%
To cattle shead	Rs. 10,000
To Develop the Land to each acre	Rs. 10,000
To invest in agriculture to each acre	Rs. 10,000
To daily wages	Rs. 80
To Transportation Charges	Rs. 10,000

Every submergible tribal family should be provided employment to one in each family.

To compensate land to land besides government lands, private lands also should be acquired, by paying the market rate which the government decides. Private lands should be acquired 5 to 10% depending on the necessity from the beneficiaries under these projects who have got above 2.5 acres of land. The government should follow the direction in solving the problems of submergible people as the beneficiaries will be glad to have their lands under these projects because they may get regular crops and they may not suffer with droughts and value of their lands will be doubled, in future. In the same manner the people who are loosing their properties, lands, and houses also should feel happy with the compensation given by government.

3. The Necessity of CWC Acceptance

The acceptance of CWC is necessary. Then neighbouring states Chhatishgarh and Orissa who accepted at the time of Bachawath Tribunal are opposing now, may be it is political. Even then because it is the recommendation of the Bachawath Tribunal to construct Polavaram at the height of 150 ft. which is supreme there is every scope to CWC to accept.

4. The Permission of Environment and Forest Departments

The permission of environment has been secured. To issue the permission by the forest department the procedure is in process.

So far no project had been constructed in India after taking environment and forest, departments permission in advance. In a process of construction of the projects these permissions used to be secured.

On the construction of Almatti A.P. Government appealed in the Supreme Court to stay the construction on the issue of lacking of environmental permission. Supreme Court din't stayed it on this ground. Hence, all these are flimsy arguments.

Another point also has to be mentioned here that some environmentalists are saying in the submergence of Polavaram the forest area is very limited. When compared with the benefit of that forest area to environment the benefit with Polavaram Project to environment is more. With the water that will be stored in the reserviour, the crops that grows in 7.20 lakh acres of up land areas, 45 T.M.C. that will be transferred to drought-prone areas like South Telangana and Rayalaseema districts etc., the crops those grow there, with dry lands becoming wet, with hundreds of kilometres the water runs in the canals, with all these besides the production of food-grains and other agriculture produce to people, the benefits to environment also is remarkable.

On Alternatives to Polavaram

1. The Lift at Eluru

A canal from Dhavaleshwaram flows to Eluru for irrigation. An other Canal from Vijayawada flows to Eluru with Krishna water for irrigation. Both these canals joins at Eluru. Some are suggesting instead of Polavaram if a lift is arranged at Eluru to Godavari canal the Water may go to Krishna Delta through Krishna canal. Experts said because Krishna canal is down towards Eluru from Vijayawada the water will not flow to Krishna Delta with a lift at Eluru to Godavari canal. Under right canal of Polavaram which has to carry 17500 Cusecs of water is no comparison, with the lift proposal at Eluru. It cannot serve even 1/20 of its purpose.

2. The Reduction of the Height of the Polavaram Dam

The reduction of the height of the Polavaram Project has been proposed by Sri T. Hanumantha Rao (retired Chief Engineer). In his proposal itself he said the design of Polavaram Project and the place are the best if it could be constructed. Because of the opposition from some circles to construct this project due to submergence of considerable tribal population, when it cannot be constructed his proposal to reduce the height may be considered.

As per his proposal the project should be constructed at the height of 135 feet instead of 150 ft. At this reduced height no water flows in to either right or left canals. To utilize the water at this height lifts should be arranged.

An other point is that even at the height of 135 feet also only 25 submergible villages could be saved out of 276 villages. At this height the production of electricity also will be reduced to nominal.

When yearly at average 2500 T.M.C. of water is being wasted in to the sea when in the drought-prone districts of South Telangana and Rayalaseema the farmers are committing suicides is it not necessary to construct Polavaram at 150 feet height to reserve 75 TMC water to use in Rabi season.

In the state as mentioned above to all the lift irrigation projects of drought-prone areas the necessity of electricity is approximately 2500 MW. If Polavaram is constructed 960 MW of cheap electricity could be utilized to all these projects. Otherwise not, only to all these lift projects thermal power which is more costly has to be used, but also it happens to use approximately 500 MW of costly power to Polavaram lift. After investigation by experts from all aspects announced that the construction of Polavaram at the height of 150 feet is a must.

3. *Sabari-Dummagudam Alternative*

Sabari-Dummagudam alternative has been proposed by Sri M. Darma Rao (a retired Chief Engineer). As per this proposal a barrage has to be constructed on river Sabari at the level of 300 feet. A reserviour on Sokileru also should be constructed and the water from Sabari should be transferred to this reserviour. One more barrage on Sabari also should be constructed at the level of 150 ft.

All this water should be utilized to East Godavari and Vizag districts where the water through the left canal of the Polavaram has to be utilized. On this proposal expert committee opined besides technically unpracticable the submergence in A.P. may be less but in Chhatisgarh and Orissa it may be more, for which they will not accept, and the expert committee refused it.

Another proposal by him is that through Dummagudam water could be used to West Godavari and Krishna districts for irrigation and to Krishna Delta. The water which is planned to use through right canal of Polavaram may be compensated with this. But 56 km, tunnel should be drilled as per this proposal which is highly costly and unpracticable. As mentioned above at least we must use 75 TMC water through Polavaram to Rabi crops and the necessity of production of electricity also is essential.

Is Polavaram obstruction to Godavari Delta?

Not only Polavaram is obstruction to Godavari Delta but also it is a safeguard. If the upper states on river Godavari will construct the projects to utilize all the water which was allotted to them, there is every scope to Godavari Delta to face the scarcity of water. Then Polavaram is the only protection to Godavari Delta. Otherwise they may also have to face the same fate of scarcity of water as the Krishna Delta farmers faced for the past 4 years when Allmatti projects etc., were constructed on river Krishna by the upper states, because Polavaram was not constructed.

Until now after using the allotted 263.60 TMC of water in Godavari Delta yearly 10 to 20 TMC remains. After using sufficiently to Godavari Delta every year at average 2500 TMC is going into the sea. From all aspects Polavaram is not at all obstruction to Godavari Delta but a protection.

Pulichintala

Pulichintala Reserviour is being constructed on river Krishna, 85 km, up stream of Prakasam barrage. It's announced capacity is 45 TMC. Out of this 9 TMC is evaporation loss. Thirty-six TMC will be used for irrigation in Krishna Delta. There is no separate irrigation under this project. Because Prakasam barrage is not a reserviour it is a balancing reservriour to Krishna Delta. Even then some are opposing this project on some pleas. One among such is that Pulichintala is useful in Krishna Delta for third crop. Is it a fact?

1. Could Pulichintala supply irrigation water to third corp in Krishna Delta? 13.05 lakh acres is the irrigated land in Krishna Delta. The water allotted to Krishna Delta by Bachawat Award is 181.2 TMC. Out of this 161 TMC is to Khariff crop. When this much water is essential to first crop how 36 TMC which will be supplied through Pulichintala is useful to third crop also? Even to one crop, i.e. to Kharif also only 22.36% it is useful. If transplantation takes place with this water, if there are rains and the water flows through Krishna river then only, the Kharif crop could be grown.

2) There is another propaganda that Polavaram or Pulichintala only one may be sufficient to Krishna Delta. As it has been mentioned above, to Krishna Delta 161 TMC is essential to only crop i.e. khariff. From Polavaram 80 TMC will be supplied. And through Pulichintala 36 TMC will be supplied. All together it is 80 + 36 = 116 TMC. Even then 161 – 116 = 45 TMC is deficit to only one crop. That deficit may be adjusted by following Rational Methods in using the water.

   Recently the irrigation engineers and agricultural scientists proved if 1/3rd of the water which is being used until now to paddy is reduced the yield is more. And if "SRI" Paddy is grown only half of the water which is being used until now is sufficient and the yield is more. By practising all such rational methods it could be adjusted. When one observes all these facts, it is upseared to use the water of Pulichintala to the IIIrd crop of Krishna Delta.

3. Instead of Pulichintala a project below the Joining point of Muneru in Krishna river may be constructed:

   In general a reserviour will be constructed on rivers in-between hills. Because the expenditure will be less and submergence of cultivating lands and people is also less. If a dam like Pulichintala size has to be constructed in plain areas the expenditure will be five to ten times more than at Pulichintala. The submergence of cultivating lands and people also will be more than

2 to 5 times. Hence, Pulichintala is a proper place to construct a project. The proposal to construct Pulichintala is 130 years age old one. Previously it was planned to construct to use 75 to 150 TMC of water but with the idea to reduce the submergence it is being constructed to the capacity of 45 TMC.

There is one more point also that the height of Pulichintala is 53 metres and the height of Polampalli Dam site on Muneru is 68 metres. Hence the water from Muneru could be diverted to Pulichintala on gravity. That is why without any unnecessary expenditure Pulichintala should be constructed and the water of Muneru also could be utilized through Pulichintala.

4. **Instead of Pulichintala to construct 5 barrages:-** The proposal to construct 5 barrages instead of Pulichintala has been made by Sri T. Hanumantha Rao (a retired Chief Engineer). The live capacity of Prakasam Barrage is 2.3 TMC and could be used 3.071 TMC. The barrages may not be constructed bigger than this. But even if we presume that these barrages may be constructed with more capacity it may be used 5 TMC from each barrage. Through all these 5 barrages it could be used 25 TMC. At Prakasam Barrage the evaporation loss is 4 TMC. If we presume that at each one of these barrages the evaporation loss as only 2 TMC total 10 TMC will be the evaporation loss. Net it could be used only 15 TMC from these 5 barrages. Whereas from Pulichintala 36 TMC could be used besides there is 9 TMC evaporation loss. Hence the proposal of 5 barrages is useless as per the expert opinion.

5. **Is there the necessity of Pulichintala for the meager flow from above Pulichintala:-** Above Pulichintala after allotting to the projects on musy 11.86 TMC remains. Some are raising the doughts to this meager water is there the necessity of Pulichintala with the capacity of 45 TMC? The water of Krishna had been allotted to each state by Bachawat Award taking into consideration the total flow of water on 75% dependability is 2060 TMC. It means

approximately at average every alternative year there are floods in river Krishna. So that flood water could be saved in Pulichintala and could be used in seaon. There is an other scope also to use Pulichintala as more beneficial. In Muneru after allotting to the existing projects 41.89 TMC remains and in Paleru 4.85 TMC remains. All together this 46.74 TMC could be diverted to Pulichintala on gravity as mentioned above. Hence, from all aspects Pulichintala is essential. 36 TMC of Pulichintala water which could be used to Krishna Delta could be saved above Nagarjunasagar and could be used in the drought-prone districts of South Telangana and Rayalaseema.

6. **On Submersion:-** The submersion area in Pulichintala will be reduced from 35580 acres to 29761 acres by constructing safety bunds. Out of this 18032 acres are private *patta* lands. Seven villages will be submerged completely and five will be partial. Reasonable and justifiable compensation should be paid to all the submergible people and this project should be constructed.

Dommagudam

Dommagudam project was brought into the agenda as a demand by Sri Kolli Nageshwar Rao at the time of his indefinite hunger strike started from 22nd March, 1999 demanding the construction of projects on river Godavari to utilize the water particularly to Telangana and in A.P. On 24th March for 6 hours it was discussed in the assembly and adopted a resolution to construct all the projects including Dummaguam on river Godavari.

An authority was framed under the Chairmanship of the Chief Minister as a part of implementation of these demands. The authority published a booklet on 24-5-1999. As per that booklet the strength of century-old Anikut at Dummagudam which was constructed for the purpose of navigation should be tested and strengthened, and the height should be raised at the first stage to supply water to 10000 acres in Khammam district. At second stage the water should be supplied to 30,000 acres. At third stage 52,000 acres should be irrigated, and 400 MW of power also should be produced.

The previous government which implemented the policies of the World Bank, as they have not constructed any major irrigation project, they have not constructed Dummagudam also.

But the present Congress Government announced to construct Dummagudam Project as a part of other projects.

As per the project report of Dummagudam in the first phase the water should be drawn near Kotulakonda from Godavari and it should be supplied for irrigation in Khammam district to 1.30 lakh acres, in Tiruvuru and Nuzvidu constituencies of Krishna district, to 30,000 acres and in Chintalapudi and Denduluru constituencies of West Godavari District to 40,000 acres. In Krishna and West Godavari Districts the water will be supplied mainly in Tammileru basin.

Recently the first phase has been shifted to foreshore of Polavaram and named it as Indira Sagar Lift Scheme and the Chief Minister Dr. Y.S. Rajasekhar Reddy performed land prayer (*bhoomi pujan*).

After it is changed as Indira Sagar Lift Scheme the Rytu Sangam is demanding to extend the supply of water to 2.00 lakhs acres instead of 70,000 acres in Krishna and West Godavari Districts. In this scheme 35,000 acres also included to distribute irrigable lands to submergible tribals in Polavaram Dam in the R & R programme of land to land scheme.

After this phase of Dummagudam is shifted to Polavaram the second stage of Dummagudaem i.e. Pamulapally may be changed as stage one. The government announced a policy that, to all up lands in Khammam district irrigation water should be supplied because the submergence is more under Polavaram Dam in this district.

As it was mentioned above to supplement to the scarcity of water in Nagarjunasagar, to divert 135 TMC to 198 TMC of Godavari Flood Water to Nagarjunasagar also will be implemented through Dummagudam.

Including Dummagudam water the below given water could be used in drought-prone districts.

135 to 198 TMC of Godavari Water transferred to NSP

45 TMC out of 80 TMC transferred from Polavaram to Krishna Delta

36 TMC of Pulichinthala used to Krishna Delta.

20 TMC of Bhima which was allotted from Krishna Delta

236 to 299 TMC total could be used.

This water will be useful to the projects which are often drought-prone districts of South Telangana, Rayalaseema, Praksasam and Nellore districts. Hence, Dummagudam has become one among the integrated irrigation projects of A.P.

When Nagarjunasagar is supplemented with flood water of Godavari through Dummagudam, when through Polavaram and Pulichintala Krishna Delta is stabilized then even 44,000 cusecs are drawn from Pothireddypadu and 117000 cusecs may be drawn from upstream of Nagarjunasagar in Krishna river there will not be any problem. This is a balanced scheme. And this is useful to the integrated irrigation development of A.P. such an ideal scheme is being opposed by some individuals and some political parties on some plea.

The below given are the causes said by those who are opposing Dummagudam:

If the Godavari Water is shifted to Nagarjunsagar through Domaguddam it is a loss to all North Telangana Districts. Is it a fact?

In Godavari the dependable water is 3,000 TMC, with flood water it is 4000 TMC. In 1980 Bachawat Tribunal distributed to A.P. 1480 TMC. Out of this so far A.P. is using 720 TMC only. In the neighbouring states also in Godavari basin the cultivating lands are less and hills and forest areas are more. That is why the use of water for irrigation in those states also is less. Hence dependable and flood water all together yearly at average 2500 TMC is going in to the sea.

In Krishna basin the cultivating lands are more and the water is less. Hence the Khosla Committee in 1951 recommended to transfer 350 TMC of Godavari Water into Krishna basin. In 1961 Gulhati Commission also said the same thing. Finally Bachawat Tribunal recommended to transfer 80

TMC water from Polavaram to Krishna Delta. Even then we could not construct this project so far.

One point should be considered here that to all North Telangana districts, to some extent Godavari water was allotted as per Bachawat Award. Because Godavari is at lower level and the lands of Telangana are at higher level without lifts Godavari water cannot be utilized to Telangana lands. From Sriramsagar the water could be used through gravity. But the water is less in that part of Godavari. The water is plenty in Godavari after the confluence of pranahita and Indravati. in to Godavari. There it is not possible to use water through gravity. Inchampally is a dreamy and ideal project in the minds of Telangana people. Bachawat Tribunal also spent so much time in bringing the agreement in between the raiperian states to construct Inchampally. If this project is constructed 1.57 lakh acres will be irrigated and 2.39 lakh acres will be submerged. This submergence also 91,000 acres is in A.P., where as 1.48 lakh acres is in neighbouring states. At present they are not accepting to construct this project who had accepted before Bachawat Tribunal. That is why to compensate Inchampally, Gangaram (Chokkarao) lift scheme is being constructed.

Pranahita-Chevella lift scheme is a big and ideal lift scheme not only in Andhra Pradesh but also in India. 160 TMC water may be utilized through this scheme. The estimated cost of this project is Rs. 10,000 crores. And proposed irrigation is 12 lakh acres. This project is accepted to construct recently and it is under investigation.

Second stage of Sriram Sagar and Flood Flow Canal etc. are being constructed. It is also announced to construct Inchampally with reduced height to use as a lift scheme. Through all these projects the government announced to supply necessary irrigation water to North Telangana districts also.

The water which will be transferred from Godavari to Krishna basin approximately half of the water will be used in South Telangana Districts which are often drought-prone. The government is announcing with all facts that through these projectd on Godavari most of the lands in Telangaana will be irrigated. Total estimated expenditure on the projects in the state is Rs.93,278 crores. In Coastal Andhra Rs. 18,340.53 crores, in Rayalaseema it is Rs. 11,170.33 crores. In Telangana it is Rs.63333.18 cores. The expected irrigation to be created in the state is 73.16 lakh acres. And 22.41 lakh acres will be stabilized. In Costal Andhra through 19 projects it is 27.92 lakh acres. In Rayalaseema through 10 projects it is 10.87 lakh acres. In Telangana through 22 projects it is 34.37 lakh acres. If it is studied and observed it seems that the state government gave all importance to construct Telangana projects besides constructing the necessary project in all over the state.

In practice in the construction of some project it seems there is some delay. The government is saying for example Dummagudam announced to the construct recently. Particularly Pranahita-Chevella is announced very recently. For investigation of any project sometime is essential. They are saying that they are constructing Gangaram, Yellampally, S.L.B.C., Kalwakurthy, Nettampadu, Bhima, second stage of SRSP and flood flow canal projects etc. The statement of the government seems to be factual. But even then taking into consideration of the historical backwardness of Telangana, investigation of Dummagudam and Pranahita-Chevella, projects should be completed on war footing. The projects of backward areas such as Telangana and Rayalaseema should be constructed on war footing.

In the neighbouring state Karnataka there may be serious political differences, but they have constructed Almatti Dam without exposing to outside. In A.P. some are obstructing the construction of the projects only from political angle, which is harmful to the development of our state.

At present the tribunal is in sitting on the disputes of Krishna water. Already Karnataka complained against 11 projects of A.P., which are in construction. And also it complained and demanded a share of water in river Krishna for the water which will be used by shifting from Godavari to Nagarjunasagar as they had got a share in the water which will be transferred from Polavaram to Krishna Delta. If it happens it is a big loss to our state.

There may be the acts of transperency. Even then in every family, every body's life, in every state and in every nation there will be some secretes. If such issues are exposed to the public there will be un-repairable loss to the state as well to the nation. Keeping in mind all the experiences that how Andhra area was exploited when it was in Madras State and how Telangana was exploited and kept backward in Nizam State and should cooperate in the development of A.P. and in construction of the projects which are the major contributors in development of the state.

Above all the people must be alert. The people must think and be united above any political difference and support the construction of the irrigation projects in A.P. which are the backbones for the development of A.P. The suicides of the farmers are more in drought-prone areas and less under project areas. Hence, through the construction of these projects the suicides of the farmers could be controlled to some extent. The future of the state will be flourished.

4

Future of Irrigation Policy in A.P.

N.B. REEDY AND D. PULLA RAO

At present one obvious means which can be need to reduce the dependence on monsoon is to strengthen conjuctive irrigation network in A.P. The sources of water potentially available for use in a given area, consist of local rain fall, water stored in aquifers underground water in streams and rivers, flowing through its territories, and water brought from reservoirs by diverting water flows outside its boundaries. How much is in fact available, or can be made available depends on geography and geology, technology and economic consideration. Access to assured irrigation (both surface and groundwater) can act as a substitute for any deficiency in natural rainfall, besides being a must for crop husbandry in rain deficient track and can result in the adaptation of profitable cropping pattern which cannot be taken up when there is uncertainity with regard to water availability for cultivation. In the present situation the irrigation policy and extention of irrigation facilities to other regions should not effect the old stabilized aycuts under Krishna and Godavari barrages.

This paper aims to examine the following objectives:

1. To examine the growth of irrigation in all three regions since the formation of the State.
2. To analyse the coverage of irrigated area in NSA.
3. To examine the possibility of reducing rice area without effecting the present outturn.

Realising the importance of irrigation in agricultural development of the state, it has been accorded high priority in successive plans by successive governments in A.P.

The major and minor rivers flowing through the state numbering about forty, carry about 18.45 m.h.m. of water into the Bay of Bengal. Of this the Krishna and Godavari rivers account for about 16.0 m.h.m. Even though most of the water goes unutilized by run off into the Bay of Bengal these rivers stand as major irrigation sources in A.P. Several lakes like Kolleru, Ramappa and tanks like 'Pakala', 'Cumbum', Kanigiri, Osmansagar and other minor tanks are also important in serving the state's irrigation needs. In future providing quality of irrigation for changing technologies in both food and non-food crops production, the state should adopt a realistic approach towards irrigation development in an integrated manner on par with ultimate irrigation potential available in the state expressed by various commissions, committees and experts. The Second Irrigation Commission has estimated the ultimate irrigation potential of the State as 103 lakh hectares of which 65 lakh hectares are under major and medium irrigation sources. The National Commission on Agriculture (1976) also estimated the gross area irrigated by 2025 as 102 lakh hectares. The Central Water Commission (1981) estimated that ultimate irrigation potential of the state to be 92 lakh hectares of which 50 lakh hectares are under major and medium sources and 42 lakh hectares under minor sources.

According to these estimates, the state has to decide on the appropriate target for additional irrigation potential that can be created.

Progress of Irrigation

Expenditure

Leaving the previous years (1955-56 to 1989-1990), expenditure on irrigation development, the state has spent Rs.84,900 lakhs, and Rs.8,35,481 lakhs under plan and non-plan revenue expenditures for the period 1990-1991 to 2003-2004 for major and medium irrigation heads. The capital expenditure is Rs.12,10,047 lakhs and Rs. 201 lakhs under plan and non-plan.

The Receipts of Irrigation

The revenue receipts received by the Government under major and medium irrigation during this period stood at

Rs.52,368 lakhs and under minor irrigation Rs.6,496 lakhs. Based on these figures it was estimated that per rupee (100 paise) revenue expenditure on major medium and minor irrigation, the return was only five paise, i.e. 100 : 5.

Irrigation Development under Broad Indicators

The growth of irrigation in Andhra Pradesh can be studied by certain broad indicators. To begin with it examined the behaviour of Gross Irrigated Area (GIA), Net Irrigated Area (NIA) and Area Irrigated more than once (AIMO) on the one hand, the behaviour of GCA, NSA and ASMO on the other. The data for three regions and the state relating to the above variables for the period 1955-56 to 1982-83 (A), and 1983-84 to 2003-2004 (B) were presented in Table 1. To analyse the growth of irrigated area in the state and all the three regions, i.e. Coastal Andhra, Rayalaseema and Telangana, compound growth rates are computed for the above-mentioned variables. It is revealed from the data that NIA increased from 27.67 lakhs hectares during 1955-58 to 41.26 lakh hectores during (trennum) 2000-2003. The GIA increased from 33.14 lakh hectares to 50.73 lakh hectares in there periods. In all the three regions in the State, the NIA and GIA increased in the above periods.

Table 1: Area Irrigated by Region

(In lakh ha)

REGIONS	NIA			GIA		
	1955-58	1980-83	2000-03	1955-58	1980-83	2000-03
Coastal Andhra	16.60	19.60	20.38	19.41	24.39	26.31
Rayalaseema	3.67	4.79	5.97	5.03	6.10	7.42
Telangana	7.40	10.38	14.91	8.70	13.75	17.00
Andhra Pradesh	27.67	34.77	41.26	33.14	44.24	50.73

Source: Statistical Abstracts of A.P. (From 1955-56 to 2004-05) triennium average.

To know the growth of irrigated area in the state compound growth rates were calculated for the periods 'A' and 'B'. There is an increase in irrigated area in the state but compound growth rate reveals that there is positive growth during the period 'A' and 'B' in the State and Regions. But during the period 'B' there is negative growth in Coastal Andhra.

The same trend is revealed in GIA in Table 2. The compound growth rates for NSA, GCA, ASMO are presented in Table 3. The NSA during the period 'A' showed a dismal growth, i.e. 0.01 per cent in Coastal Andhra region and other two regions recorded negative growth rate. During the period 'B' except in Telangana, all other regions showed positive growth in NSA. The growth rate for GCA showed negative growth in Rayalaseema and Telangana for the periods 'A' and 'B' respectively. On the whole, during the period 'B' the GCA recorded 0.12 per cent in the state.

Table 2: Compound Growth Rates of NIA, GIA, AIMO, [1955-56 to 1982-83 (A) 1983-84 to 2003-04 (B)]

Regions	NIA		GIA		AIMO	
	A	B	A	B	A	B
Coastal Andhra	0.97	-0.41	1.13	-0.25	1.85	0.60
Rayalaseema	1.41	1.20	1.28	1.37	1.35	1.43
Telangana	1.31	1.64	2.19	1.83	5.38	2.84
Andhra Pradesh	1.12	0.49	1.46	0.68	2.80	1.41

Source: Statistical Abstracts of A.P. (1955-56 to 2003-2004).

Table 3: Compound Growth Rates of NSA, ASMO, GCA [1955-56 to 1982-83 (A) 1983-84 to 2003-04 (B)]

Regions	NSA		ASMO		GCA	
	A	B	A	B	A	B
Coastal Andhra	0.01	1.92	1.51	1.23	0.28	0.27
Rayalaseema	-0.55	0.18	-0.41	3.36	-0.61	0.41
Telangana	-0.01	-0.58	4.92	2.39	0.26	-0.22
Andhra Pradesh	-0.14	0.10	2.03	1.75	0.06	0.12

Source: Statistical Abstracts of A.P. (1955-56 to 2003-2004).

The compound growth rates for area under different sources were calculated for the period 'A' and 'B'. It is revealed from

Table 4 that the growth of canal irrigation in the State decreased in 'B' period when compared to 'A' period. Among the regions Telangana registered high percentage growth under canal irrigation, 3.94 per cent and 2.87 per cent followed by Rayalaseema 2.70 per cent and 2.72 per cent and in Coastal Andhra 1.19 per cent and 1.21 per cent. During 'B' period all these regions including state, registered low growth rate. The compound growth rate of area under tank irrigation showed negative growth in all these regions. The growth of area under well irrigation showed positive growth in both the periods. But in Coastal Andhra, the percentage growth was lower during 'B' period when compared to 'A' period. The area under other sources registered positive growth in the state. But in Coastal Andhra there is negative growth rate during 'A' period and in Rayalaseema it was negative during 'B' period.

Table 4: Compound Growth Rates of Different Sources of Irrigation [1955-56 to 1982-83 (A) 1983-84 to 2003-04 (B)]

Regions	Canals		Tanks		Wells		Others	
	A	B	A	B	A	B	A	B
Coastal Andhra	1.19	1.21	-0.83	-1.60	5.03	2.70	-0.44	4.03
Rayalaseema	2.70	2.72	-2.02	-3.49	3.53	3.90	0.18	-2.48
Telangana	3.94	2.87	-1.26	-3.56	4.47	5.77	1.46	0.73
Andhra Pradesh	1.65	1.58	-1.13	-2.48	4.33	4.49	0.29	2.23

Source: Statistical Abstracts of A.P. (1955-56 to 2003-2004).

The ratios of NIA/NSA and GIA/GCA are analysed in all the three regions and the state. These ratios indicate the extent of NSA and GCA served by irrigation. It can be seen from the Table 5 that there is an increase in these ratios in 1980-83 (trennium) when compared to 1955-58 (triennium). In 2000-2003 it decreased to 0.2502 from 0.3211 triennium 1980-83). The same trend was recorded in respective regions.

The intensive use of irrigation and cropping intensity are presented in Table 6. The intensity of irrigation increased in Coastal Andhra and in A.P. State in respective periods as shown in the table. In Telangana though there is an increase in intensive use during 1980-83 it decreased in the end period. But in Rayalaseema there was continuous decrease of intensity of irrigation recorded. There was continuous decrease in cropping intensity in all three regions and state.

Table 5: Region-wise Ratios

REGIONS	YEAR	NIA/NSA	GIA/GCA
Coastal Andhra	1955-58	0.4644	0.4652
	1980-83	0.5486	0.5363
	2000-03	0.5399	0.5231
Rayalaseema	1955-58	0.1224	0.1572
	1980-83	0.1849	0.2208
	2000-03	0.0690	0.0834
Telangana	1955-58	0.1584	0.1785
	1980-83	0.2226	0.2670
	2000-03	0.3675	0.3586
Andhra Pradesh	1955-58	0.2456	0.2707
	1980-83	0.3211	0.3549
	2000-03	0.2502	0.2718

Source: Statistical Abstracts of A.P. (1955-56 to 2003-2004).

Table 6: Intensity of Irrigation and Cropping

(Percentage)

Regions	Year	Irrigation	Croping
Coastal Andhra	1955-58	117.26	117.05
	1980-83	124.48	127.34
	2000-03	129.17	133.32
Rayalaseema	1955-58	137.08	106.69
	1980-83	127.29	106.56
	2000-03	124.12	102.70
Telangana	1955-58	116.84	103.64
	1980-83	132.45	110.46
	2000-03	113.99	116.82
Andhra Pradesh	1955-58	119.78	108.70
	1980-83	127.25	115.09
	2000-03	122.95	113.18

Source: Statistical Abstracts of A.P. (1955-56 to 2003-2004).

The foregoing analysis reveals that there is an increase in irrigated area on protective principle (under Crown rule in India) in all three regions and State. But there is no indication of utilization of irrigation water under productive principle. This was evident from Intensity of Cropping and Intensity of Irrigation. Irrigation under canals and tanks showed declining trend. In fact tank irrigated area showed negative growth rate. On the other hand the State's agriculture, to meet its irrigation needs, depends upon groundwater sources but assurance of these sources will depend upon assurance in power supply. Thus the government expenditure (revenue expenditure) to some extent capital expenditure did not serve the A.P. farmer to draw his crop plans free from uncertainity and risk from water scarcity and power shortage. Of course there are other risks like fake seeds, spurious pesticides and fertilizers.

Policy Suggestions

The following are the policy suggestions:

Efficient use of available irrigation waters: Both surface and groundwater, should be utilized in conjuctive manner.

The old *warabandhi*, 'rotation system' and 'turn' procedures should be adopted to protect standing crops in all seasons.

In this regard the Water Users' Associations should function effectively free from political attachments. The forgotten command area development programme should be revived in all river basins in the State. In this regard the silt in the present reservoirs should be cleared. The canals bunds should be cemented to improve carrying capacity and to minimize page loss. Finally the cropping patterns (seasonal crops) should be followed on current monsoon and reservoir water level. In this regard the Water User Associations should take leading step. In this regard there is much scope to reduce rice area without effecting the present outturn by adopting 'SRI' Vari cultivation. The field experiments, and farmers experiences from 'SRI' Vari cultivation reveals that the per acre output, water use, seed use and the absence of inorganic fertilizers reveals that there is much scope to save water and land which can be diverted to other crops. For instance per acre, 16 to 26 per cent water and 0.25 acres land can be saved when compared to the present rice cultivation practices.

Thus the Government can adopt the policy of allocating water resources by helping farmers to adopt the new systems in crop production where ever production is profitable. More over old water bodies and reservoirs, canals and tanks should not be neglected.

REFERENCES

Irrigation Development in A.P. (Miner), 1987-88.

Ramanjaneyulu, 'SRI' Vari Cultivation – My Experiences, *Annadata, December 2005*.

Reddy, N. Bhaskara, *Economics of Conjunctive Irrigation in Canal Command Area*, Anmol Publications, New Delhi. 1992.

Satyanarayana, T.V., G. Subba Rao, D. Sreenivas, K.N.RA Kumar, and S. Malleswari. Rice Cultivation with Less Quantity of Water: A Scientific Analysis, *Annadata,* September 2005.

Second Irrigation Commission Report 1972.

Statistical Abstracts of A.P. (1955-56 To 2004-05).

5

Irrigation Policy – Need for Holistic Approach

P. NARASIMHA RAO AND P. SRINIVAS

Agriculture sector in the state is providing employment to 70 per cent of the 8 crore population directly or indirectly. In recent period, the declining share of agricultural sector in state gross domestic products, its impact on livelihoods of the people living in agricultural sector has become a matter of serious debate. The distress conditions in the rural areas is a matter of serious concern for policy makers and others who are concerned with the sector. The share of agricultural and allied sectors in gross domestic product was 53.4 per cent in 1960-61 and it has come down to 21 per cent in 2003-04 while the proportion of people living on agricultural sector remain same for the past fifty years.

The importance of irrigation for agricultural development has been well-recognized. The role of irrigation in drought proofing cover against fluctuating pattern of rainfall and its adverse effects on agricultural production have been well appreciated. Creation of irrigation infrastructure has been the central in strategies for agricultural development for the State and Central Governments for the past five decades.

Though irrigation expansion has been chosen as the prime engine in the strategy of agricultural development and poverty alleviation, irrigation requirements are growing with growing population. These strategies have failed to meet the growing demand for irrigation, in spite of huge expenditures made in this sector. The irrigation expenditure has been the largest expenditure (both plan and non-plan expenditure) item in the budgets over the years. For the past 50 years, state has spent on an average more than 20 per cent of the total plan expenditure on irrigation sector besides large amounts of non-plan expenditure (Table 1). In recent years the average share of plan expenditure on irrigation in the total plan expenditure is about 30 per cent. However, this huge expenditure under various five year plans (Table 2) does not seems to be effective in terms of their economic return and spread of irrigation.

Table 1: Plan Outlay in Irrigation Sector

(Rs. in crores)

Year	Irrigation Sector Expenditure	Total Plan Expenditure in share of	Total Plan Expenditure Irrigation Sector
1956-57	8.70	25.91	33.6
1960-61	17.75	51.37	34.6
1970-71	28.22	91.70	30.8
1980-81	153.02	471.52	32.5
1982-83	152.56	555.98	27.4
1988-89	329.31	1398.53	24.2
1990-91	314.55	1465.53	21.5
1995-96	652.50	2869.38	22.7
1996-97	689.51	3052.26	22,6
1997-98	796.24	3604.20	22.1
1998-99	931.49	4971.97	18.7
1999-2000	1075.23	4528.53	23.7
2000-01	1305.13	6717.12	19.4
2001-02	1125.68	7968.95	14.1
2002-03	1487.00	8314.87	17.9
2003-04	1701.10	9688.54	17.6
2004-05	4221.60	13291.20	31.8

Source: Andhra Pradesh Annual Plan 2004-05.

Inadequate supply of water for irrigation has been the severe problem for the most of the farmers in the state. There are only very few districts where level of irrigation is reasonably sufficient. In most parts of the state, supply of water for crop cultivation has become a constant concern as the canal irrigation is unequally distributed across the state. As a result of failure of monsoon every year in one part or some parts of the state, farming become unavailable due to regular crop losses. These conditions have created crisis in agricultural sector as a result farmers has resorted to suicide. One of the major causes for this state of conditions is low performance of irrigation sector.

The most important reasons for the low efficiency of this sector that are reported are: (1) High cost of major and medium projects due to their faulty location and designs, (2) escalation of cost of projects due to the delay in completion of projects, (3) neglect of minor and traditional systems and over emphasis on major irrigation and (4) neglect of maintenance of existing systems and high priority to the construction of new projects.

In spite of the huge expenditure made in this sector, it has failed to provide cover against fluctuating pattern of rainfall. The problem has been aggravated by the spate of droughts for the past ten years as the rainfall has been substantially less than normal over the most of the period. The serious of continuous droughts has affected surface and groundwater sources. Its impact can be seen in the prevailing agrarian conditions in the Andhra Pradesh for the past few years. These conditions in irrigation sector along with the general deterioration of conditions in agricultural sector, the pressure for irrigation water from farmers become so strong that it became a political issue in the 2004 election for Legislative Assembly. The Congress party coined its focus on new irrigation projects and carried out election campaign mainly on irrigation projects. After assuming office the Chief Minister Dr. Y.S. Rajasekhara Reddy has announced to complete the construction of 26 new projects with an outlay of Rs.45,000 crores in within five years and it has gone to Rs.90000 crores. Later, the proposal is to create additional irrigation to 65 lakh acres. Given the magnitude of the expenditure in irrigation sector and its role in agricultural development, it is necessary to examine the implications of this expenditure on irrigation sector in terms of its sustainability, spread of irrigation, its effectiveness and more importantly the rational of this focus on major and medium projects. In order to understand the implications of this programme it is necessary to examine the trends in irrigation and problems of irrigation sector in the state.

The sustainability of the irrigation projects (present ongoing and proposed) is based on the ultimate irrigation potential of the state and estimated water resources. Ultimate irrigation potential of the state has been estimated by different committees in different periods. There is wide variation in these estimates. The Second Irrigation Commission (1972) has estimated this as 103 lakh hectares of which 65 lakh hectares under major and medium irrigation and remaining under minor irrigation. At the same time state government has estimated it as 87 lakh hectares. The National Commission on Agriculture (1976) has estimated that the gross area that can be irrigated by 2025 as 102 lakh hectares. The Central Water Commission (1981) estimated that ultimate irrigation potential of the state is 92 lakh hectares, where 50 lakh hectares under major and medium schemes and 42 lakh hectares under minor schemes. As for the engineering experts' estimates the surface and groundwater resources can irrigate 92 lakh hectares. At present (as for the Planning Commission data) the potential utilized by the end of ninth plan is 50.64 lakh hectares out of the potential created 53 lakh hectares. This means that even by taking the lowest estimation of 87 lakh hectares, the additional irrigation that can be possible is for only 34 lakh hectares from all sources. If we consider, the surface water availability in all the river basins together in the state and its utilization for the existing, on going and proposed prospects (Table 2) many river basins come under dark category. The total water availability from all river basins is 2764 TMC, out of it 2011 TMC are allotted to already completed projects and 221 TMC is allotted to the on going projects considering the estimated drinking water need as 81 TMC the water available for the present proposed projects is 461.290 without considering dependable water availability. There is deficiency of 213 TMC after completing the proposed projects without considering dependability. If consider the dependable water availability, there will be a deficiency of 424 TMC after completing the projects (Table 2).

Table 2: Water Utilization in Andhra Pradesh

Sl. No.	Basin	Water availability (T.M.C)	Designed water utilization for completed projects (T.M.C)	Designed water utilization for ongoing projects (T.M.C)	Designed water utilization for proposed projects (T.M.C)	Drinking water utilization (T.M.C)	Total water utilization (TMC)	Balance water (T.M.C)
1	2	3	4	5	6	7	8	9
1.	Bahudha	2,290	1,867	0,000	1500	0,012	3,379	-1,089
2.	Mahendratanaya	4,876	12,552	0,010	0,060	—	12,622	-7,746
3.	Pundi Minor Project	1,444	1,767	0,100	0,015	—	1,882	-0,438
4.	Noupadu Minor Project	4,599	10,022	0,140	—	—	10,162	-5,563
5.	Vasandhara	48,002	21,358	9,000	7,460	0,031	37,849	10,153
6.	Nagavali	48,400	51,560	7,300	11,300	0,454	70,614	-22,214
7.	Peddagedda	2,533	6,829	—	0,020	—	9,849	-4,316
8.	Kandivalasagedda	1,917	1,793	—	—	—	1,793	0,124
9.	Champavathi	8,350	11,292	0,080	4,145	0,310	15,827	-7,477
10.	Gostani	8,616	7,973	—	—	0,055	8,028	0,588
11.	Madhuravaada	1,148	1,867	—	—	—	1,867	-0,719
12.	Narvagedda	1,610	5,517	0,060	—	—	5,577	-3,967
13.	Anakapalli Minor Project	1,235	2,382	0,270	—	—	2,652	-1,417
14.	Sarada	12,596	17,756	1,,573	—	0,090	19,419	-6,913

15.	Varaha	7,218	5,254	1,110	—	—	5,364	1,854
16.	Tandava	10,717	9,655	0,060	—	0.155	9,870	0,847
17.	Pampa	3,415	1,592	—	—	—	1,592	1,823
18.	Suddagedda	3,642	2,063	—	—	—	2,063	1,579
19.	Eleru	23,379	9,684	9,185	0,040	4,930	23,839	-3,460
20.	Godavari	1480,000	755,703	36,804	636,815	45,787	1,476,100	3,891
21.	Errakalva	32,415	12,604	4,103	—	—	16,707	15,706
22.	Tammileru	9,644	12,063	1,360	0,260	—	13,683	-4,039
23.	Ramileru	2.080	0,894	0,028	0,050	—	1,224	0,856
24.	Budameru	10,800	11,973	—	—	—	11,973	-1,173
25.	Krishna	811,000	802,315	92,230	189,380	25,196	1109,121	-298,121
26.	Romperu	6,603	4,477	—	—	—	4,477	2,126
27.	Gundlakamma	20,479	12,807	0,130	12,600	0,127	25,664	-5,185
28.	Musi, Gundlakamma Madhya Minor Drainages	2,125	0,880	—	—	—	0,880	1,245
29.	Musi	5,133	2,757	—	2 882	—	5,639	-0,506
30.	Paleru	5,817	3,985	0,040	—	—	4,025	1,792
31.	Maneru	11,450	14,082	—	0,050	0,047	14,179	-2,729
32.	Kandaleru	4,425	3,906	—	0,100	—	4,006	0,419

(contd.)

Table 2 (concld.)

1	2	3	4	5	6	7	8	9
33.	Pennar	98,649	128,936	58,125	0,750	3,021	196,832	-98,183
34.	Upputeru	16,580	12,243	—	0,050	—	12,293	4,287
35.	Svarnamukhi	17,331	14,284	0,130	0,685	3,021	16,053	1,278
36.	Kaalangi	8,689	5,911	—	—	—	5,911	2,778
37.	Araneyir	6,379	6,576	0,100	—	—	6,678	-0,299
38.	Kortaliyar	5,233	4.199	—	—	—	4,199	1,034
39.	Palar	16,596	16,779	0,310	0,060	0,515	17,664	-1,068
40.	Ponnayar	1,179	0,770	0,100	—	—	0,870	-0,691
Total		2764,504	2011,929	221,600	674,222	81,684	3189,435	-424,931

Source: Chief Engineer of Irrigation, Government of Andhra Pradesh.

This reveals that there is no realistic estimation of water resources available in the state. In this context, state has to decide an appropriate target of irrigation potential that can be sustainable. The strategy for irrigation development in the state has to be designed considering realistic picture of water resources available. Present level of utilization and problems faced so far. The main objective of irrigation development strategies should be efficient use of available water resources and not as a means of receiving and widening elected support.

To evaluate the implications of present irrigation development strategy, it is necessary to examine the problems of irrigation sector for the last five decades in the state. The progress in irrigation to be analyzed through the changes in land use pattern, as it determines its sustainability in the long run. There have been marginal changes in land utilization in the state between 1955-56 and 2004-05 (Table 3). Land use pattern is more or less stable for the last fifty years. The net sown area declined marginally from 112.9 lakh hectares in 1955-56 to 103.27 lakh hectares in 2004-05.

However, cropping intensity increased during the same period. While copping intensity increased in 70s and 80s it is almost stagnant in 90s. After 90s the cropping intensity is very low for a state like Andhra Pradesh when compared to other states. The percentage of gross cropped area that is irrigated increased from 26 per cent in 1955-56 to 40 per cent in 2004-05. The growth in the percentage of gross cropped area that has irrigation facility for a period of fifty years seems to be very low, inspite of huge expenditure under various plans. This points out that large parts of the area in the state need to be provided irrigation facilities.

The net irrigated area increased from 27.47 lakh hectares during 1955-58 to 38.81 lakh hectares in 2004-05, grown at the rate of 0.68 per cent per annum during period. The gross irrigated area increased from 31.99 in 1955-56 to 49.84 lakh hectares in 2004-05, increasing at an average rate of 1.1 per annum.

The development of irrigation in the state during the period accompanied by the change in the relative importance of different sources of irrigation (Table 4). While canal and tank irrigation has been the major source initially. Tube well

Table 3: Net Area Irrigated and Intensity of Irrigation in Andhra Pradesh

(Area in Hectares)

Year	Gross cropped area	Net area sown	Gross irrigated area	Net irrigated area	GIA as %of GCA	NIA as % of NAS	Intensity of irrigation	Intensity of cropping
1955-56	12301889	11290181	3199916	2746984	26.01	24.03	85.84	108.96
1960-61	12751804	11405767	3472138	2909096	27.22	25.50	83.78	111.80
1970-71	13347385	11734771	3313017	4222552	24.82	35.98	127.45	113.74
1980-81	12281695	10738094	3462720	4341561	28.19	40.43	125.38	114.37
1990-91	13192714	11021786	5369677	4305478	40.78	39.06	80.18	119.70
1995-96	13042981	10637213	5304007	4123424	40.66	38.76	77.74	122.62
1996-97	13410147	10834172	5782246	4394919	43.11	40.56	76.00	123.78
1997-98	12134911	9845867	5158081	3944602	42.50	40.06	76.47	123.25
1998-99	13624671	16978139	6092074	4538485	44.71	41.34	74.49	124.11
1999-00	13023038	10610025	5745883	4384124	44.12	41.32	76.30	122.74
2000-01	13545263	11114642	5916147	4527729	43.67	40.73	76.53	122.74
2002-03	13625000	9615000	4536195	3613664	36.29	37.58	79.66	141.71
2003-04	12518000	10118000	4781000	3634000	38.19	35.92	76.01	123.72

Source: Directorate of Economies and Statistics Government of Andhra Pradesh.

irrigation has emerged as the predominant source of irrigation in the later years. Tank irrigation has significantly declined and the area under canal irrigation has increased form 13 lakh hectares in 1955-56 to 17.30 lakh hectares in 2004-05. The area under wells and tube wells has increased from 2.14 lakh hectares to 25.63 lakh hectares in 2004-05. This growth in area under irrigation came from private investment. While canal irrigation is stagnant in coastal Andhra after 80s, there is a drastic shift in the composition of irrigation in Telangana and Rayalaseema. The well irrigation has replaced tank irrigation and become major source of irrigation in both Telangana and Rayalaseema. Even in Coastal Andhra tank irrigation has been replaced by well irrigation. The share of well irrigation in the net irrigated area has been increasing while that of canal irrigation is declining. These trends have to be taken into account while designing the strategy for sustainable irrigation development in the state.

Table 4: Irrigated Area Different Source in Andhra Pradesh

(Area in lakh of ha)

Year	Canal	Tanks	Tube Wells	Other Wells	Other source	Total
1955-96	12.92	10.68	0.0	2.14	1.03	26.75
1960-61	13.31	11.51	0.0	3.57	6.33	34.72
1970-71	20.31	12.85	0.94	6.83	1.30	42.23
1980-81	21.29	9.77	1.91	9.34	1.11	43.42
1990-91	23.11	11.07	15.34	11.59	2.23	59.16
2000-01	22.02	7.98	15.34	11.59	2.23	59.16
2001-02	20.89	6.34	15.75	10.45	2.07	55.49
2002-03	14.52	4.52	16.01	8.78	1.51	45.36
2003-04	15.13	5.38	17.01	8.72	1.57	47.81
2004-05	17.30	5.05	17.50	8.13	1.77	49.87

Source: Directorate of Economics and Statistics Government of Andhra Pradesh.

Despite major plan investments in irrigation, irrigation sector is facing number of problems. An investment of Rs.9342 crores has been spent under various plans (Table 4) on both major and medium (Rs.8735 crores) and on minor (Rs.1004.10

crores) irrigation projects. As a result, the addition potential created is 17.71 lakh hectares under major and medium and 5.9 lakh hectares under minor irrigation projects. The cost of creation of irrigation potential per hectare under major and medium irrigation projects is three times that of minor irrigation. As per the Planning Commission (Ninth Five-year Plan: 1997-2002) per cent of the potential to ultimate potential created under minor irrigation sources is 48. Remarkably, 52 per cent of the ultimate potential is yet to be taped, under minor irrigation resource. The cost of creation of additional potential under minor irrigation projects is low and economical, when compared to major and medium projects. This has not been recognized properly.

The major problem in irrigation sector is unutilized irrigation potential. The optimum utilization of potential created at the cost of the other sectors should be the main aim of the irrigation strategy in the state. But, there is a big gap between the potential created and utilized in the case of major and medium projects. While the potential created under major and medium and minor projects is 53.31 lakh hectares. The net irrigated area has never exceeded 40 lakh hectares, only in two years has exceeded (Table 3). There is gap of 13 lakh hectares between potential created and utilized. This gap has been increasing from 5th Plan onwards. This is a matter of serious concern in view of the magnitude of funds allotted to this sector. This may due to the lack of funds for maintenance and neglect on the part of the government.

The irrigated area under groundwater sources has increased from 2.14 lakh hectares in 1955-56 to 25.63 lakh hectares in 2004-05. Initially, open wells are the sources of groundwater, later tube wells have become major source of groundwater utilization. While the area under bore wells is 17.5 lakh hectares, the area under other wells is 8.13 lakh hectares. The sustainability of these wells as per the reports is at stake. Nearly 50 per cent of the wells are subject to risk and uncertainty which depend upon the groundwater levels. The groundwater situation in some regions is alarming. The problem is more serious in Rayalaseema and some parts of the Telangana. While the growth in the number of wells is increasing, area irrigated under each well is declining as per the government reports. An increasing stress on groundwater resources is reflected. Watershed development is the only option to make these wells sustainable. Earlier some attempts have been made in this direction during TDP regime and later it was given low priority. Since 50 per cent of the present area irrigated in the state depends on the groundwater source and large potential for future development lies on ground source, watershed development, needs priority in the irrigation development strategy.

Tank irrigation occupies a strategic place in state irrigation sector as the functioning of well irrigation to a large extent depends upon the tanks. The development of minor irrigation sources, exploitation of groundwater potential are closely related. These are more than 70000 tanks of which most are under poor condition. The area irrigated under tanks declined from 10.62 lakh hectares to 5.05 lakh hectares in 2004-05. The decline in the tank irrigation over the years is due to government neglect and high priority to the construction of new major and medium projects rather than maintaining the existing traditional systems. The origin of neglect of tank irrigation began with when the large farmers in the command area of tanks has shifted to groundwater sources. Telangana has largest potential under tank irrigation, accounts for 44 per cent of the total tanks in the state followed by Coastal Andhra, Rayalaseema regions with highest dependency on groundwater and lowest number of tanks, created alarming situation in groundwater levels. The increasing cost of providing additional irrigation potential in the major and medium irrigated projects, the environmental and other social impacts like displacement of human population though light on the need for revival of traditional water systems and its development in future strategy. This linkage between the renewal of traditional tanks and groundwater has to be recognized.

Conclusion

In the light of these experiences, a cautious approach is necessary in the present programme of constructing 26 new projects, in view of the water resource potential, poor performance of existing projects and environmental and other considerations. Therefore, a comprehensive policy on irrigation covering modernization of existing systems, tank rehabilitation, development of minor irrigation source with particular emphasis on conservation of groundwater and promotion of optimum and efficient use of groundwater and surface water resources should be prepared for optimum utilization of resources.

The irrigation policies have to be more open and sensitive to the social, environmental and regional imbalances. This is essential because of the gracious regional conflict. The concerns with the problem of displacement people, the impact of degradation in the catchment areas on the sustainability of reservoirs, the relative merits of large verses small projects and poor maintenance, low capacity utilization of existing projects. Moreover, different ways of utilizing water resources and its distribution have different impacts in terms of both productivity and distribution of benefits.

It is necessary to explicitly examine alternative designs and their consequences in terms of displacement, environmental effects, productivity and its distribution. The present practice of evaluating the viability of project proposal on the basis of single design and keeping the whole process strictly within the files of government is to be given serious thought.

The effectiveness of these measures will be greatly enhanced if steps were taken to make process more transparent and open to public scrutiny. There should be transparency in the design of each project, its scope, the proposed and water use. A crediable mechanism should be evolved such as public hearings, though which effected parties and seek clarifications, rouse objections alternative suggestions. The project planners should clarify the doubts and objections before a project proposals considered for appraisal by the government or financial institutions. Political parties should suggest institutionalized mechanisms for ensuring transparency in the on going irrigation policies.

6

Role of Groundwater Markets in Addressing Efficiency and Equity in Irrigation*

M.G. CHANDRAKANTH AND M. SHAMALADEVI

Preamble

The total volume of water on the earth is around 1400 million cubic kilometres, which can cover the earth 3 kilometres deep. However, 97.3 per cent of this water is salt water, while only 2.7 per cent is fresh water, useful for drinking and irrigation. Of this fresh water, 75.2 per cent is frozen in Polar Regions, 2.2 per cent is available as surface water in lakes, rivers, atmosphere and moisture, and 22.6 per cent is available as groundwater (Mukherji, 2005). Thus, there is greater scope for groundwater irrigation than surface water irrigation all over the world and India and Karnataka are no exception to this. Although, the use of groundwater in India has been from time immemorial, the real impetus to its use for irrigation came after independence with the launching of planned development programme. Breakthrough in groundwater irrigation came with the advent of high yielding variety (HYV) technology and modern groundwater extraction technology. These modern technologies are complementary to each other and together result in higher productivity and production. Groundwater irrigation has therefore become the most crucial and fast-growing segment in irrigation sector.

---

*Information System Directorate Performance Overview, 1996, Water and Related Statistics, Central Water Commission, Government of India, New Delhi, p.1.

Groundwater is an endemic scarce resource for irrigation enabling increase in cropping intensity extending to rabi and summer seasons, diversifying cropping pattern and supporting farming systems even. Unlike surface water irrigation, which forces a near uniform crop pattern and not so much of diversification, groundwater promotes diversified crop pattern and virtual diversification in farming systems due to relative flexibility in water management with the farmer. Thus, *prima facie*, a groundwater farmer is relatively more efficient than his surface water counterpart, even with the inherent uncertainty in striking groundwater in irrigation wells. Scope exists largely for groundwater irrigation.

Groundwater Development in India

Although development of groundwater potential took major strides in the past three decades, only one-third of groundwater potential has been developed in India and Karnataka too (GOI, 1995). There are large areas in the State and the country, where substantial reserves of groundwater are yet to be developed and brought to productive use While our recent literature highlight the problems of over-exploitation of groundwater and resultant externalities, which are doubtless in several parts of the county, the major issue in groundwater development ensuring equity and efficiency in the use of groundwater.

Karnataka's economy is predominantly agrarian in nature. About 78 per cent of the cultivated area is totally rain fed depending on the mercy of rain God. In addition, Nearly 97 per cent of the area is covered with hard rocks consisting of Granites, Schists, Gneisses, where recharge is below 10 per cent of the rainfall and groundwater availability is relatively poor, in relation to the alluvial Indo-Gangetic plains in the north. Both rain fed and irrigated agriculture in Karnataka is totally dependent on timely and well-distributed rainfall. Groundwater extraction for irrigation is mainly through dug wells, dug-cum-bore wells and bore wells. The total number of irrigation wells in the state is estimated to be 8,73,322 and the total groundwater draft is 28,02,706 ha meters in 1999 (Department of Mines and Geology, Government of Karnataka, 2004). It is estimated that out of the 380 watersheds in the state, 21 are characterized as 'over-exploited', 16 as 'critical' and only 296 as 'safe' (Department of Mines and Geology, Government of Karnataka, 2004). The nature and properties of the hard rocks restrict groundwater recharge capacities to around 10 per cent. Of late, there has been spurt in the number of bore wells in the hard rock areas of Karnataka state and the rate of well failure is around 0.5 rendering groundwater exploitation risky and capital intensive. In hard rock areas, groundwater scarcity manifests in the form of (i) increased depth of water-table, (ii) decrease in well yield over time and (iii) increase in the proportion of failed wells.

Emergence of Groundwater Markets

Due to increasing rate of irrigation well failure and increasing investment requirement in sinking and operation irrigation wells, the financial capacity of owning and operating such irrigation wells obviously is with those who can afford the risky and bulky investment. Thus, ownership of modern irrigation wells is skewed towards large farmers. In Indo-gangetic plains, skewness in owning irrigation wells is lower than that in hard rock areas of southern peninsula where water-table is low, requiring higher initial investment. The other reasons for skewed ownership of irrigation wells is the skewness in distribution of holdings and fragmentation. A farmer must have captive irrigable command area of a certain minimum size to earn a decent return on investment. Despite the norms of the isolation distance imposed especially while granting long-term institutional loan for drilling of irrigation well/s. These norms do not distinguish between early and latecomers to irrigation and the brunt fall on the late coming small and marginal farmers to groundwater irrigation. Even with such norms, the well failure rate is increasing unabated.

Considering the relatively risky and bulky investment in irrigation wells, groundwater market offers limited economic opportunity for equitable access to groundwater irrigation to resource poor small and marginal farmer buyers for irrigation and domestic purpose.

About 90 per cent of domestic water needs are met by groundwater in India. In recent years in Karnataka, evidence suggests that groundwater markets are slowly developing as niche markets endemic in a few pockets. Groundwater markets for non-agriculture purposes, mainly for domestic use, are developing in the semi-urban fringes meeting the needs of urban and semi-urban areas. The groundwater market for agriculture purpose is highly localized and largely are need based. The groundwater pumped out and sold for agriculture purpose is of much larger volume, but the seller realizes much lower value for groundwater than that sold for non-agriculture purpose. The earliest formal references of water selling can be traced to late sixties.

Groundwater market for agriculture, generate benefits to buyers such as higher and risk-free income flows throughout the year by contributing to increased cropping intensity, changing cropping pattern in favour of high value – low water intensive crops and use of modern farming technologies. Wheat yield per hectare for non-tubewell owners was marginally lower than tubewell owners. Farmers using purchased groundwater obtained higher yield per hectare than tubewell owners. Average yield of wheat and paddy was greater for farmers using their groundwater from wells followed by buyers from farmers owning tubewells, and buyers from state tubewells. Water markets offer an opportunity to small and marginal farmers who own a WEM to increase WEM utilization for what their own land would not permit and thereby to spread its overhead cost over a larger command area. These markets also cause for upward revision of wages and larger employment opportunities throughout the year for farmers and laborers.

Water Markets in India

Mukherji (2004) in her work on the spread and extent of irrigation rental market in India (1976-77 to 1997-98), has used the National Sample Survey Data from 31st, 48th and 54th rounds. The pump rental market implied water market, irrigation services market and hiring in of irrigation services, where farmer owning well and pump hires out or sells water to other farmers. According to the study, in 1976-77, there were 6.5 million pumps, of which 10.4 per cent were rented, irrigating 0.8 million ha (mha) out of the total 17 mha of lift irrigated land. Water market was widespread in eastern region, and here 38 per cent of pumps were rented, accounting for 38 per cent of net area irrigated. But in central and western India, 10.5 per cent was irrigated through water market (Table 1).

In 1976-77, 4.9 per cent of net lift irrigated area was irrigated through water markets, In 1997-98, out of the 64.9 m.ha. net irrigated area, 31 per cent was irrigated through water markets, marking a 20 times increase in area under water markets. The eastern states of India have the highest water market where more than 60 per cent of the rural households participate, followed by northern (41%), western (26%) and southern (23%) states. In India, the electric and diesel pumps are equally distributed. The total value of agricultural output produced in water markets which also includes contribution of other inputs fertilizer, land, labour and capital. Mukherji (2004) calculated this by multiplying area irrigated through pump rental market (ha) with average value of agricultural produce (Rs/ha) in each state. In 1990s, area irrigated through water market generated a whopping value of Rs 150 billion. The study noted an apparent east-west energy-water divide. The eastern states had abundant water and diesel pumps, while the western states had water scarcity and electrical pumps.

Equity Issues in Water Markets

Mukherji's study indicates that about 48 per cent of the pumpsets (irrigation wells) is owned by small farmers (1 to 2 ha) and medium farmers (2 to 4 ha). Out of the country's 82 million farming households, 30 per cent (25 million) reported participating in water markets. Among them, 75 per cent (18.5 ml households) were marginal farmers (Table 2). The water market grew from less than 1 mha in 1976-77 to 20 mha in 1997-98.

Groundwater Market in Karnataka

In what follows we present the results of a study based on primary data from Karnataka regarding groundwater markets. This study explores efficiency and equity in groundwater markets in hard rock areas of peninsular India (in Karnataka) considering farmers using water for irrigating their land and selling groundwater for agriculture purpose (FSWFA, n=30), farmers using water for irrigating their land and also selling for non-agriculture purpose (mainly for silk

Table 1: Net Area Irrigated in Water Market, Own Irrigation, Pump Rented and Percentage of Farmers Participating in Water Market

Sl. No.	State	1976-77 (NSSO 31st round) 1976-77			1997-98 (NSSO 54th round) 1997-98		
		Net area Irrigated Through hired Irrigation Services (mha)	Net area irrigated through own irrigation services (mha)	Percentage of pumps rented services (mha)	Net area irrigated through hired irrigation services (mha)	Net area irrigated through own irrigation services	Percentage of households reporting hiring in irrigation
A	B	C	D	E	F	G	H
1	Andhra Pradesh	0.03	0.74	7.41	1.41	3.73	33.76
2	Karnataka	0.02	0.36	6.57	0.54	3.42	16.56
3	Kerala	0.02	0.17	37.19	0.03	0.43	7.18
4	Tamil Nadu	0.02	1.03	2.41	0.41	1.69	24.64
5	Southern India	0.09	2.3	6.10	2.39	9.27	23.13
6	Bihar	0.46	1.34	31.19	3.40	3.01	68.56
7	Orissa	0.02	0.16	42.78	0.30	0.86	27.24
8	West Bengal	0.12	0.36	50.61	1.59	0.96	67.20
9	Eastern India	0.30	1.86	38.1	5.29	4.83	60.83
10	Haryana	0.04	0.83	4.74	0.58	1.69	38.52
11	Punjab	0.05	1.65	3.07	0.28	2.13	19.26

12	Uttar Pradesh	0.12	6.13	2.57	6.73	6.65	66.52
13	Northern India	0.21	8.61	3.1	7.59	10.47	40.83
14	Gujarat	0.02	0.93	2.35	NA	NA	NA
15	Rajasthan	0.05	1.49	7.99	1.48	5.46	27.79
16	Madhya Pradesh	0.09	0.62	24.26	1.91	6.48	29.55
17	Maharashtra	0.12	0.92	14.78	0.44	3.39	17.69
18	Western and Central India	0.28	3.96	12	3.83	15.33	25.6
19	All India	0.87	16.73	10.37	20.29	44.59	46.33

Source: Aditi Mukherji: The Spread and Extent of Irrigation Rental Market in India, 1976-77 to 1997-98: What Does the National Sample Survey Date Reveal?, *IWMI-TATA water policy research highlight 7*, 2005.

filatures/domestic purpose) (FSWFNA, n=15), and comparing their efficiency of water use with farmers who are not selling/ buying water but using their groundwater on their own farm (FNSW, n=30), and farmers who are buying groundwater for agriculture purpose (FBWFA, n=30). Buyers of water for non-agriculture purpose (BWFNA, n=15) are also studied. This study in EDZ (Eastern Dry Agroclimatic zone) of Karnataka has intensive groundwater market/s (GWM) in Sidlaghatta taluk as reflected in high initial investments on bore wells, high risk of well failure and increasing demand for groundwater for agriculture and non agriculture purposes. This study is aimed to reflect the differential groundwater use efficiencies among farmers with the hypothesis that FSWFNA are relatively more efficient than (i) FSWFA, (ii) FBWFA, and (iii) FNSW.

Table 2: Proportion of Farmers Participating in Water Market in India

Size-class category (ha)	Number of households hiring irrigation services (millions)	Percentage of households hiring irrigation services
Below 0.50	12.4	49.5
00.51-01.00	6.0	24.1
01.01-02.00	4.1	16.6
02.01-04.00	1.8	7.2
04.01-10.00	0.6	2.4
10.01 & above	0.1	0.2
All	24.9	100.0

Source: Aditi Mukherji: The Spread and Extent of Irrigation Rental Market in India, 1976-77 to 1997-98: What Does the National Sample Survey Data Reveal?, *IWMI-TATA water policy research highlight* 7, 2005.

Water Extraction

Bore-well was the predominant groundwater extraction structure in study area as all the 93 functioning wells in the sample, were bore wells. There were no functioning dug wells. Yield of bore well was estimated by recording the number of seconds to fill a bucket (of known volume) of water and then linearly extrapolated. Volume of groundwater sold for agriculture by FSWFA (= volume bought by FBWFA) in acre inches is obtained as (yield of well of farmer selling water in Gallons per hour (GPH) × (frequency of irrigation per month of the buyer) × (duration of the buyer's crop in months)/22611. Volume of water sold for non-agriculture purpose by FSWFNA is obtained as (no. of tankers filled per day) × (tanker capacity in liters) × (no. of days of water sold in a month) × (no. of months where water was sold in a year) × (4.54 liters per gallon)/22611 gallons per acre-inches. For FSWFA total groundwater extracted includes water used on their own farm plus the water sold for agriculture to buyers. For FSWFNA, total water extracted includes water used on their own farm plus the water sold for non-agriculture purposes.

Cost of Production

Largely, farmers in reality paid no power tariff and accordingly no variable costs are incurred by farmers in pumping groundwater other than repairs and maintenance and theoretically there are no charges towards cost of irrigation. However, due to frequent failure of irrigation wells due to cumulative interference externality and other factors, farmers are forced to invest on additional wells. Thus annual cost of irrigation in this study is construed as = Amortized cost of irrigation well + Amortized cost of conveyance + Amortized cost of pump set and electrical installation + annual cost of repairs and maintenance. The amortization is over the average life of irrigation wells. Labour cost of irrigation was merged with cost of other cultural operations. Annual cost of irrigation pertains to each irrigation well and is added across all the wells on the farm. This total cost of irrigation is then appropriated over individual crops according to the volume of groundwater used in each crop. Thus, Cost of irrigation per acre – inch = [Total amortized cost of irrigation on the farm]/[total acre-inches of water used in that year]. The cost of irrigation for each crop is the cost per acre-inch of water multiplied with the number of acre-inches of water applied to each crop. Negative externality (per well) is considered as Amortized cost per functioning wells minus amortized cost per well.

Economic Profile of Farmers in Groundwater Market

Considering FSWA 40 per cent belonged to marginal and small farmers. However, among FSWNA 70 per cent were small farmers. Among FBWFA 70 per cent belonged to marginal and small category. Thus, groundwater sale for agriculture is by both large farmers (60%) and marginal and small farmers (40%). Average size of holding of farmers in groundwater market is below 5 acres, being 2.17 acres for FSWFNA 3.45 acres for FBWFA and 4.71 acres for FSWFA. The hypothesis that groundwater sales are usually by large farmers was not tenable (**Table 3**).

Table 3: Land-holding by Farmers in Water Markets in Sidlaghatta Taluk, Karnataka (2003-04)

Sl. No.	Particulars	FNSW (n=30)	FSWFA (n=30)	FBWFA (n=30)	FSWFNA(n=15)
1	Total land holding size (acres)	6.12 (100)	4.71 (100)	3.45 (100)	2.17 (100)
2	Dry land area (acres)	3.00 (49.00)	2.00 (42.46)	2.87 (83.18)	0.42 (19.35)
3	Area irrigated by irrigation well (acres)	2.23 (36.43)	2.03 (43.09)	0.37 (10.72)	1.60 (73.73)
4	Area under Orchards (mango / eucalyptus)	0.89 (14.54)	0.68 (14.43)	0.21 (6.08)	0.15 (6.91)
5	No. of Marginal farmers (below 2.5 acres)	2 (6.67)	4 (13.34)	8 (26.67)	3 (20.00)
6	No. of Small farmers (2. 5 to 5 acres)	8 (26.67)	8 (26.67)	13 (43.34)	9 (60.00)
7	No. of Large farmers (above 5 acres)	20 (66.66)	18 (60.00)	9 (30.00)	3 (2.00)
8	Total	**30** (100)	**30** (100)	**30** (100)	**15** (100)

Note: Figures in parentheses are percentage to total.

Note: FNSW: farmers not selling water, FSWFA: farmers selling water for agriculture purpose, FBWFA: farmers buying water for agriculture, FSWFNA: farmers selling water for non-agricultural purposes.

FBWFA had 83 per cent of land as dry land. Though FSWFNA had smaller holding, 74 per cent was under irrigation. Groundwater sellers sold water promoting equity in access to groundwater for small farmers and also for large farmers who could not invest on irrigation wells. FSWFNA had smaller holding size of 2.17 acres and invested in irrigation wells, as they were located in urban outskirts and has the advantage of increasing demand for water for non-agriculture purposes.

Features of Irrigation Wells

FBWFA suffered the highest failure rate of wells and eventually resorted to buying groundwater from neighbouring farmer-seller. Though gross irrigated area per well was five acres and average age of wells was 9 to 10 years, across all categories variation existed in area irrigated by wells in each category as functioning wells varied from 8 wells for 30 FBWFA to 46 wells for 30 FNSW. Negative externality per well was the highest for FBWFA (Rs. 4061) while for others it ranged from Rs. 1500 to Rs. 1900. Plight of FBWFA has been reduced by FSWFA resulting in equity through groundwater market. The amortized cost per well (functioning well) ranged from Rs. 13483 (Rs. 15725) to Rs. 15547 (Rs. 17544) for different categories.

Sources of Income in Groundwater Market

Mulberry a hardy low water perennial is the major crop preferred by farmers in groundwater market. FBWFA had 87 per cent of irrigated area under mulberry followed by FSWFA (70%), FSWFNA (64%) and FNSW (56%). Area under other crops such as tomato, chilies, carrot, beetroot and potato, which require relatively more water, was higher for FNSW over other categories of farmers.

For FSWFA, FNSW, FSWFNA, income from irrigated farming ranged from 20 to 30 per cent of the annual income, while for FBWFA, the irrigated farming contributed 15 per cent (**Table 4**). FSWFA realized 17 per cent of income from sale of groundwater, FSWFNA realized 41 per cent. FSWFA sold higher volume of 47 acre inches per farm for agriculture, and realized lower returns (of Rs. 29,069 per farm), compared to FSWFNA who sold half the volume sold by FSWFA (25 acre inches) but realized an income (Rs. 85000) more than twice that of FSWFA. Thus, end use price of groundwater and not so much the volume of water sold, is the key in shaping marginal productivity of groundwater. Groundwater for non-

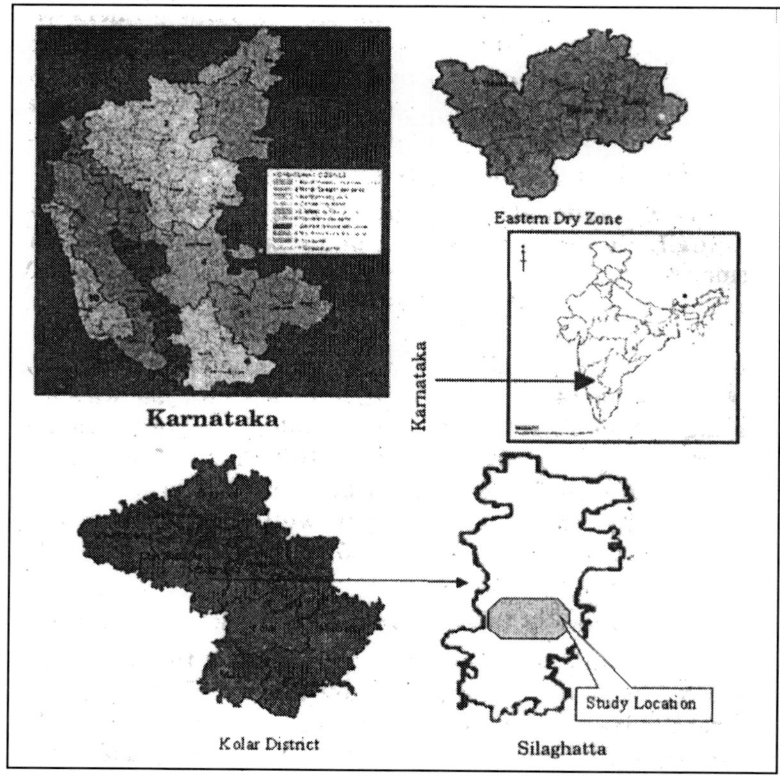

Fig.1: Map of groundwater market area in Karnataka

agriculture purposes like silk filatures and domestic use fetched higher price compared to agriculture purpose. Sale of groundwater by FSWFA added contributed to 17 per cent of the gross returns is equivalent to the contribution by dairy. FBWFA, FNSW and FSWFA derived 30 to 40 per cent of their total returns from sericulture. Dairy is the main source of income for FBWFA, which accounted 46 per cent of net returns.

Economics of Irrigation

The net return per acre of GIA is the highest being Rs. 18345 for FSWFNA followed by Rs. 17009 for FNSW, Rs. 16173 for FSWFA and Rs. 7208 for FBWFA (**Table 5**). FBWFA are relatively more agronomically efficient in using water for

Table 4: Sources of Farm Income in Groundwater Market in Sidlaghatta Taluk, Karnataka (2003-04)

(Net returns in Rs. Per farm per year)

Source of income per farm	FNSW (n=30)	FSWFA (n=30)	FBWFA (n=30)	FSWFNA (n=15)
Size of holding (acres)	6.12	4.71	3.45	2.17
From Farming (irrigated agriculture)	47149 (30.98)	41584 (24.58)	10683 (14.90)	43783 (20.96)
From Dairy	26884 (17.67)	29485 (17.42)	32965 (46.01)	9154 (4.38)
From Sericulture	61426 (40.37)	58691 (34.69)	20431 (28.51)	45500 (21.78)
From Sale of groundwater	—	29069 (17.18) from selling 1396 acre inches for irrigation	—	85000 (40.69) from selling 368.46 acre inches for non-agriculture purpose
From other sources (business, job)	16666 (10.95)	10334 (6.10)	7563 (10.56)	25428 (12.17)
Total annual income per farm	152125 (100)	169163 (100)	71642 (100)	208865 (100)

Note: Figures in parentheses show percentage to total.

Table 5 : Economics of Irrigation in Groundwater Market in Sidlaghatta Taluk, Karnataka (2003-04)

Sl. No.	Particulars	FNSW (n=30)	FSWFA (n=30)	FBWFA (n=30)	FSWFNA (n=15)
1	Cropping intensity (percent)	174.8	201.7	163	244.2
2	Gross irrigated area per farm (acres)	6.38	6.20	3.65	5.54
3	GW Marketing per acre of GIA (acre inches)		7.50 sold	10.77 purchased	5.04 sold
4	Water extracted per well (acre inches)	107.58	127.16	74.00	81.55
5	GW used on per farm basis (acre inches)	164.96	131.53	66.26	36.66
6	GW used per acre of GIA (acre inches)	25.91	21.21	15.41	15.64
7	Amortized cost of irrigation per acre inch of groundwater from owned irrigation well (Rs.)	131	122	182	189
8	Amortized cost per well (Rs.)	14058	15547	13483	15427
9	Net returns per farm (Rs.)	108575	100275	31114	89283
10	Net returns per acre inch of Groundwater used (Rs./acre inch)	658	762	470	1217
11	Net returns per acre of GIA (Rs.)	17009	16173	7208	18345

irrigation than FSWFA, using 15.41acre inches when compared to 21.21 acre inches by FSWFA per acre of gross irrigated area. Both FSWFNA and FBWFA were agronomically the most efficient as they used around 15 acre inches per acre. The net return per acre-inch of groundwater used for irrigation was the highest for FSWFNA, followed by FNSW, FSWFA and FBWFA.

Returns from Sale of Groundwater

Considering the options for the groundwater farmer to use groundwater and sell it as well, FSWFA realized Rs. 762 per acre-inch of groundwater, while they realized Rs. 624 for every acre-inch of groundwater sold, hardly a difference of Rs. 138 per acre-inch (**Table 6**).

Table 6 : Net Returns from Water Sales in Groundwater Market in Sidlaghatta Taluk, Karnataka (2003-04)

Particulars	FSWFA (n=30)	FBWFA (n=30)	FSWFNA (n=15)
Net returns per farm (Rs.)	100275	31114	89283
Net returns per farm including returns from sale of groundwater (Rs.)	129344	-	174283
Net returns (per farm) from selling groundwater per year (Rs.)	29069	-	85000
Net returns per acre inch of water from farming (Rs./acre inch)	563	470	912
Net returns per acre inch of groundwater from farming and sale of groundwater (Rs/acre inch)	726	-	1780
The addition to the net returns per acre inch of groundwater extracted (Rs.)	163	-	868
Net returns per acre inch from using own water in farming (Rs./acre inch)	762	-	1217
Notional price realized per acre inch of groundwater sold (Rs./acre inch)	624*	-	6910**

FSWFA, by selling water, realized almost the same return (Rs. 624) as they could realize by using groundwater on their farm (Rs. 762). Thus, FSWFA realizes an additional Rs. 624 per acre inch purely by selling groundwater and this difference of Rs. 138 per acre inch is not substantial to cover the additional risks and uncertainty in groundwater extraction. Notional price realized by FSWFA and FSWFNA per acre-inch of groundwater is Rs 624 and Rs 6910 respectively. This whopping difference of Rs 6286 is due to end use pricing.

Economics of Water Buying for Irrigation

The cost of purchased water for agriculture forms about 50 per cent of the net return. The FBWFA, are irrigating 4.29 acres using purchased water for every acre of irrigated area from their irrigation well. Their gross irrigated area from purchased water is 3.5 acres, realizing a net return of Rs. 470 per acre inch of purchased water which amounts to a net return of Rs 7208 per acre of gross irrigated area. For FBWFA irrigation cost is two to four times higher than the cost incurred by other categories. Accordingly, unable to bear the risk of well failure and associated externalities, FBWFA felt appropriate to buy water for irrigation. Both FSWFA and FSWFNA, sold about 25 per cent of groundwater extracted by them but realized differential net return due to the price differential obtained, a strong function of the end use.

End-use Price Determines the Pay Off to Groundwater

FSWFNA selling for silk filatures and for domestic purposes, and FSWFA sold around 25 per cent of their groundwater extracted. The estimated price realized by FSWFA is Rs. 624 per acre inch as they sold for irrigation while FSWFNA realized ten times this price, since they sold groundwater for non-agriculture purposes (silk filatures / domestic use) (Fig. 2). The FSWFNA extracted around 45 per cent lower groundwater extracted by FSWFA, but realized 192 per cent higher net return than FSWFA. End use and end use price play a key role in determining volume of groundwater extracted, sold and revenue realized in water market.

Estimated Price of groundwater according to end-use

Groundwater price ranged from $1/3^{rd}$ to $1/4^{th}$ of the gross value of produce cultivated using the purchased groundwater.

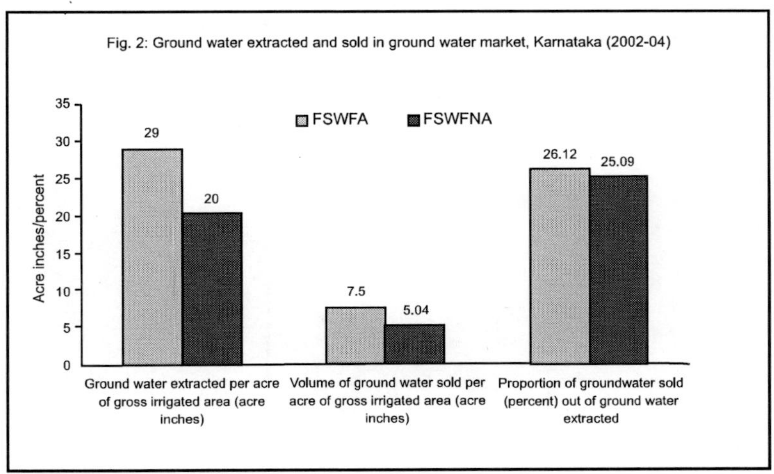

Fig. 2: Ground water extracted and sold in ground water market, Karnataka (2002-04)

In this crop share basis, the estimated price of groundwater in agriculture ranged from Rs. 567 to Rs. 656 per acre inch (**Table 7**). At the amortized cost of Rs. 122 per acre inch of groundwater, the price to amortized cost ratio ranged from 4.65 to 5.37 across different crops. Price of groundwater for non-agriculture purposes, ranged from Rs. 4 to Rs. 6.9 per 100 liters of water for purposes like household use, hotels and silk filatures (**Table 8**).

REFERENCES

Deepak, S.C., 2004, "An economic analysis of groundwater markets in eastern dry zone of Karnataka", Unpublished MSc. (Agri Econ) thesis, Deptt. of Agri. Economics, UAS, GKVK, Bangalore.

Kei, Kajisa and Sakurai Takeshi, 1999, *Price determination under bilateral bargaining with multiple modes of contract: A study of groundwater market in India* (from google.com).

Mukherji, Aditi, The Spread and Extent of Irrigation Rental Market in India, 1976-77 to 1997-98: What Does the National Sample Survey Data Reveal?, *IWMI-TATA water policy research highlight* # 7, 2005.

Saleth, R.M., 1994, *Water institutions in India - Economics, Law and Policy*. Commonwealth Publications, New Delhi.

Shah, T., 1991, Water markets and irrigation development in India. *Indian Journal of Agricultural Economics*, **46**(3): 335-348.

Table 7: Estimated Price of Water in Different Crops in Groundwater Market, Sidlaghatta Taluk, Karnataka (2003-04)

Crop and crop share	Yield of the crop (tonnes/ acre)	Ground water bought and used acre (acre inches)	Estimated value of groundwater used per acre = market value of crop share quantity (Rs.)	Estimated price of groundwater sold for agri-culture in Rs. per acre inch	Amortized cost per acre inch of ground-water	Estimated price-amortized cost ratio
Mulberry (1/3)	8.56	5.4	3420	3420/5.4= 633	122	5.19
Tomato (1/4)	23.30	19	12460	12460/19=656	122	5.37
Potato (1/4)	6.21	12	6800	6800/12=567	122	4.65
Carrot (1/4)	6.06	11	6795	6795/11=617	122	5.06
Beetroot (1/4)	6.82	9.5	6014	6014/9.5=633	122	5.19

Table 8: Price of Groundwater Purchased for Non-agricultural Purposes in Groundwater Market in Urban Fringe Sidlaghatta Town, Karnataka (2003-04)

Groundwater buyers	No. of groundwater buyers in the sample (n=15)	Groundwater purchased in litres per day	Groundwater bill(Rs/day)	Price per 100 litres of ground-water (Rs)	Justification regarding the groundwater price
1. Silk filatures	08 (53.66)	1400	95	6.90	Power tiller driven tankers are the main mode of transporting water with tanker capacity ranging from 1400-1500 litres per tanker
2. Hotels	04 (26.34)	1100	70	6.40	Bullock drawn, cart mounted tankers are the main mode of transport, the tanker capacity ranging from 250 to 375 liters.
3. House holds	03 (20)	400	20	4.00	Bullock drawn, cart mounted tankers are the main mode of transport with tanker capacity ranging from 250 to 375 liters

Note: Price of the tiller mounted tankers ranges from 90 to 100 Rs per load.

7

Irrigation Reforms – Qualitative Change in Irrigation Management

P. SRINIVAS AND R. VENKATA RAO

Andhra Pradesh is leading in introducing reforms in irrigation sector. It has started introducing reforms in 1980s. In 1984, the Andhra Pradesh Government passed the Andhra Pradesh Irrigation and Command Area Development Act, 1984, which authorized the creation of Command Area Development Authorities and Pipe Committees. These Pipe Committees were formed under the CAD Programme for the internal distribution of water below the minor outlet and the maintenance of the micro network. The pipe committees, however, proved to be unsustainable and powerless. The water supply at the minor outlet was not reliable because of lack of coordination between the irrigation department. The pipe committees were too small to have any say in the maintenance of the main system. They had neither clear cut rights and responsibilities nor any means to raise resources. They lasted as long as they had the support of the Command Area Development Department and become non-functional once this support was with drawn.

In 1997, the state embarked on an ambitious programme of reforms in its irrigation sector. As a large agriculture state, irrigation management has been revolutionized by transferring responsibility for the operation and maintenance of irrigation schemes to the water users or farmers. In total 10,292 WUAs has been formed. The reforms witnessed a lot of changes on the role of Irrigation Department is gradually shifting from service provider to facilitator. At the same time, it has witnessed some resistance from irrigation officials by opposing the reforms.

The WUAs and 174 Distributory Committees (DCs) were created through the democratic process of elections. Reforms has made the Irrigation Department accountable to farmer organizations. The irrigation reforms made the water charges increased by 3 times and linked the money collected to the costs of operating and maintenance of the irrigation systems.

The eight years of irrigation reforms is expected to bring revolutionary changes in irrigation sector. The irrigation reform programmes aimed at making irrigation sector accountable to users. Reforms have to go a long way in making the irrigation sector sustainable. The WUAs has to become sustainable by raising funds for operation and maintenance on their own to achieve the goal of reforms.

In this background, the experiences gained so far need to be analysed systematically so as to evolve suitable approaches. Although some of the studies for the country and for Andhra Pradesh is made in this area, most of these are descriptive and deal with experience of the one or two associations, they are confined to a separate projects locate in a different agro-economic region of the state. Most of them are based on secondary information. They are government reports, which concentrate on administrative and procedural aspects. They do not provide any assessment of the working of the farmers associations and the impact of WUA on farm production and productivity. Most of the studies made so far concentrated more on process of formation and less on the impact. There is no comprehensive study on Andhra Pradesh that provides any quantitative information on the impact of water user associations through a standard scientific methodology. All the studies are made when the reform process is in the initial stages. In this backdrop, there is a need to make a comprehensive study on the impact of the irrigate reforms in Andhra Pradesh covering all the agro-climatic regions.

The key objective of irrigation reform programme was to improve the efficiency of irrigation systems. The parameters can be used to measure the efficiency of irrigation are in terms of qualitative and quantitative aspects. This paper is confined to measure the impact of reforms in qualitative terms with respect to distributional, organizational and functional aspects.

Sampling Design and Methodology

Andhra Pradesh is divided into three zones on the basis of agro-climatic conditions and levels of development and socio-economic conditions of the people. The study area is divided into three zones such that there is homogeneity in respect of the above variables. Agro-climactic variables are critical to the success or failure in the performance of an irrigation system. The performance indicators like organizational functions of the institution largely depend upon the socio-economic variables. Similarly the performance indicators like production, productivity, income and area irrigated largely depends upon the agro-climatic conditions. Basing on these variables the study area is divided into three zones such that there is near homogeneity in the above variables with each zone. Although the constraint is that it is not possible absolute homogeneity in all respects. From each of the zone, one major, one medium and minor irrigation systems are selected at random. In major irrigation three WUAs, one from upper head, one from middle and one from tail end, in medium irrigation two WUAs, one from head reach and one from tail end were selected at random. Since, only one WUA is formed for each of minor irrigation systems that WUA is selected from minor irrigation system. Multi-stage random sampling is used at every of stage of selection. From each association, 15 farmers on an average were selected as respondents. The selection of farmers was done by method of stratified random sampling so as to provide representation to all categories of farmers within the project area under study. To get feedback from farmers from different locations of the cropped area, equal number of farmers was selected at random as far as possible from head, middle and tail end. Impact of WUA was analyzed at micro and macro level. At micro level, the impact is analyzed by comparing the agricultural status of the farmers in terms of the above variables as prevailing before formation of association with that after formation, which was taken immediately preceding year of the survey viz. 2004-05 (in some cases and 2005-06 in other cases). At macro-level, the impact of WUAs on agricultural economy of the concerned area was analyzed by comparing the period before and after formation. The present study is concentrated on the impact of WUAs in terms of distributional, organizational and functional aspects which are presented in the rest of the paper.

Equity in Distribution of Irrigation Water

The equity in distribution of irrigation water reflects the effective functioning of WUAs. The response of the farmers towards the equity in distribution of water by WUAs presented in Table 1. The analysis of the study reveals that about 62.5 per cent of the farmers were of the opinion that the water was distributed equally in the command area of WUAs followed by the farmers (21.85%) who did not respond about these functional aspect and the remaining (15.5%) were negatively responded.

The earlier studies on irrigation in Andhra Pradesh indicated that the large category and upper caste farmers have a greater share of water in the government managed irrigation systems. But contrary to this in the WUA managed irrigation systems the water has distributed equally to more people in the command area of the WUA.

By region wise, the study indicates that the distribution of water is assumed to be efficient and equitable in Telangana and Andhra regions than Rayalaseema. It may be due to political interferences in Rayalaseema region which might be effect the water management and distribution among the water users of WUAs.

In the case of projects, the water distribution among minor irrigation systems seems to be more efficient than the major and medium irrigation systems. This reflects that in minor irrigation systems, the WUAs are functioning effectively and this may be due to command area of the WUAs in minor irrigation systems is less than the major and medium irrigation systems. This becomes easy to coordinate all the members of the WUA in an effective way by the Presidents.

Conflict Management after Formation of WUAs

One of the main objectives of the formation of Water Users Associations is to minimize or eliminate the disputes among the farmers in the distribution of water in different reaches of command area of WUA. The response of the farmers towards the disputes after formation of WUAs is given in Table 2. The data reveals that 70 per cent of the farmers were of the opinion that there are no disputes among the WUA members and 22.5 per cent of the farmers confirmed that the disputes are decreased and only 7.4 per cent of the farmers were of the opinion that the disputes were still persisting.

The study also indicates that the level of disputes in the major irrigation systems is low (33.4 per cent) when compared to the medium and minor irrigation systems. By the above information it can be concluded that the water management in the major irrigation systems is efficient and equitable and the presidents of WUAs in these irrigation systems are more aware of their functions and powers.

By region-wise, the study observed that the level of disputes has decreased significantly after formation of WUAs in Andhra region than the Rayalaseema and Telangana. This reveals that the adequacy of water is prevalent in Andhra region due to efficient management of water by the President of WUA. It can also be observed that the Presidents of WUA in Andhra region were elected unanimously in majority of the WUAs in the study area whereas in Telangana and Rayalaseema region this is less than Andhra region. This shows evidently that the coordination and cooperation of water users to the Presidents towards the effective functioning of WUAs in Andhra region than the other two regions of the State.

Transparency in the Activities of WUAs

Transparency in the activities done by WUAs is one of the key principles of participatory irrigation management. In order to strengthen the confidence and reliability over the functioning of WUAs, various activities undertaken by WUAs have to be informed to all water users in the area of operation. Some of the results obtained in the study area over the transparency of WUAs are discussed here.

Dissemination of Information to Water Users

Widespread information to the water users in the command area about various works undertaken by WUAs is essential to make the sustainability of these institutions. Dissemination of information on different works undertaken by WUAs is given in Table 3. The table reveals that 57 per cent of the farmers in the command area of WUAs have replied that they have been informed in advance by WUAs whereas 43 per cent of farmers felt that they were not informed.

The above information reflects that most of the works undertaken by WUAs are done by the prior consent of the water users of the respective WUA. Majority of the farmers preferred distribution of broachers and regular general body meetings are the means to disseminate the information to the water users. They felt that in the initial stages of formation of WUAs a chunk of amounts were spent on number of rehabilitation and other works. But after the reelections for WUAs the percentage of works undertaken by the WUAs are very low. This reemphasized that the government should have take deliberate steps in this regard.

By region wise, in Andhra region greater number of people complained that they are not receiving adequate information regarding the works undertaken by WUAs whereas the number of people complained is less in Rayalaseema and Telangana region. In case of projects, in medium irrigation projects majority of water users reported that they have been informed in advance about the works taken by WUAs while in major and minor irrigation system this becomes slow. However, this varies by region and in some cases the dissemination of information is well in major and minor irrigation systems also.

Prioritisation of Works undertaken by WUAs

For operation and maintenance of irrigation systems the government has laid down some procedures for undertaking the repair works by the WUAs. According to 1997Act, before undertaking the works it should have conducted a walkthrough survey of the system in the command area of WUA.

The study reveals that 82.3 per cent of the farmers felt that walk through survey was essential to underlying the repair works on the system, the extent to which the funds made available could be utilized properly.One of the important indicators for the effective functioning of WUAs is the quality of works done by them. The response of the farmers towards the quality of works undertaken by WUAs is given in Table 4. The data revealed that majority of the farmers expressed that distinct improvements has taken place in the command area of WUAs after the completion of works undertaken by WUAs. However, they felt that the quality of works was medium and there is a need to improve the quality for the sustainability of the irrigation systems.

A good number of the water users in three regions of the state as well as in all types of projects replied that the quality of works taken up by WUAs is medium and they felt that the government should take appropriate steps to improve the quality. They reported majority of the works taken up by the WUAs were repair of canals followed by formation and raising the height of the bunds and removal of silt and maintenance. The farmers also reported that de-siltation of canals underlying greater accessibility of water to tail end areas when compared to the situation before the formation of WUAs. The number of hours for the access of water to the tail-enders was decreased considerably by ensuring equitable distribution of water in the command area of WUA.

Transparency in the Utilization of Funds

The size of WUA affects the fund allocation, as fund allocations are on per acre basis. Major source of funding is from the government followed by water charges allocated to WUAs. The response of the farmers towards the utilization of funds is given in Table 5. The data shows that 67.4 per cent of the farmers replied that the WUAs have utilized the funds in a precised manner by prioritizing the works through walkthrough survey and the remaining were responded negatively. This clearly indicates that the procedures laid down by government in utilization of funds were strictly followed by WUAs.

By region wise, it is observed that in Telangana, majority of the water users replied that the WUAs have utilized their funds allotted to them in a proper way than the other regions of Andhra and Rayalaseema. This is evident that in Telangana region the procedures laid down by government in utilization of funds is effectively enforced by WUAs.In case of projects, the utilization of funds in minor irrigation systems by the WUAs is efficient in terms of repairing the breached bunds, de-silting of canals despite of low allocations to minor irrigation system, whereas in major and medium irrigation systems, the transparency in utilization of funds is less and this implies that the office bearers of the WUAs in major and medium irrigation systems are engaged in corrupt and dishonest in the utilisation of funds.

Farmers' Participation in Management of Irrigation Systems

Participatory irrigation management turns around the sharing of responsibility in the management of irrigation systems. Various forms of participation in the management of irrigation systems were analyzed in the study area were presented below.

Participation of Farmers in the Election of Office Bearers of WUAs

The participation of farmers in electing the presidents and managing committees of WUAs is reflected the involvement of water users in the area of operation of WUA. The percentage of farmers who used their voting rights in electing WUAs was given in Table 6. By examination of the table, it is revealed that 53 per cent of farmers exercised their voting rights and 25 per cent of the farmers have not used their voting right. The study also indicates that 24 per cent of the WUA Presidents are elected by unanimously and this is prevalent in minor irrigation systems. The involvement of farmers in a large number in electing the office bearers of WUAs may be showed the fact that the farmers are distressed by the performance of irrigation department and shows their desire to manage the system on their own.

Participation of Farmers in Social Audit

Accountability is one of the most important parameters of PIM. The WUAs are accountable to farmers in their command area for providing irrigation services. According to the provisions of APFMIS Act, at the end of every irrigation season the WUAs have to conduct social audit. The participation of farmers towards the auditing of funds utilized the WUAs is given in the Table 7. The data indicates that almost all the water users (98.5 per cent) have the opinion that the social audit was essential along with the financial audit and only 1.5 per cent of the farmers are of the opinion that the audit is not essential. In the case of projects, every member of WUA in medium and minor irrigation systems felt that the audit is essential whereas in major irrigation systems, only four per cent of the farmers of the opinion that the audit was not essential.

Form the above, it can be concluded that whatever the funds received should be audited at the end of the working season by an agency appointed by the government. The performance of WUAs in terms of financial and social audit would help to create confidence and reliability among the water users towards the functioning of these institutions.

Farmers Participation in Collection of Water Charges

One of the principle objectives of introducing PIM was to increase the collection of water charges. The government has intended to make the WUAs as financially self-sufficient by its own resources in the form of water charges and other financial sources. The opinion of the farmers in collection of water charges is presented in the Table 8. The data reveals that nearly 88 per cent of the farmers voluntarily came forward to pay the water charges whenever the revenue officials came for the payment and 9.6 per cent of them paid the water charges only when they are repeatedly contacted for payment and 2.5 per cent of the farmers are not paying the water charges.

By region wise, the study indicates that the percentage of farmers who paid the water charges voluntarily in Telangana region is low when compared to the Andhra and Rayalaseema regions while in the case of projects the water users of medium irrigation projects are more cooperated in the revenue department in collection of water charges than the major and minor irrigation projects. This is evident that the farmers in the command area of medium irrigation projects are getting reliable and assured irrigation compared to major and minor irrigation projects.

From the above, it can be concluded that the devolution of powers regarding collection of water charges by WUAs is assumed to be essential for the self – sufficiency and sustainability of the institution. Further, the farmer opined that if the water is assured and reliable, cent per cent of water charges can be ensured.

Forms of Participation of Farmers in Execution of Works

Participatory irrigation management was introduced in the state to involve the farmers at every stage of management of irrigation systems in the area of operation. Through involving the actual stakeholders in the management irrigation systems, the government has supposed to make the WUAs gradually strong as economically and socially. The different forms of participation by the farmers in the execution of works are presented in the Table 9. From the data, it can be seen that the farmers contribution in the form of cash in the execution of works is less than 5 per cent and the percentage of farmers who are contributed in the form of labour is 32.96 per cent and surprisingly 62.2 per cent of the farmers are not responded about the participation in various works undertaken by WUAs. This clearly indicates that the mandatory 15 per cent contribution in works is not adhered in the entire sample of WUAs. The reason for this is continuous drought situation prevailed in the state and the other reason for the absence is that allocation of funds by the government in last three years is very low and this approach made the farmers almost adamant about the participation in works undertaken by WUAs.

By region-wise the performance of WUAs in terms of contributing voluntary labour is high in Telangana by representing 42.2 per cent and it is followed by Andhra and Rayalaseema region by forming 31 and 25.5 per cent respectively. While the performance in terms of contribution in the form of cash is high in Andhra region by forming 10 per cent whereas it is 3.3 per cent and 1.1 per cent in Rayalaseema and Telangana regions. This is evident from the above that the majority of farmers in Telangana region were small and marginal whereas in Andhra and Rayalaseema region they are less. The absence of farmers in the execution of works in Rayalaseema region is high when compared to Andhra and Telangana regions. This may be due to political interference and prevalence of anti-social groups, which made the people become absentees in the works.

In the case of projects, the people contribution in the form of labour is high in medium irrigation projects whereas in major and minor irrigation projects it is less. As against this, the percentage of farmers who contributed in the form of cash is high in minor irrigation systems when compared to the major and medium irrigation projects.

The performance of farmers in terms of participation in the execution of works is very poor in minor irrigation systems whereas it is less in the major and medium irrigation systems. The reason seems to be that in minor irrigation systems the allocation of funds is insufficient for the operation and maintenance works. This approach of inadequate funds may be indirectly effects the participation of farmers in the execution of works.

Conclusion

From the above analysis, it is clear that the WUA have formed very successfully as institutions for executing activities for improved maintenance and repair of the channels by alleging rulers from government. Their presence has been quite encouraging and effective in case of equitable water distribution. The philosophy of the present policy makers dealing with water has not changed despite the success story of the process of irrigation reforms. Water resources management by stake holder has taken a back seat in the present *Jalayagnam*. Though the basic philosophy of WUA is to transform the planning and implementation of irrigation development programmes to stake holders. There are deviations in the process. For sustainability of the Water User Associations (WUAs), even though adequate ground and the required environment are created, there is a need to look into the weaknesses and remedies there after. More importantly, a regular monitoring mechanism has to be put into operation to initiate corrective measures as and when needed. Training has to be a continuous process to build up the skills and capacities of the WUA to meet the day to day challenges. The final arrangement is for carrying the process of irrigation reforms, which are necessary and inevitable.

Summing up in the words of Dantwala (1947), "Institutions are not built in a day. Their streamlined exterior hardly gives any idea of the toil and sweat invested in the spade-work. The evolution of institutions is not mere history; it is an object lesson for the builders of tomorrow. Trial and error, not omniscience, go to the building of an institution. The journey is as thrilling as the journey's end. Perhaps, there is no end, but a continual process of growth and adjustment. This process of adjustment with concrete situations makes a fascinating study. Institutions cannot lag behind the exigencies of a situation, nor can they shoot ahead of times without causing serious maladjustment. Posterity may smile at the obvious crudeness of yesterday's institutions. Possibly it cannot always view them in historical perspective. A few years hence the apparently perfect institutions of today may be as anachronistic in the context of tomorrow as those of yesterday are in the context of today."

Table 1: Responses of Farmers Towards the Equity in Distribution of Water by WUAs

Response of Farmers	Andhra				Rayalaseema				Telangana				Total
	Major	Medium	Minor	Total	Major	Medium	Minor	Total	Major	Medium	Minor	Total	
Equity in	23	22	13	58	23	16	12	51	36	15	9	60	169
distribution	(51.1)	(73.3)	(86.6)	(64.4)	(51.1)	(53.3)	(80.0)	(56.6)	(80.0)	(50.0)	(60.0)	(6.6)	(62.5)
No equity in	13	6	-	19	10	4	-	14	4	3	2	9	42
distribution	(28.8)	(20.0)	-	(21.1)	(22.2)	(13.3)	-	(15.5)	(8.8)	(10.0)	(13.3)	(10.0)	(15.5)
No response	9	2	2	13	12	10	3	25	5	12	4	21	59
	(20)	(6.6)	(13.3)	(14.4)	(26.6)	(33.3)	(20.0)	(27.7)	(11.1)	(40.0)	(26.6)	(23.3)	(21.85)
Total	45	30	15	90	45	30	15	90	45	30	15	90	270
	(100)	(100)	(100)	(100)	(100)	(100)	(100)	(100)	(100)	(100)	(100)	(100)	(100)

Table 2: Responses of the Farmers Towards the Disputes after Formation of WUAs

Disputes among farmers	Andhra				Rayalaseema				Telangana				Total
	Major	Medium	Minor	Total	Major	Medium	Minor	Total	Major	Medium	Minor	Total	
Increased	2	-	-	2	3	2	-	5	-	-	1	1	8
	(4.4)			(2.2)	(6.6)	(6.6)		(5.5)			(6.7)	(1.1)	(2.9)
Decreased	2	4	2	8	5	6	7	18	27	3	5	35	61
	(4.4)	(13.3)	(13.3)	(8.8)	(11.1)	(20.0)	(46.7)	(20.0)	(60.0)	(10.0)	(33.3)	(38.8)	(22.5)
Remained as it was in past	-	-	-	-	5 (11.1)	4 (13.3)	2 (13.3)	11 (12.2)	1 (2.2)	-	-	1 (1.1)	12 (4.4)
No disputes	41	26	13	80	32	18	6	56	17	27	9	53	189
	(91.1)	(86.6)	(86.7)	(88.8)	(71.1)	(60.0)	(40.0)	(62.2)	(37.7)	(90.0)	(60.0)	(58.8)	(70.0)
Total	45	30	15	90	45	30	15	90	45	30	15	90	270
	(100)	(100)	(100)	(100)	(100)	(100)	(100)	(100)	(100)	(100)	(100)	(100)	(100)

Table 3: Dissemination of Information on Works Undertaken by WUAs

Information	Andhra				Rayalaseema				Telangana				Total
	Major	Medium	Minor	Total	Major	Medium	Minor	Total	Major	Medium	Minor	Total	
Disseminated to farmers	10 (22.2)	17 (56.6)	12 (80.0)	39 (43.3)	35 (77.7)	13 (43.3)	10 (66.7)	58 (64.4)	26 (57.7)	21 (80.0)	9 (60.0)	56 (62.2)	153 (56.6)
Not disseminated to farmers	35 (77.7)	13 (43.3)	3 (20.0)	51 (56.3)	10 (22.2)	17 (56.6)	5 (33.3)	32 (35.5)	19 (42.2)	9 (30.0)	6 (40.0)	34 (37.7)	117 (43.3)
Total	45 (100)	30 (100)	15 (100)	90 (100)	45 (100)	30 (100)	15 (100)	90 (100)	45 (100)	30 (100)	15 (100)	90 (100)	270 (100)

Table 4: Response Towards the Quality of Works Undertaken by WUAs

Quality of Works	Andhra				Rayalaseema				Telangana				Total
	Major	Medium	Minor	Total	Major	Medium	Minor	Total	Major	Medium	Minor	Total	
High	6	5	2	13	6	1	2	9	-	-	1	1	23
	(13.3)	(16.6)	(13.3)	(14.4)	(13.3)	(3.3)	(13.3)	(10.0)			(6.7)	(1.1)	(8.5)
Medium	27	19	11	57	30	23	13	66	43	26	12	81	204
	(60.0)	(63.3)	(73.3)	(63.3)	(66.6)	(76.6)	(86.7)	(73.3)	(95.5)	(86.6)	(80.0)	(90.0)	(75.5)
Low	4	3	-	7	6	3	-	9	1	2	1	4	20
	(8.8)	(10.0)		(7.7)	(13.3)	(10.0)		(10.0)	(2.2)	(6.6)	(6.7)	(4.4)	(7.4)
Can't say	8	3	2	13	3	3	-	6	1	2	1	4	23
	(17.7)	(10.0)	(13.3)	(14.4)	(6.6)	(10.0)		(6.6)	(2.2)	(6.6)	(6.7)	(4.4)	(8.5)
Total	45	30	15	90	45	30	15	90	45	30	15	90	270
	(100)	(100)	(100)	(100)	(100)	(100)	(100)	(100)	(100)	(100)	(100)	(100)	(100)

Table 5: Responses of Farmers Towards the Utilization of Funds

Funds Utilization	Andhra				Rayalaseema				Telangana				Total
	Major	Medium	Minor	Total	Major	Medium	Minor	Total	Major	Medium	Minor	Total	
In Precise Manner	25 (55.5)	17 (56.6)	14 (93.3)	56 (62.2)	33 (73.3)	15 (50.0)	14 (93.3)	62 (68.8)	36 (80.0)	19 (63.3)	9 (60.0)	64 (71.1)	182 (67.4)
Not in precise manner	9 (20.0)	11 (36.6)	-	20 (22.2)	8 (17.7)	4 (13.3)	-	12 (13.3)	6 (13.3)	8 (26.6)	1 (6.7)	15 (16.6)	47 (17.4)
Don't know	11 (24.4)	2 (6.6)	1 (6.7)	14 (15.5)	4 (8.8)	11 (36.6)	1 (6.7)	16 (17.7)	3 (6.6)	3 (10.0)	5 (33.3)	11 (12.2)	41 (15.1)
Total	45 (100)	30 (100)	15 (100)	90 (100)	45 (100)	30 (100)	15 (100)	90 (100)	45 (100)	30 (100)	15 (100)	90 (100)	270 (100)

Table 6: Farmers Who Use Their Voting Power in Electing WUAs

Category	Andhra				Rayalaseema				Telangana				Total
	Major	Medium	Minor	Total	Major	Medium	Minor	Total	Major	Medium	Minor	Total	
Farmers who used their voting power	24 (53.3)	26 (86.6)	-	50 (55.5)	21 (46.6)	17 (56.6)	-	38 (42.2)	31 (68.8)	24 (80.0)	-	55 (61.1)	143 (53.0)
Farmers who did not used their voting power	6 (13.3)	4 (13.3)	-	10 (11.1)	24 (53.6)	13 (43.3)	-	37 (41.1)	14 (31.1)	6 (20.0)	-	20 (22.2)	67 (25.0)
By unanimous	15 (33.3)	-	15 (100)	30 (33.3)	-	-	15 (100)	15 (16.6)	-	-	15 (100)	15 (16.6)	(24.0) (24.0)
Total	45 (100)	30 (100)	15 (100)	90 (100)	45 (100)	30 (100)	15 (100)	90 (100)	45 (100)	30 (100)	15 (100)	90 (100)	270 (100)

Table 7: Response of Farmers Towards the Auditing of Funds

Response Category	Andhra				Rayalaseema				Telangana				Total
	Major	Medium	Minor	Total	Major	Medium	Minor	Total	Major	Medium	Minor	Total	
Audit is essential	44 (97.7)	30 (100.0)	15 (100.0)	89 (98.8)	43 (95.5)	30 (100.0)	15 (100.0)	88 (97.7)	44 (97.7)	30 (100.0)	15 (100.0)	89 (98.8)	266 (98.5)
Audit is not essential	1 (3.3)	-	-	1 (1.1)	2 (4.4)	-	-	2 (2.2)	1 (2.2)	-	-	1 (1.1)	4 (1.4)
Total	45 (100)	30 (100)	15 (100)	90 (100)	45 (100)	30 (100)	15 (100)	90 (100)	45 (100)	30 (100)	15 (100)	90 (100)	270 (100)

Table 8: Opinion of Farmers in Collection of Water Charges

Water Charges	Andhra				Rayalaseema				Telangana				Total
	Major	Medium	Minor	Total	Major	Medium	Minor	Total	Major	Medium	Minor	Total	
Pay voluntarily	38	28	15	81	41	27	13	81	35	28	12	75	237
	(84.4)	(93.3)	(100.0)	(90.0)	(91.1)	(90.0)	(86.7)	(90.0)	(77.7)	(93.3)	(80.0)	(83.3)	(87.7)
Pay on request	2	2	-	4	4	3	1	8	9	2	3	14	26
	(4.4)	(6.6)		(4.4)	(8.8)	(10.0)	(6.7)	(8.8)	(20.0)	(6.6)	(20.0)	(15.5)	(9.6)
Not paying	5	-	-	5	-	-	1	1	1	-	-	1	7
	(11.1)			(5.5)			(6.7)	(1.1)	(2.2)			(1.1)	(2.5)
Total	45	30	15	90	45	30	15	90	45	30	15	90	270
	(100)	(100)	(100)	(100)	(100)	(100)	(100)	(100)	(100)	(100)	(100)	(100)	(100)

Table 9: Forms of Participation of Farmers in WUAs

Nature of Participation	Andhra				Rayalaseema				Telangana				Total
	Major	Medium	Minor	Total	Major	Medium	Minor	Total	Major	Medium	Minor	Total	
Contribution of 15%	5 (11.1)	1 (3.3)	3 (20.0)	9 (10.0)	1 (2.2)	1 (3.3)	1 (6.7)	3 (3.3)	- -	1 (3.3)	-	1 (1.11)	13 (4.8)
Contribution of Labour	17 (37.7)	10 (33.3)	1 (6.7)	28 (31.1)	11 (24.4)	7 (15.5)	5 (33.3)	23 (25.5)	13 (28.8)	19 (63.3)	6 (40.0)	38 (42.2)	89 (82.9)
Not responding	23 (51.1)	19 (63.3)	11 (73.3)	53 (58.8)	33 (73.3)	22 (73.3)	9 (60.0)	64 (71.1)	32 (71.1)	10 (33.3)	9 (60.0)	51 (56.6)	168 (62.2)
Total	45 (100)	30 (100)	15 (100)	90 (100)	45 (100)	30 (100)	15 (100)	90 (100)	45 (100)	30 (100)	15 (100)	90 (100)	270 (100)

8

Transferring Irrigation Management Responsibility in Andhra Pradesh: Performance of the Water Users' Associations

B. CHINNA RAO AND K. MADHUBABU

Background

Andhra Pradesh is one of the river states in South India and is endowed with numerous rivers like Godavari, Krishna, Pennar and Vamsadhara and other minor river basins. The State has a total irrigation potential of 4.80 m.ha. Irrigation and drainage have always been accorded priority in plan allocations by the government. Despite massive investments in the irrigation sector, the irrigated area has shown declining trend in several major commands, due to insufficient allocations for the maintenance of irrigation schemes, poor cost recovery of water charges, limited user involvement, low quality of agriculture etc,. resulting in a gap ayacut[1] of 4.78 lakh hectares. To remedy this situation, Government of Andhra Pradesh has taken the historic decision to transfer management of all irrigation systems to farmers' organizations in January 1996.

In the year 1996-97 several consultations were held with farmers of the major project areas, District Collectors, press, universities, legislators and parliamentarians to evolve a strategy for the constitution of farmers' organizations in the irrigation sector. Farmers in Andhra Pradesh have marginal and small land-holdings ranging from 0.01 to 1.5 hectares and the complexity of irrigation systems varies from, minor irrigation tanks etc., to major irrigated commands. Further the indiscriminate use of water by the head-reach farmers is depriving the same to the tail-enders with water logging and salinity almost being a common phenomenon in most of the irrigation projects. The result of the series of consultations led to the enactment of the Andhra Pradesh Farmers' Management of Irrigation Systems Act, 1997 (APFMIS Act, 1997) embodying the concept of Participatory Irrigation Management. To bring more transparency in the working of the Farmers Organizations the amendments to the Act are brought out through Act 7 of 2003 in April 2003.

Andhra Pradesh's own experiment in water management demonstrates the power of people's participation. Also, the state's own legislation (like APFMIS Acts, 1997 and 2003) in relation to local bodies provides same basis for people's participation. Today, the state is leading in its irrigation reforms in India.

The Problem

Irrigation is a crucial factor in agriculture and there is a crisis in the management of surface irrigation because of the huge investment requirements, project implementation problems, the need and expenses for maintenance, institutional difficulties in distribution and environmental concerns. There is also a crisis in the management of groundwater because of excessive exploitation and inadequate recharge of the water-table in many areas. The technical and economic solutions to these problems are well-known and often simple. But their participative institutional management in the political economy is becoming very difficult and posing serious challenges. A change in irrigation management where by farmers take over the management of operation and maintenance, while government agencies mainly focus on developing and improving the management of the systems have been proposed by irrigation experts. These ideas have led to the promotion of Participatory Irrigation Management (PIM).

Some of the findings reported on this, though still at very initial stage, are quite encouraging. It was reported that the PIM leads to significant increases in the efficiency of water use and the value of irrigated agricultural production. Another significant benefit to farmers reported was considerable saving in time to obtain water. There has also been a more equitable water distribution and therefore reduction in conflicts. This in turn has led to more understanding and goodwill in the farming community. Reduction in the water logged area was also reported in a few cases, since farmers are found to be taking more care and spending money on repair and maintenance. The physical structures are reported to be maintained in good condition and willful damage to the structure is reduced considerably. Reduction in time spent for water distribution, easier conflict resolutions are some of the other positive features reported. These are initial reports from various locations in Andhra Pradesh and require wider and better examination.

These are the results of the studies conducted in various locations in Andhra Pradesh. Most of the studies focused only on a specific aspect of irrigation. They are also subjected to certain methodological limitations. The studies covering comprehensively all the aspects of irrigation covering a wider area are limited. In this paper, an attempt has been made to evaluate the PIM in Andhra Pradesh covering a wider area under three irrigation systems namely major, medium and minor.

II

OBJECTIVES AND APPROACH

The major objectives of the paper are:

i) To examine if the devolution of power to the WUAs has taken place in the state.

ii) To examine if the WUAs have contributed towards regular water supply, efficiency in water use, collection of water charges and operation and maintenance of water delivery systems.

iii) To examine if there is any change in the performance/ pattern of agriculture and well-being seen by the beneficiaries.

iv) Identify constraints in the active implementation of PIM, problems in the coordination between the WUAs and the irrigation agencies, and ways to remove the constraints including training needs and proper organization structure. It will seek to identify parameters of success.

Methodology

This paper makes an initial assessment of the working of Participatory Irrigation Management including the Water User Associations (WUAs) in the state of Andhra Pradesh by selecting a sample of areas irrigated by canals and tanks respectively. Tanks were selected in Chittoor district while canal irrigated areas were selected from command areas of Godavari delta system for major irrigation in East-Godavari district and Tatipudi reservoir for medium irrigation system in Vizianagaram district. Specially, it attempts to find out to what extent Participatory Irrigation Management has contributed to the following areas: efficiency of water use by reducing supply side inefficiencies, increase in agricultural and managerial efficiency, the benefits achieved by Participatory Irrigation Management in resolving head-tail and land based in equity in accessing water and facilitate conflict resolution. Both primary and secondary data are used for the purpose of the study. The primary data are collected from a sample of 135 farmers of different categories, 30 farmers from major irrigation and 45 farmers from medium irrigation of canal irrigated areas and 60 farmers from four Water User Associations under the minor irrigation tanks. Irrigation department and the institutions (nine WUAs) under different irrigation systems have provided the relevant data for the study. The reference year of the study is 2003-04 and data are collected during 2004-05 season.

III

EFFECTIVENESS OF WUAs

Observations from Case Studies of Selected WUAs

As seen from the case studies of selected WUAs under different irrigation systems in Andhra Pradesh, the performance of the WUAs in deltas under major irrigation are in a better position, particularly in solving the major problems infested with the drainage. The WUAs in these delta regions came as a boon to execute essential works and check the system operation and maintenance. Farmers have taken enormous interest in WUAs and their activities, mainly to boost up production levels. Funds for WUAs, DCs and PCs came as a boon to delta regions. Heavy machines were used to desilt main canals, branch canals and distributories and essential structures were also constructed in some places and repaired in many places. This massive work was visible to land owners. All this had facilitated a smooth flow of water and paddy yields were increased in both the seasons.

The WUAs under medium irrigation systems in the state are relatively in small number (around 4% of the total WUAs) have been trying to compete the WUAs under major irrigation. But with limited fund allocation, these WUAs could not attend the long pending irrigation works in their jurisdiction. Inadequate budget allocations for the operation and maintenance of irrigation have led to poor maintenance and unsatisfactory service over the years. The major problem is deficit of laskers (water man) in all WUAs to look after the distribution of water and minimize the wastage of water.

Tank WUAs under minor irrigation constitute 81 per cent of the total WUAs in the State. The overall performance of most minor irrigation tanks is more sensitive to droughts and cyclones due to small size. Their deficient maintenance under the I & CADD has resulted in losses and decline of irrigated areas. Most of the tanks are 100 to 400 years old. They are constrained by siltation in the tank bed and reduction in the inflows even the rainfall is good. As a result, more tanks in Chittoor district have been converted into percolation tanks over the last 10-15 years due to fast depletion of groundwater table and siltation of the tank bed. Gradually farmers have shifted to groundwater usage from the earlier practice of tank irrigation.

It seems, there is discrimination in allocation of funds among the three irrigation systems. The funds provided by Government to major and medium irrigation sources were in lakhs of rupees every year, but the tank WUAs are getting the funds only in thousands of rupees. The major irrigation WUA focuses only on operation and maintenance and repairs of the distribution system in its command, while the tank-WUA has to take care of both the source (including tank structures) and distribution system. There was an imbalance in the fund allocation pattern, as most of the tank WUAs in the study area have complained. Indeed, field officials of the minor irrigation department endorsed this view, and suggested modification in the present allocation pattern to encourage tanks rehabilitation.

IV

RESPONSE OF THE HOUSEHOLDS ON THE STRUCTURE AND FUNCTIONING OF THE WUAs

This section examines the response of the farmer households on the structure of the WUAs and the role of various functionaries in working of these water institutions. A comparative analysis based on the farmers' response on devolution of powers to WUAs before and after formation of these bodies is carried out.

Role of Functionaries/Socio-Economic Groups in the Functioning of WUAs

The massive process of farmers' empowerment needs considerable skills in social engineering and irrigation department is the agent of change through out the process. But, for further consolidation of these transformations, the participation of other functionaries like NGOs, village panchayats, various committees formed formally or informally at the village level are very essential and imminent. In this section, the response of sample farmer households on the role of these functionaries under three irrigation systems is examined.

The data indicate that, the managing committee of the WUA, the I&CADD, the large farmers, upper caste people and the farmers at different reaches are actively involved in the functioning of the WUAs at various levels. The other bodies of the government, semi-government, co-operative, NGOs and the other socio-economic groups including the youth in the villages are not involved with the activities of the WUA and moreover they feel that it is not their concern. This is a common phenomenon found and people's participation in WUA (other than the farmers under the respective irrigation system) in a popular sense is absent.

Major Irrigation

Table 1 shows that under major irrigation system, 70 per cent of the farmers respond that the president and the managing committee take active part in the functioning of the WUAs. 86 per cent have reported that the competent authorities (I&CADD) were found co-operating actively with WUAs and individual farmers, in water regulation, cleaning and maintenance of the irrigation network. More than 93 per cent respond that all categories of farmers including the small and marginal were actively participate at various levels in WUAs. 80 per cent of the head-reach farmers and 63.33 per cent of tail-end farmers also actively work for the WUAs. The other groups like landless agricultural labour, women, village secretary, co-operative credit society, sarpanch and any religious or caste group do not participate in the activities of WUAs and more than 95 per cent of the sample households expressed that these groups do not involve with the functioning of WUAs.

Medium Irrigation

The WUAs under medium irrigation system also are functioning on the same lines as of major irrigation and the response of the sample farmers is similar to that of the major irrigation system. Though the executive committee members take active (84.44%) part in the meetings, almost all the activities which relate to the WUA's management are being carried out by the president (91.11%). 73.33% of the farmer members reported as active and show co-operative behaviour on various functions of the WUAs. Ninety-five per cent of the large farmers and 66% of the small and marginal category actively involve with the activities of WUA. Eighty-two per cent of farmers from upper caste and upper income groups play a crucial role in the WUAs. The percentages of head reach and tail-reach farmers constitute 97.78% and 86.67% respectively and they share the responsibilities of WUAs and its functioning.

Since the irrigation department is the principal agency of the government that coordinates the functioning of the WUAs, 91 per cent of the sample farmers reported its active role in the present irrigation system. All the remaining agencies of

Table 1 : Role of Various Functionaries/Socio-economic Groups in the Functioning of the WUA—Major

Particulars	Percentage of Households Reporting	As Percentage of Reporting Households			
		Very Active	Active	Passive	None
1. General Body	100.00	3.33	63.33	33.33	-
2. Chairman	100.00	43.33	56.67	-	-
3. Managing Committee	100.00	30.00	70.00	-	-
4. Members	100.00	16.67	66.67	16.67	-
5. Non-members	83.33	-	8.00	4.00	88.00
6. Secretary	63.33	-	10.53	-	89.47
7. Other staff	70.00	-	4.76	28.57	66.67
8. Any other individual (Specify)	63.33	-	5.26	5.26	89.47
9. Government Officials	100.00	3.33	86.67	3.33	6.67
10. Panchayat	100.00	-	6.67	73.33	20.00
11. Sarpanch	100.00	-	6.67	63.33	30.00
12. Cooperative Credit Society	100.00	-	-	3.33	96.67
13. Cooperative Marketing Society	100.00	-	-	3.33	96.67
14. Other local institutions	100.00	-	-	10.00	90.00
15. Any particular religious group (specify)	96.67	-	-	6.90	93.10

16. Any particular caste group (specify)	100.00	-	-	6.67	93.33
17. Any other specific group (specify)	100.00	-	-	6.67	93.33
18. Women	100.00	-	-	3.33	96.67
19. Poor	96.67	-	-	3.45	96.55
20. Middle Income	100.00	-	43.33	13.33	43.33
21. Upper Income	96.67	-	62.07	6.90	31.03
22. Large/medium farmers	100.00	-	93.33	3.33	3.33
23. Small/marginal farmers	100.00	-	93.33	3.33	3.33
24. Landless	100.00	-	-	40.00	60.00
25. Labour/wage earners	100.00	-	-	13.33	86.67
26. Livestock owners	100.00	-	-	10.00	90.00
27. Tribals	73.33	-	-	4.55	95.45
28. Upper Caste	100.00	-	30.00	13.33	56.67
29. Lower Caste	100.00	-	13.33	30.00	56.67
30. Scheduled Castes	100.00	-	-	26.67	73.33
31. Head Reach Farmers	100.00	-	80.00	16.67	3.33
32. Tail Reach Farmers	100.00	-	63.33	33.33	3.33
33. Youth	96.67	-	-	24.14	75.86
34. Any other (specify)	-	-	-	-	-

(contd.)

Table 1(Contd): Role of Various Functionaries/Socio-economic Groups in the Functioning of the WUA—Minor

Particulars	Percentage of Households Reporting	As Percentage of Reporting Households			
		Very Active	Active	Passive	None
1. General Body	100.00	2.22	66.67	31.11	-
2. Chairman	100.00	2.22	91.11	6.67	-
3. Managing Committee	100.00	2.22	84.44	13.33	-
4. Members	100.00	2.22	73.33	24.44	-
5. Non-members	100.00	-	-	42.22	57.78
6. Secretary	100.00	-	13.33	66.67	20.00
7. Other staff	95.56	-	30.23	16.28	53.49
8. Any other individual (Specify)	100.00	-	-	4.44	95.56
9. Government Officials	100.00	-	91.11	4.44	4.44
10. Panchayat	100.00	-	2.22	17.78	80.00
11. Sarpanch	100.00	-	2.22	17.78	80.00
12. Cooperative Credit Society	100.00	-	-	2.22	97.78
13. Cooperative Marketing Society	100.00	-	-	2.22	97.78
14. Other local institutions	100.00	-	-	-	100.00
15. Any particular religious group (specify)	95.56	-	2.33	2.33	95.35

16. Any particular caste group (specify)	100.00	-	4.44	6.67	88.89
17. Any other specific group (specify)	97.78	-	-	-	100.00
18. Women	100.00	-	-	-	100.00
19. Poor	100.00	-	-	-	100.00
20. Middle Income	100.00	-	24.44	66.67	8.89
21. Upper Income	100.00	-	82.22	8.89	8.89
22. Large/medium farmers	100.00	-	95.56	4.44	-
23. Small/marginal farmers	100.00	-	66.67	33.33	-
24. Landless	100.00	-	-	44.44	55.56
25. Labour/wage earners	100.00	-	2.22	8.89	88.89
26. Livestock owners	100.00	-	-	-	100.00
27. Tribals	100.00	-	2.22	-	97.78
28. Upper Caste	100.00	-	82.22	6.67	11.11
29. Lower Caste	100.00	-	24.44	57.78	17.78
30. Scheduled Castes	100.00	-	2.22	24.44	73.33
31. Head Reach Farmers	100.00	-	97.78	2.22	-
32. Tail Reach Farmers	100.00	-	86.67	13.33	-
33. Youth	100.00	-	-	26.67	73.33
34. Any other (specify)	-	-	-	-	-

(contd.)

Table 1(Concld.): Role of Various Functionaries/Socio-economic Groups in the Functioning of the WUA—Minor

Particulars	Percentage of Households Reporting	As Percentage of Reporting Households			
		Very Active	Active	Passive	None
1. General Body	100.00	-	63.33	36.67	-
2. Chairman	100.00	-	73.33	26.67	-
3. Managing Committee	100.00	-	70.00	30.00	-
4. Members	100.00	-	61.67	33.33	5.00
5. Non-members	100.00	-	3.33	30.00	66.67
6. Secretary	100.00	-	6.67	28.33	65.00
7. Other staff	100.00	-	-	18.33	81.67
8. Any other individual (Specify)	100.00	-	1.67	8.33	90.00
9. Government Officials	100.00	-	55.00	11.67	33.33
10. Panchayat	100.00	-	1.67	15.00	83.33
11. Sarpanch	100.00	-	1.67	10.00	88.33
12. Cooperative Credit Society	100.00	-	-	8.33	91.67
13. Cooperative Marketing Society	100.00	-	-	6.67	93.33
14. Other local institutions	100.00	-	-	3.33	96.67
15. Any particular religious group (specify)	100.00	-	-	1.67	98.33

16. Any particular caste group (specify)	100.00	-	-	5.00	95.00
17. Any other specific group (specify)	100.00	-	-	5.00	95.00
18. Women	100.00	-	-	8.33	91.67
19. Poor	100.00	-	-	5.00	95.00
20. Middle Income	100.00	-	46.67	13.33	40.00
21. Upper Income	100.00	-	50.00	13.33	36.67
22. Large/medium farmers	100.00	-	51.67	15.00	33.33
23. Small/marginal farmers	100.00	-	50.00	16.67	33.33
24. Landless	100.00	-	5.00	5.00	90.00
25. Labour/wage earners	100.00	-	-	3.33	96.67
26. Livestock owners	100.00	-	-	3.33	96.67
27. Tribals	100.00	-	-	3.33	96.67
28. Upper Caste	100.00	-	46.67	5.00	48.33
29. Lower Caste	100.00	-	46.67	5.00	48.33
30. Scheduled Castes	100.00	-	38.33	13.33	48.33
31. Head Reach Farmers	100.00	-	53.33	8.33	38.33
32. Tail Reach Farmers	100.00	-	45.00	15.00	40.00
33. Youth	100.00	-	5.00	6.67	88.33
34. Any other (specify)	-	-	-	-	-

government and non-governmental are not involved with the functions of the WUAs under medium irrigation schemes. The general feeling of non-farmer groups is that land and water management programmes are exclusively meant for the farmer community.

Minor Irrigation

Role of various institutions/groups in the functioning of the WUAs formed under minor irrigation (tank system) are said to be poor and not fully involved in the better management of tank irrigation in Andhra Pradesh. Here also the same groups have paid attention in the activities of WUAs as mentioned in the earlier systems of irrigation, but the participation rate is considerably low. The net benefit from tank irrigation to the beneficiaries is comparatively lower than under the major and medium projects. Efficient water management and agriculture development could not be achieved due to frequent droughts under tank irrigation in the sample areas of the study. About 70 per cent of the sample farmers reported that the president and the T.C. members actively involve in WUA activities and 55 per cent respond towards the irrigation officials' coordination with the WUAs. Irrespective of the incomes and farm sizes, 50% of the users from these groups participate in various functions of the WUAs whenever needed. The participation of others like sarpanch, co-operatives, landless, wage labour, tribals, youth, women and the poor is not reported by the sample farmers and people from these groups were totally missing in the WUAs functioning.

Devolution of Power to WUAs

The basic foundation of the irrigation reform process is the WUA. The reform is aimed at empowering farmers and reducing the role of the irrigation agency. At the primary level powers like maintenance of the system, conflict resolution, record keeping, etc., have been delegated. There is accountability of the irrigation department towards the WUA. The reforms have substantially shifted the responsibility for maintenance functions. This section deals with the devolution of powers and decision making by WUAs in water management considering the situation prior to WUA formation and at present. Response of the sample farmers on these issues is analysed under different irrigation systems.

Table 2 shows the devolution of powers/decision making by the WUAs in activities like planning, implementation, revenues, conflict resolution and agricultural development, which come under the purview of the WUAs under new set up of irrigation reforms in the state. From the field observations it was found that all the works undertaken were identified by the elected bodies and also executed by them without the mediation of contractors or any other intermediary. The interaction was directly between the WUA and competent authority, who is from the irrigation department. The institutional structure of PIM has provided a forum for the users and the agency to come together and discuss irrigation issues, which was absent earlier.

The major and medium irrigation areas are the real beneficiaries of the irrigation reforms and the WUAs formed under the command areas are satisfied with the devolution of powers and they could exercise the powers in water management by taking decisions independently.

Just before the formation of the WUAs, planning for capital investment, providing resources for investment, execution of structures, release of water and its distribution, maintenance and repairs and stopping misuse of water etc., were under the control of the irrigation department mainly in case of major and medium irrigation projects. This is supported by the field data and the respondents revealed that 100% of the above powers were rested with the irrigation Department. The crop pattern only was decided by the farmers.

Now the situation has changed and the WUA bodies could decide themselves about the issues related to irrigation and solve them. About 70 per cent of user farmers revealed that decisions with regard to planning for capital investment, providing resources for investment and actual capital investment in irrigation structures were taken jointly by the bodies of WUAs and the I.D. About 80 per cent of member farmers opined that the planning for release of water and actual release of water under major and medium commands are in the hands of I.D. Pricing of water and collection of dues

Table 2 : Devolution of Powers/Decision Making —Major

Decision/Activity	Just Before WUA Formation					PRESENT				
	%age of HHs Reporting	Govt Body	WUA/ Farmers	Joint	Others	%age of HHs Reporting	Govt Body	WUA/ Farmers	Joint	Others
		As %age of Reporting Households					As %age of Reporting Households			
Planning for capital investment in irrigation structures	100.00	100.00	-	-	-	100.00	16.67	23.33	60.00	-
Providing resources for investment	100.00	100.00	-	-	-	100.00	23.33	10.00	66.67	-
Actual capital investment in irrigation structures	100.00	100.00	-	-	-	96.67	24.14	13.79	62.07	-
Assessment of water availability	100.00	100.00	-	-	-	100.00	80.00	6.67	13.33	-
Planning for release of water	100.00	100.00	-	-	-	96.67	79.31	10.34	10.34	-
Actual release of water	96.67	100.00	-	-	-	96.67	89.66	6.90	3.45	-
Distribution of water among farmers	100.00	93.33	-	6.67	-	96.67	-	100.00	-	-
Pricing of water received	100.00	100.00	-	-	-	96.67	96.55	3.45	-	-
Pricing of water distributed to farmers	100.00	100.00	-	-	-	96.67	96.55	-	3.45	-
Collection of dues from farmers	100.00	100.00	-	-	-	96.67	100.00	-	-	-
Decision on maintenance/ repair requirement	100.00	100.00	-	-	-	100.00	-	96.67	3.33	-

Providing resources for maintenance/ repair	100.00	100.00	-	-	-	100.00	-	36.67	63.33	-
Implementation of maintenance/ repair	100.00	100.00	-	-	-	100.00	-	93.33	6.67	-
Monitoring use of water	100.00	100.00	-	-	-	100.00	-	96.67	3.33	-
Stopping misuse/ waste	100.00	96.67	3.33	-	-	96.67	-	89.66	10.34	-
Action on misusers	90.00	96.30	3.70	-	-	96.67	3.45	86.21	10.34	-
Crops to be grown	93.33	21.43	75.00	3.57	-	90.00	-	96.30	-	3.70
Others	3.33	100.00	-	-	-	-				

(contd.)

Table 2(Contd): Devolution of Powers/Decision Making —Medium

Decision/Activity	Just Before WUA Formation					PRESENT				
	%age of HHs Reporting	Govt Body	WUA/ Farmers	Joint	Others	%age of HHs Reporting	Govt Body	WUA/ Farmers	Joint	Others
		As %age of Reporting Households					As %age of Reporting Households			
Planning for capital investment in irrigation structures	100.00	100.00	-	-	-	100.00	66.67	2.22	31.11	-
Providing resources for investment	100.00	100.00	-	-	-	100.00	71.11	-	28.89	-
Actual capital investment in irrigation structures	100.00	100.00	-	-	-	100.00	68.89	-	31.11	-
Assessment of water availability	100.00	97.78	2.22	-	-	100.00	93.33	4.44	2.22	-
Planning for release of water	100.00	97.78	2.22	-	-	100.00	91.11	8.89	-	-
Actual release of water	100.00	97.78	-	2.22	-	100.00	97.78	2.22	-	-
Distribution of water among farmers	100.00	91.11	2.22	6.67	-	100.00	2.22	97.78	-	-
Pricing of water received	100.00	100.00	-	-	-	100.00	60.00	40.00	-	-
Pricing of water distributed to farmers	100.00	100.00	-	-	-	100.00	100.00	-	-	-
Collection of dues from farmers	100.00	100.00	-	-	-	100.00	100.00	-	-	-

Decision on maintenance/ repair requirement	100.00	100.00	-	-	-	100.00	-	100.00	-	-
Providing resources for maintenance/ repair	100.00	97.78	-	2.22	-	100.00	48.89	22.22	28.89	-
Implementation of maintenance/ repair	100.00	100.00	-	-	-	100.00	13.33	86.67	-	-
Monitoring use of water	100.00	97.78	-	2.22	-	100.00	4.44	95.56	-	-
Stopping misuse/ waste	100.00	97.78	-	2.22	-	100.00	8.89	91.11	-	-
Action on misusers	100.00	100.00	-	-	-	100.00	33.33	66.67	-	-
Crops to be grown	95.56	30.23	69.77	-	-	93.33	7.14	92.86	-	-
Others (Specify)	-									

(contd.)

Table 2 (Concld.): Devolution of Powers/Decision-making —Minor

Decision/Activity	Just Before WUA Formation					PRESENT				
	%age of HHs Reporting	Govt Body	WUA/ Farmers	Joint	Others	%age of HHs Reporting	Govt Body	WUA/ Farmers	Joint	Others
		As %age of Reporting Households					As %age of Reporting Households			
Planning for capital investment in irrigation structures	100.00	100.00	-	-	-	100.00	100.00	-	-	-
Providing resources for investment	100.00	100.00	-	-	-	100.00	100.00	-	-	-
Actual capital investment in irrigation structures	100.00	100.00	-	-	-	100.00	100.00	-	-	-
Assessment of water availability	100.00	100.00	-	-	-	100.00	91.67	8.33	-	-
Planning for release of water	100.00	100.00	-	-	-	100.00	63.33	31.67	5.00	-
Actual release of water	100.00	100.00	-	-	-	100.00	50.00	41.67	8.33	-
Distribution of water among farmers	100.00	100.00	-	-	-	100.00	38.33	55.00	6.67	-
Pricing of water received	100.00	100.00	-	-	-	100.00	100.00	-	-	-
Pricing of water distributed to farmers	100.00	100.00	-	-	-	100.00	100.00	-	-	-
Collection of dues from farmers	100.00	100.00	-	-	-	96.67	32.76	60.34	6.90	-

Decision on maintenance/ repair requirement	100.00	100.00	-	-	-	100.00	5.00	78.33	16.67	-
Providing resources for maintenance/ repair	100.00	100.00	-	-	-	100.00	60.00	13.33	26.67	-
Implementation of maintenance/ repair	100.00	100.00	-	-	-	100.00	16.67	60.00	23.33	-
Monitoring use of water	100.00	100.00	-	-	-	98.33	33.90	40.68	25.42	-
Stopping misuse/ waste	100.00	98.33	1.67	-	-	100.00	-	100.00	-	-
Action on misusers	100.00	96.67	3.33	-	-	100.00	16.67	43.33	40.00	-
Crops to be grown	98.33	13.56	86.44	-	-	93.33	3.57	96.43	-	-
Others (Specify)	23.33	85.71	14.29	-	-	25.00	80.00	13.33	6.67	-

from the users are decided by the government. More than 90 per cent of the sample users revealed that the major decisions in connection with the repair requirement, implementation of maintenance, distribution of water, monitoring use of water, stopping misusers of water and action on misusers are the duties of the WUAs. So, some decisions are taken independently by WUAs and some jointly and the technical part of the projects are taken care by the I&CADD. Though the government suggests the appropriate crop pattern depending on the availability of water, the farmers act on their own in implementing the crop pattern in command areas. The government has no control over the crops to be grown by the water users.

Management of minor irrigation (tanks) necessitates an altogether different approach. Tank Users' associations have control both on source of water and its entire distribution system. Compared to major and medium irrigation systems, tank systems are pretty old.

In the earlier setup, i.e., prior to formation of tank-WUAs, the planning for capital investment in irrigation structures, providing resources and execution of the structures and repairs, revenue collection and monitoring use of water through laskers/*Neeruganties*, etc., were under the control of the irrigation and revenue departments of the state. The farmers forming into committees under the tank, used to stop misuse of water and some action was taken on these misusers. This was the general practice in management of tank irrigation till 1997. But under the present system of tank management, more than 90 per cent of the sample farmers report that the planning for capital investment, creation of funds for maintenance and repairs, pricing of water, collection of water charges are the duties of the I.D. and the government. Bulk of the user farmers reported that under the present system, decisions on work proposals, maintenance of repairs, distribution of water, stopping misuse of water, action on misusers were undertaken by the WUA management. However, changes in crop pattern under the tanks depend upon the availability of water in time. Farmers are the decision makers on crops to be grown by adopting effective management of water.

V

IMPACT OF WUAs

Impact of WUAs on Farm Economy of Sample Households

As from the field observations, it is found that the only shift in the cropping pattern induced by the reforms is to reinforce the cultivation of wet crops, like rice. The farmers are inclined to shift to rice wherever possible. The interesting question is that this is justified by the lack of any feasible alternative, which has comparable ease of cultivation and economic returns. The argument put forward by the farmers in favour of persisting with rice cultivation is that the soil gets addicted to rice and it is not possible to switch over to dry crops usually during a period of water scarcity.

As reflected in our analysis, there is no basis for attributing a large increase in per acre yields of the crops including rice to the institution of irrigation reforms. Limited water under canals in medium irrigation system and lower cropping intensity further underscores the need to use water for extensive cultivation to benefit the entire area.

It is to be mentioned that the usage of all the inputs increases with quality irrigation. In times of low rainfall and scarcity of water under medium irrigation systems (reservoirs), normally the input use will be low and on decrease. This is a common practice experienced by the farmers of these WUAs in many years.

The more important issue regarding WUA impact (irrigation) on cropping pattern, yields and input was its stabilizing role. Better management of the system would contribute to greater stability by ensuring timely and predictable supplies. Although it is not possible to overcome the fluctuations in natural climatic factors, controlled irrigation can often mitigate the adversity. However, no such impact was in evidence. It is also a little early for such impact to become visible.

Impact of WUAs on General Economy of the Selected Areas

In general, it can be concluded that the farmer managed WUAs have created the infrastructure like construction of culverts and small bridges across the canals, formation of roads to the fields connecting the villages, improving the drainage system to arrest the water logged conditions in deltas. All these improvements are part of the infrastructure development of the areas and could be achieved in a short time due to the advent of WUAs. This paper brings out that it is too early to talk about the contributions of WUA to economic development of area as the process of implementation is just falling in line. Obviously, there is greater need to strengthen them in terms of people's participation and involvement. Self-sufficiency and resource strength is central to the sustainability of the institutions and also to the development of the areas. It appears that institutions (WUAs) would be effective if the economic gains are substantial.

Major Problems faced by the WUA Members in Terms of its Functioning

Major Irrigation

Past experience with operation and management would suggest that inadequate attention paid specially to the farm level irrigation water management is one of the major reasons for low performance of the major irrigation projects. The field date reveals that 96.67 per cent of reporting households have expressed about inadequate field channels, 53.33 per cent report lack of training to field staff, 65.52 per cent were not satisfied in devising water distribution rules, 73.33 per cent face problems during the period of water scarcity and 53.33 per cent revealed the problems with regard to limited control over water flow. These are some of the major technical and administrative problems came in the way in functioning of the WUAs under major irrigation.

Regarding the economic problems, high cost of maintenance, lack of financial support, lack of freedom to determine water rates are reported to be the major problems by majority of members. Inadequate maintenance, non-availability of water at canal, poor quality of water, conflicts among the members, lack of quality planting material, complaints from tail-enders, lack of investment credit with the farmers are the problems faced by the WUAs occasionally. But these are not serious problems in case of major projects.

Social factors are more complex. It was revealed that conflict about pricing of water, water table receding, non-payment of water charges, lack of member co-operation, lack of leadership and lack of members' willingness to take up management functions are not faced by any of the WUAs in major projects and have been expressed by majority of the users.

The hurdles and difficulties in the process of transformation are many and complex, but, they are not insurmountable in case of major irrigation WUAs.

Medium Irrigation

Major problems faced by the WUAs under medium irrigation as expressed by 80 per cent of the sample households are; non-availability of water at the source, conflicts in quantity and timing of water, inadequate field channels, lack of financial support, complaints from tail-enders and lack of training to the field staff. These water control activities necessitate both technical and organizational aspects of water management. Devoid of organizational structure requiring users' participation, technical changes cannot be brought into use with positive results to meet the desired objectives.

It is to be mentioned that majority of members face the problems in functioning of WUAs in this sub-sector of irrigation, though occasional, are very important aspects in respect of poor quality of water (80%), lack of government support in funding (73.33%), lack of mechanism to control water use (91.11%), problems in devising water distribution rules (88.89%), problems during scarcity of water (62.22%), limited control over water flow (91.11%) and with regard to lack of members' willingness to take up management functions (68.89%).

Inadequate maintenance, high cost of maintenance, lack of members' co-operation, pricing of water, water table receding fast, lack of consensus in deciding crop pattern, non-payment of water charges, lack of leadership etc are not considered as problems to WUA's functioning that are reported by a large proportion of beneficiaries under the system.

The uncertainty of timing and volume of supplies at the individual farmers level, below the channel outlets, is considerably greater under medium irrigation projects.

Minor Irrigation

A more serious problem is regarding the functioning of tanks in A.P. At the state level 65 per cent of the tanks are under repair, which account for 75 per cent of the area irrigated by tanks. Effectively only 25 percent of the tank ayacut (command area) is being irrigated. The decline, quantitative as well as qualitative, in tank irrigation may explain the low groundwater development in some regions in the state.

Non-availability of sufficient irrigation water in tanks and poor quality of water are the very major problems expressed by more than 90 per cent of sample households in tank-WUAs.

Inadequate maintenance of the system, lack of members' co-operation, lack of funding, complaints from tail-enders are some of the major problems, which the sample farmers tried to express. Conflicts among the users in respect of timing of water and quantity of water distributed are said to be occasional problems as revealed by about 45% of the reporting households because of small size of the command and small number of irrigators under minor irrigation system.

Other problems like pricing of water, complaints from tail-enders, lack of leadership, payment of water charges etc., can be overcome with the help of the members, provided better water availability in tanks. Hence, majority of the farmers felt that these are not obstacles for functioning of the associations under minor irrigation system.

In the larger social interest minor irrigation needs to be protected, maintained and enhanced. There are regions where promotion of minor irrigation would be more effective, economically, ecologically and socially in the coastal areas of A.P.

User Members' Assessment on the Success of WUA

As reflected in our analysis, the reform process initiated in irrigation sector in particular does not seem, as yet, to have made any major changes to bring additional areas under irrigation or increase in revenue collection or an increase in crop production. Apart from this, the success of WUAs is attributed mainly to the availability of external funding and the sustainability of the programme is critically linked with the availability of resources (K.V. Raju). Besides, investments may not bear any fruit, as this money is not productively invested in terms of social capital development. This, inturn, blocked the hard decisions envisaged in the reforms, such as implementation of user charges effectively (Ratna Reddy).

In this section, the user members' assessment about the performance of WUAs is examined. At the moment these WUAs seem to be working well especially in canal commands. In majority of the cases it is found that, these institutions paid attention on water distribution and succeeded to extend the irrigation to the tailend locations while minimizing the conflicts among the users. However, these benefits are not reflected in the data related to minor irrigation WUAs. Success of WUAs is linked with the funding, as little effort is being made to make them self sufficient or financially independent and the same problem has been expressed by large proportion of user members in the command areas.

The user members' assessment on the success and the financial health of these WUAs is made for each irrigation system separately. The field data show that majority of the sample holdings expressed their satisfaction over the functioning of the WUAs that are formed in command areas. But a large proportion of households in minor irrigation (Tank-WUAs) have expressed their dissatisfaction over the functioning of these groups and 65 per cent of users quantified them as poor. However, the rest of the reporting households were satisfied with the functioning of WUAs and it is mostly from the channel fed-WUAs. This indicates that the regions with relatively better water availability show some what better performance than regions with scarce water.

The success of the WUAs in command areas is attributed to a large to the equal distribution of water to all reaches, number and quality of irrigation works that are completed during the period, judicious use of funds and in solving the disputes among users in times of scarcity of water.

It is to be mentioned that a considerable per cent of reporting households in various WUAs were not aware of the financial position of the institutions. About 36.66 per cent of sample holdings from major irrigation WUAs have expressed their unawareness about the finances of the institution. A large proportion of sample water users i.e. 76.66 per cent of minor, 62.22 per cent of medium, and 23.33 per cent of major sources of irrigation revealed that the WUAs are poor in financial resources. It seems that only ¼ of the sample holdings across the WUAs have expressed their satisfaction over the finances.

The approach at the policy level seems to be to sustain WUAs through injecting more funds (borrowed). User contribution has not really materialized, as it goes against political interests. As a result, economic efficiency gets least priority though talking about it is in vogue. The sustainability of WUAs is in danger once the funds dry up. So, the institutional arrangements (WUAs) need to be autonomous and strengthened in terms of finances and administration. In the short run, the WUAs should be made responsible for collection water charges, making them transparent as well as accountable. In the long-run, WUAs should move towards volumetric pricing and efficient use of water, including shifts in cropping pattern.

User Members' Suggestions for Improving the Functioning of the WUA

Major Irrigation

Suggestions made by sample households of various WUAs on specific problems, devolution of powers for better functioning of these institutions are analyzed. According to the data, no major problems were identified by 63.33 per cent of sample households in major irrigation WUAs. Where as only a small per cent (16.66) of users point to the water distribution as deficient to tail-end areas. A majority of the user members (83.33%) expressed satisfaction with regard to the devolution of powers. They further opined that though the devolution of powers to WUAs is adequate, the powers exercised will be critical when the financial strength of the association is weak.

Majority user members felt that, technical and finances are the major factors that contribute for success of WUAs. About 53% reported about the necessity of field staff, more locks and mid dams for efficient distribution of water and another 23.33 per cent of the users expressed that the success of WUAs is linked with the funds.

The data suggests that technical and financial matters are key for success of WUAs; a large proportion of the users in major commands suggested that the government needed to share up funding; WUAs should also be enabled to generate funds on their own through right to auctioning grass, trees and collection of cess from fishing rights given to them. They were of the view that WUAs be allowed to fix and collect water charges. More technical staff (which is deficient now) is to be recruited to attend the engineering works that are proposed by the WUAs. This may help to speed up completion of pending and also new works to improve the flow of irrigation and to minimize the wastage of water in distribution.

Medium Irrigation

As per the data, nearly 30 per cent of the sample households did not express any major problem regarding the functioning of the WUAs. But the water distribution under medium irrigation system is not as good as the major irrigation commands. The available water is used for drinking purpose to towns in addition to the irrigation. So, the users face water deficiency in some periods during the crop season. This has been expressed by 26.66% of the user members; especially the tail-enders who often face the situation. Another major problem expressed by nearly 30 per cent of these sample households is financial constraints to the WUAs to attend to a number of maintenance works under the system. They further viewed that the devolution of powers to these WUAs is quite adequate, provided the finances.

Major factors/requirements for the success of WUA that has been expressed by majority of users are more technical/ field staff to attend operation and distribution of water (35.55%) and allocation of more funds and proper utilization (37.78%). These two are the important factors that contribute much for the successful functioning of water institutions.

Some of the important suggestions made by the user members for better functioning of WUAs while keeping in view the present situation are more water to be diverted to irrigation purpose instead of supplying water to meet the requirements of nearby towns. A majority of them (53.33%) suggested proper maintenance of distributory channels to minimize the water wastage, and more funds are to be allocated to attend these improvements have been stressed by nearly 30 per cent of the members. The common observation was that there was general enthusiasm about implementing PIM and keenness to improve the irrigated area and crop yields.

Minor Irrigation

Decades of siltation, poor organization and management, decline of compulsory labour contribution in maintenance work, inadequate operation and maintenance budget from government, meager revenue from tank based activities, growth of wells in tank command areas and well owners reduced interest in tank management and encroachments have contributed to their decline.

As revealed from the data the functioning of the tank-WUAs is not as smooth as the WUAs that run in command areas. The major contributions for this unsatisfactory functioning of these institutions are natural calamities like drought and cyclones. In the absence of availability of good irrigation, number of problems may have come up especially in the fragile resource regions. In the sample areas of the study, the tank-WUAs are not said to be functioning satisfactorily and the sample households have mentioned, frequent droughts (76.92%), financial constraints to WUAs (65%), deficient maintenance of tanks (55.50%) and encroachments of tank beds (30%) as the major constraints for good irrigation in their operation. They are satisfied with the devolution of powers to WUAs but these are linked with the finances available with the institution.

The user members opined that major factors that may contribute for the success of WUAs are feeder channels to be provided (42%), regular maintenance of tanks (68%) and need to bring the balance between minor, medium and major irrigation systems through judicious fund allocation (65%). They further mentioned that minor irrigation sources of tanks should be treated in an integrated fashion.

The following suggestions were made by the sample households to improve functioning of the WUAs:

i. WUAs should be made vibrant and responsive

ii. Desiltation of tank beds to store more water and

iii. Financial constraints to WUAs to be removed to make them self sufficient and financially independent.

Thus, judging the WUAs from rather subjective and not easily quantifiable data, it is found that by and large the associations established in command areas of major and medium irrigation systems are working satisfactorily. The WUAs formed under minor irrigation, mostly of un-assured irrigation conditions need special attention by the government as well as participants to make them vibrant and responsive. The programme is said to be success only when the WUAs established in minor irrigation sector work efficiently in water management as more than 80 per cent of total WUAs in the state come under this category.

Principal Findings

1. A WUA is created by delineating a portion of the command area under an irrigation system. Essential works under the system are identified by local farmers.
2. For identified works, technical estimates are prepared by the competent authority and are executed by the WUA; this has considerably enhanced quality of works and duration of work execution; farmers are satisfied with works quality.
3. Complaints on water supply and system break downs are quickly resolved. Procedural delays are reduced. Department officials quickly access problem areas and are able to resolve with WUAs/DCs.
4. Social equity has increased; rights and responsibilities are getting clearer during the process. Conflict resolution is easy and quick.
5. Drainage system improved under major irrigation.

6. Empowerment of farmers; they are more articulate now.
7. Irrigated area increased mainly in tail reaches by 10 to 15 per cent.
8. Now users have role in works identification, prioritization and execution.
9. In some places, the major gains are removal of encroachments, particularly in tank-bed areas.
10. In the process of users identifying and execution of works, lot of attention has been laid on users' needs like cattle path ways, washing steps for women in canal systems, removal of encroachments, clearing shrubs and silt for smooth flow of water till the tail reach.
11. WUA and DC presidents are not very clear about their future activities and the potential of these organizations to carry out allied activities.
12. Government grants have remained the sole source of funding for most of the WUAs with little (or no) efforts having been made to mobilize own resources.

Recommendations

1. The question of financial sustainability of WUAs in the absence of external inflow of resources is very critical and needs to be faced squarely. There is an immediate need to bring the balance between minor, medium and major irrigation systems through judicious fund allocations and make the institutions self sufficient or financially independent.
2. Substantial increase in quantum of area under irrigation has not taken place due to lack of interest in water regulation functions by WUAs. This has to be taken care by the farmers as well as the officials.
3. The contributing factors are essentially the legal status of the WUA and freedom to decide its functioning. The weaknesses, which need to be taken care are political interference, presidents of WUAs turning out to be contractors, lack of operational plans etc,.

4. Women form a negligible percentage in PIM activities in A.P. So, more women are to be involved in WUAs activities as women constitute a major proportion of agricultural workers, especially in irrigated agriculture.
5. A majority of WUAs were of the view that they must have the right to fix and collect water cess and should also be enabled to generate funds on their own through right to auctioning grass, trees and collection of cess from fishing rights.
6. The WUAs formed under minor irrigation, mostly of un-assured irrigation conditions need special attention by the government as well as the users to make them vibrant and responsive. The programme is said to be success only when these groups work efficiently in water management as more than 80 per cent of total WUAs in the state come under this category.

9

Growth and Development of Irrigation: An Overview

K. DASARATHARAMAIAH AND
D. SREENIVASA RAO

Irrigation plays protective and productive role in agricultural production. The major function of irrigation is to mitigate the impact of irregular, uneven and inadequate rainfall. Irrigation supplements supply of rainwater, parti-cularly in a country like India where rainfall is concentrated mostly in the south-west monsoon months of June-September. The additional supply of water makes possible double and multiple copping. Irrigation has paved beneficial to the agri-cultural development of a country. In fact, irrigation formulates the lifeline for sustained successful agriculture. Irrigation is everything in India, water is more valuable than land.

Irrigation and Agriculturral Development

Irrigation is deemed necessary for the maximum production of most farm crops, especially in the arid and semi arid regions. To cut short imports, self-sufficiency in food grains is very necessary. This can be achieved, besides putting various inputs in the fields, through increasing irrigation facilities. Different crops require different quantities of water supply through out their growing period. For example, grain crops require maximum supply during the time of heads are formed, while sugarcane, cotton, chillies, requires more water. The total water requirement of crops varies from 10.6 acre inches for mustard, to 95 acre inches for sugarcane. The water needs for other crops are, linseed 12.7 acre inches; barley 14.1; oats 14.4 wheat 14.8, maize 17.8 jowar 25.7 groundnut 26.1 potato 26.7 chilies 38.8, tobacco 39.2 and cotton 41.7 acre-inches.

When the required quantity of water is not available through natural water supply, irrigation has to be resorted to considerable advantages of the soil, sunshine and climate. Development of adequate and dependable irrigation facility is very essential to banish famines as a result of drought conditions. Irrigation alone supplies dependable and timely supplies of water. In the absence of irrigation, the farmer cannot take risk to invest for other agricultural inputs, that contribute to increased productivity. Thus, irrigation plays a crucial role in the country's agricultural production strategy.

Progress of Irrigation

It would be of interest to know that the irrigated area increased from about less than a million hectares in 1800 to about 5 million hectares in 1900 and 17 million hectares in 1925. At the beginning of the Plan period (1951), the area under irrigation was of the order of 22.6 million hectares. At the end of 1969-70, about 37.68 million hectares of land were irrigated by 1973-74, 44.1 million hectares was irrigated by 1976-77. The total irrigated area rose to 7.0 million hectares. Up to 1951, 9.7 million hectares of land was irrigated by major and medium projects and 6.4 million hectares by minor irrigation works. In addition, 6.5 million hectares were being irrigated by groundwater use. At the beginning of the Fourth Plan, it was estimated that about 24 million hectares were under irrigation. Out of this, 16.9 million hectares of area was under major and medium irrigation and 7.1 million hectares under minor irrigation schemes.

Irrigation Under Five Year Plans

Agriculture and its development formed the main theme of the first five-year plan. The planning commission recognized the importance of irrigation in increasing agricultural production and assigned a very high priority to it in the first five year plan.

Expansion of irrigation facilities, along with consolidation of the existing systems, has been the main part of the strategy for increasing production of food grains. With sustained and systematic development of irrigation, the irrigation potential through major, medium and minor irrigation projects has increased from 22.6 million hectares (mha) in 1951, to about 93.95 million hectares at the end of Ninth Plan. Plan-wise irrigation potential created and utilized through major, medium and minor irrigation projects in the country is presented in Table 1. Irrigation potential created during the Pre-planed period was 22.6 million hectares and the same potential was utilized. However, over a period of time during the planning process irrigation potential utilized has less than its creation. For instance during the Seventh Plan and Ninth Plan irrigation potential created were 86.26 million hectares and 93.95 million hectares respectively. But its utilization was only 77.24 million hectares and 80.06 million hectares respectively during the same plan periods (Table 1).

Table 1: Development of Irrigation Potential (Cumulative) Through Plan Periods

S. No.	Plan Period	Potential Created (Mha)	Potential Utilized (Mha)
1	First Plan	26.26	25.04
2	Second Plan	29.08	27.80
3	Third Plan	33.57	32.17
4	Annual Plans	37.10	35.75
5	Fourth Plan	44.20	42.19
6	Fifth Plan	52.02	48.46
7	Sixth Plan	65.22	58.82
8	Seventh Plan	76.53	68.59
90	Annual Plans	81.02	72.86
10	Eighth Plan	86.26	77.24
11	Ninth Plan	93.95*	80.06*
12	Targets for Tenth Plan (2002-07)	109.11*	90.42*

Source: India 2006, Publications Division MIB, Government of India, New Delhi, 2006.

* Provisional and are subject to change.

Minor Irrigation

All Ground Water and Surface Water Schemes having a Cultivable Command Area (CCA) up to 2,000 hectares, individually are classified as Minor irrigation Schemes. Irrigation Potential created and utilized under Minor Irrigation during the various plan periods in India are presented in Table 2. From First Plan to the three Annual Plans irrigation potential creation and potential utilization were equal. After the annual plans, i.e., from VI plan to the present utilization has been less than the potential creation.

Table 2: Irrigation Potential Created and Utilized Under Minor Irrigation

Plan Period	Potential created (Mha)	Potential utilized (Mha)
First Plan	14.06	14.06
Second Plan	14.75	14.75
Third Plan	17.00	17.00
Annual Plan	19.00	19.00
Fourth Plan	23.50	23.50
Fifth Plan	27.30	27.30
Annual plan	30.00	30.00
Sixth Plan	37.52	35.25
Seventh Plan	46.61	43.12
Annual Plan	50.35	46.54
Eight Plan	53.31	48.77
Ninth Plan	56.90	49.05
Tenth Plan (2002-2007) Target	63.71	54.49

Source: India 2006, Publications Division MIB, Government of India, New Delhi, 2006.

*Importance of Minor Irrigation.

The significance of minor irrigation to country's agricultural programme is obvious. This is clear when considered against other type of major and medium irrigation. Costs of major and medium irrigation projects are very high. Minor irrigation works have been the backbone of agriculture throughout the history of India. Minor irrigation works have a short gestation period. They can be executed with comparatively small initial outlay. They are supposed to yield quicker results because irrigation water flows immediately after the completion of the work. These minor irrigation schemes also provides a large amount of disposed employment among the local people. People's participation could be counted upon for the construction of these minor works. The Government involvement by way of expenditure on these minor irrigation works is relatively small. This is mainly because of a fairly high proportion of these works are privately owned or owned by local bodies or groups.

Improvement in Water-use Efficiency

In total water use in 1990, the share of agriculture was 83 per cent followed by domestic use (4.5%) industrial use (2.7%) and energy (1.8%). The remaining 8 per cent was for other uses including environmental requirements. In a long period projection of water use, the Ninth Plan intends to bring down the total demand for water for irrigation by AD 2025 to about 74.75 per cent. For this more efficient use of water by encouraging economical and effective methods of irrigation were to be undertaken. It was estimated that by 10 per cent increase in the present level of water use efficiency in irrigation projects, and additional 14 million hectares could be brought under irrigation with existing capacities. Obviously, this required large scale education of farmers to under take more efficient water use methods. For this purpose, the Ninth Plan considered participatory irrigation management programme as the key element of strategy. State-wise and year-wise percentage of Net Irrigated area is presented in Table 3.

Irrigation Programmes in the Tenth Plan

The working group for the tenth plan has assessed that a total of 159 major and 242 medium irrigation projects would spill over into the tenth plan. Anther 89 projects known as extension, renovation and modernization projects would also spill over to the tenth plan. A further 67 major, 130 medium and 34 ERM projects would also be taken up during the tenth plan. For completion of the old projects and executing new projects the Tenth plan proposes a total outlay of Rs. 109,025 crores and hopes to create over 11 million hectares of additional irrigation potential.

Table 3: State-wise Percentage of Net Irrigated Area in Selected Years

States	1990-91	1995-96	2000.01
Andhra Pradesh	39.06	38.76	40.71
Arunachal Pradesh	20.79	19.46	25.6
Assam	—	20.58	6.22
Bihar (Inc. Jharkhand)	43.45	50.27	48.79
Chhattisgarh	—	22.25	20.60
Delhi	78.60	93.62	100.00
Goa	—	16.55	16.45
Gujarat	25.74	30.10	31.80
Harayan	72.71	76.99	83.82
Himachal Pradesh	17.07	18.49	22.70
Jammu & Kashmir	40.80	52.59	41.58
Karnataka	20.36	22.09	25.39
Kerala	14.84	15.10	17.27
Madhya Pradesh	22.06	30.01	28.26
Maharashtra	14.89	14.33	16.78
Manipur	—	46.43	46.43
Maghalaya	22.88	21.84	—
Mizoram	—	6.42	9.53
Nagaland	31.02	29.38	24.00
Orissa	30.68	33.66	33.16
Punjab	92.71	92.95	84.48
Rajasthan	23.84	31.57	30.90
Sikkim	—	16.84	17.80
Tamil Nadu	42.53	49.14	54.40
Tripura	18.51	12.64	13..2
Uttar Pradesh	60.94	67.10	72.70
West Bengal	—	34.99	43.40
India	33.61	37.55	38.70

Source: Agriculture, Centre for Monitoring Indian Economy (CMIE) November 2000 and March 2005.

Table 4: Source-wise Relative Shares of Irrigation in India in Selected Years

(Million hectares)

Years	Canals	Tanks	Wells	Other sources	Total net irrigated
1970-71	12.84	4.11	11.90	2.26	31.10
1975-76	13.79	3.97	14.44	2.38	34.59
1980-81	15.29	3.18	17.69	5.55	38.72
1985-86	16.18	2.76	20.41	2.50	41.86
1990-91	17.45	2.49	24.69	2.93	48.02
1995-96	17.12	3.11	29.70	3.46	53.40
2000-01	15.98	2.52	33.27	2.89	54.68

Source: Agriculture, Centre for Monitoring Indian Economy, CMIE, March 2005.

Table 5: Irrigated Area and Agriculture Production in India

Years	Gross Irrigated (m. ha)	Net irrigated as a % of net sown	Gross Irr. as a % of gross cropped area	Agl. Produ. (m. tons)
1970-71	38.19	22.17	23.04	108.42
1975-76	43.36	24.42	26.31	121.03
1980-81	49.77	27.66	29.83	129.59
1985-86	54.28	29.71	30.42	150.44
1990-91	63.20	33.61	34.03	176.39
1995-96	71.35	37.55	38.25	180.42
2000-01	75.14	38.75	40.18	200.00

Source: Agriculture, Centre for Monitoring Indian Economy (CMIE), March 2005.

Irrigation in Andhra Pradesh

Andhra Pradesh is naturally endowed with a substantial scope for irrigation and power because of the rivers like Krishna, Godavari, Tungabadra and Pennar. The economy of Andhra Pradesh is an agricultural based one. About 70 per cent of population derives its livelihood from agriculture. Agricultural sector has received attention in all the five year plans. Since the beginning of planning era, many efforts are being made to step up agricultural production. This is done by bringing additional area under cultivation. Further, cultivated land is put to intensive use through extension of irrigation facilities and introduction of high yielding varieties of seeds. Changing cropping pattern and increasing productivity have been largely responsible in registering increase in agricultural production in Andhra Pradesh. In Andhra Pradesh, more than 70 per cent of cropped area is under food grain crops. Rice and jowar nearly account for 60 per cent of the total area under food grain crops. Groundnut, sugar-cane, cotton and tobacco are the important non-food crops grown in Andhra Pradesh. Among the different states in India, Andhra Pradesh occupies fifth position in the total cropped area. The state ranks tenth among the major states in respect of the proportion of area under double cropping.

In Andhra Pradesh tanks and wells were the main source of irrigation till the first half of the 19th century. The government spent reasonable amounts in maintaining, repairing and improving tanks. Tanks maintenance was locked after by the public works department and revenue department. The construction of anicuts across Krishna and Godavari in 1850s heralded a new era of large scale irrigation development. In the Rayalaseema region of Andhra Pradesh, irrigation requirements for centuries were ment by 17 canals, led through the rocky banks of Tungabadra to the field. The water from rivers were supplemented by hundreds of wells. The precarious agriculture in this region was maintained by these canals and wells.

Over a period of time, these canals were neglected and they lapsed into disrepair and ruin, by the middle of the 16th century. As a result the Rayalaseema region, became almost depopulates and its cities vanished. In this region a new canal by name Kurnool and Cuddapah canal came into existence in 1863. The canal was drawn from the Tungabadra by a private company known as "The Madras Irrigation Company." Originally the canal was designed both for irrigation and navigation between Kurnool and Kadapa. The canal was designed to carry 85 cu.mt of water. After an examination, the first irrigation commission observed, "owing to original defects in the work and to the neglect of necessary annual repairs and the difficulty of getting money for expenditure on a work which had proved so un-remunerative, a large volume than 2000 cu mt cannot be passed. The revenue returns from the canal were inadequate. The revenue could not cover even the working expanses." Finally the government bought out the company and took over the canal in 1882.

Water Resources for Irrigation in A.P.

The state of Andhra Pradesh is popularly known as the "River State" the important rivers which help irrigation include Godavari, Krishna, Tungabadra, Pennar and Vamsadhara Canals, tanks, tube-wells, filter points and other well irrigated a gross cropped area of 50.57 lakhs hectares during 1983-84, accounting for 40 per cent of the gross cropped area of the state. In terms of utilization of irrigation water resources in the state, rice accounts for 77.60 per cent, groundnut for 6.60 per cent and all other crops for the remaining quantity. The total groundwater potential in the state is estimated to be 4.1 million hectare metres, out of which the present exploitation is 0.98 million hectare meters through dug wells and filter points mainly in the river basins. This leaves a balance of 3.1 million hectares as against the gross cropped irrigated area of 50.57 lakhs hectare in 1983-84, the ultimate irrigation potential of the state was estimated at 103.20 lakhs hectares.

In Andhra Pradesh various sources of irrigation played a significant role for the development of agriculture and other fields of development. The following table explains the area irrigation under various sources in Andhra Pradesh. In Andhra Pradesh, a significant decrease in the area of irrigation under tanks. This decline was compensated by significant improvement in well irrigation in the state. In spite of fluctuation in the area irrigated under different sources the gross irrigated area more or less remains constant.

As presented in Table 6, the area under canel irrigation has been fluctuating fro year to year. The reason for the is due to fluctuations in rainfall in the catchment areas of the major rivers in the state. However, the percentage of area under tank irrigation declined from 7.31 per cent in 1998-99 to 4.37 per cent in 2002-2003. But the area under tube-wells increased from 8.27 per cent of the net area sown in 1998-99 to 11.85 per cent by 2002-2003. Net irrigated area as percentage of net sown area in Andhra Pradesh declined from 40.98 per cent to 37.14 per cent from 1998-1999 to 2002-2003.

Table 6: Sources of Irrigation in Andhra Pradesh (in ha)

Source of Irrigation	2001-02	2002-03
Canals	1562413	1208538
	(14.85)	(12.42)
Tanks	567519	425677
	(5.39)	(4.37)
Tube wells	1115711	1152800
	(10.60)	(11.85)
Other wells	811727	689485
	(7.71)	(7.09)
Other sources	180498	137164
	(1.72)	(1.41)
Net irrigated area	4237868	3613664
	(40.27)	(37.14)
Net area sown	10524194	11558629

Source: GOAP: Statistical Abstract, Andhra Pradesh, Directorate of Economics and Statistics, GOAP, Hyderabad, 2004.

Note : Figures in parentheses indicate percentage to total net area sown.

Irrigation and New Challenges to Agriculture

An important constituent of the current strategy for raising agricultural production is the increasing reliance on irrigation. The strategy of Intensive Agricultural District Programme (IADP) and the High Yielding Varieties Programme (HYVP) were initially introduced only in those areas which had assured rainfall and irrigation facilities. As the scope for extending the cropped area is limited, in fact, the cropped area has ranged between 140 to 141 million ha in recent years. Greater reliance has to be placed on irrigation so as to have double or multiple cropping. The basic objective is to produce a much higher yield of grain output per hector by promoting the showing of two or more crops an irrigated land.

It has been estimated that India has around 166 million hectare of agricultural land out of which 140 million hectare of land could ultimately be irrigated by 1999 to 2000, only 95 million hectare are provided irrigation facilities. That levels still 45 million hectares of potential irrigation for the successive five year plans. According to the Irrigation Commission the cost of exploiting this potential could work out at Rs. 30,000 crores (at 1980-81) or more than Rs. 75,000 crores now (in current price). As the financial resources available to the government are limited, the Seventh and Eighth Plans took up only a few major and medium projects but laid emphasis on the completion of ongoing projects.

In order to expand irrigation facilities, the Government of India has adopted the following programmes:

a. NABARD has set up Rural Infrastructure Development Fund (RIDF) under which loans are granted to states for speedy completion of major irrigation projects.

b. The government has launched, since 1996-97, a programme called 'Accelerated Irrigation Benefit Scheme', under which the centre is providing additional central assistance by way of loans to the states for early completion of selected large irrigation and multi-purpose projects.

REFERENCES

CMIE (2005), *Basic Statistics on Agriculture*, Centre for Monitoring Indian Economy, March, Mumbai.

Dawn, B.D. (1988), 'Indian Irrigation: An Assessment,' *Economic and Political Weekly*, May 7, Mumbai.

GOAP (2004), *Statistical Abstract 2004*, Directorate of Economics and Statistics, Government of Andhra Pradesh, Hyderabad.

Mamoria, C.B. and Tripathi, B.B. (2001), *Agricultural Problems of India*, Kitab Mahal, Allahabad.

Maynard, M. Hufschmids (1993), "Water Policies and Sustainable Development," In: Asit K. Biswas, Hommed Jellai, Glen E.Stiout (Eds), *Water: Sustainable Development in the Twenty First Century*, Oxford University Press, New Delhi.

10

Irrigation of Rayalaseema "Begger Thy Neighbour Policy" in Andhra Pradesh

A. RANGA REDDY

The paper highlights backwardness of Rayalaseema's irrigation situation in the scenario of Andhra Pradesh economy.

Andhra Pradesh is a River State and an agriculture economy, which is based on dichotomy in-between irrigation and rain-fed agriculture. The total surface water of entire river systems of the State is estimated to be of the order of 2764 TMC at 75 per cent dependability. This breaks up into 1480 TMC from Godavari River system, 811 TMC from the Krishna, 99 TMC from the Pennar and the rest from 37 other small rivers. We had surplus water of 745 TMC in Godavari and Krishna water was fully harnessed through projects. Unfortunately, investment on large water resources development projects is presently seen as a panacea. Earlier projects lost their installed capacity in mid-way. Another giant project of linking Ganga-Cauvery is on pipe line. Users should be encouraged to aim at greater efficiency and productivity, through integrated use of soil moisture, local and exogenous water.

At present, a shift is needed from the present approach of equating water resource development to creation of new resources by rain water harvesting and construction of storage reservoirs. Importance needs to be given to sustainability, productivity enhancement and efficiency of water-use. Local resources by themselves are often inadequate in rain-fed areas to provide for food security. Further, due to land degradation and sub-optimal water use, it is difficult to provide the water needed to create the marketable surplus of food grains and pulses. Integration of local resources of water and land can enhance the benefit from external water by optimizing the storage options through the limited use of irrigation water over extensive area for extended commands as well as new projects.[1]

Irrigation alone cannot bring prosperity to any area. There is a big sector of landless poor in the affluent Coastal Andhra districts and other areas, they go in search of work during seasonal agricultural operations in K.C. Canal, Nizamsagar and other projects in the backward areas of Rayalaseema and Telangana regions. Many such people have also migrated to Hyderabad, in search of better income and employment and vice versa.[2]

Struggle for Irrigation

In Andhra Pradesh, out of 133.113 lakh acres of cultivated area, from irrigation department sources lakh acres (133.113) – (14.90 + 7.75) = 110.5 lakh acres, 14.90 lakh acres under Panchyat Raj Departments irrigation tanks and 7.75 lakh acres under Andhra Pradesh State Irrigation Development Corporation (APS IDC) and the balance is rain-fed (292–133.113 = 158.887) lakh acres. In all irrigated sources 46% of land is irrigated.[3]

The regions of Rayalaseema and Telangana have experienced drastic shifts in the composition of irrigation. By the 1980s well irrigation had become the dominant source of irrigation replacing tank irrigation in Rayalaseema and Telangana. The larger part of rain-fed area is affected by frequent droughts. As the droughts increase, the struggles for 'water' and politics of water have intensified in recent times. The water struggles are fought at different levels. The regional struggles of Telangana and Rayalaseema for more water are being intensified, including a demand for separate "State of Telangana". "Recently, the 'War' between the farmers of Kurnool district and Mahabubnagar district at Rajolibanda Diversion System (RDS) in effect fought between the close relatives separated only by the district boundaries and

Tungabhadra river of course, the water 'war' between Andhra Pradesh and Karnataka is never ending.

There are number of studies linking rain-fed areas and poverty, irrigation development and poverty reduction, irrigation development and industrial development. All studies generally subscribe to the theory that irrigation development has strong influence on the overall growth and regional development.

Most of the farmers' suicides are reported from drought-prone areas especially small and marginal farmers. Anantapur tops the list of farmers' suicides as a result of frequent droughts. The drought hit farmers are in the web of perpetual cycle of indebtedness and poverty for generations and are unable to getout of it. Only some assured irrigation could provide a farmer with ability to cope with such a pathetic situation.

When Telangana, Coastal Andhra political leaders are continuously fighting for their share of river waters and stabilising their ayacuts, Rayalaseema faction political leaders never voiced their resentment. Of course, good droughts are fortunes for their vote bank but not stability in politics and regional greenery. Possibly, the history of Rayalaseema made them immunised not to go for development of irrigation projects. A brief analogy is given below.

A Brief History of Rayalaseema

Satavahanas ruled Rayalaseema during 400 B.C. Kings were Vaishnavites but queens professed Buddhism. In A.D. 600, feudalism had been with high taxation and harsh punishments. Chalukyas, Kakatiyas and Reddy rulers reigned during A.D.680-1450 with Vengi, Warangal (Orugallu), Rajamahendra-varam, Kondavidu as capitals. Both Kannada and Telugu had a homogenous language. Muslims conquered and ruled Telugu land and people – Bahamani and later Kutbshahi sultans of Golconda and still later the Nizams of Hyderabad with their vassals of Kurnool, Adoni, Cuddapah and Arcot Nawabs.

Vijayanagara Rule

Rayalaseema means, the area (*seema*) ruled by the Rayas (rulers) of Vijayanagara Empire. It consisted of the present districts of Anantapur, Chittoor, Kadapa, Kurnool and Bellary which is now in Karnataka State. Under their glorious rule particularly of Sri Krishnadevaraya (1509-1529), Rayalaseema received systematic canal linked Tank irrigation and flourished with *navadhanyas*[4] and *navaratnas*. Unfortunately, Vijayanagar rulers besides a very large standing army had also encouraged military chieftains of *palems* known as Palegars. These Palegars ruled at times extremely cruel. Due to this situation some dignified and rich families migrated from Rayalaseema. Under anarchism and promiscuity, poets and reformers emerged leading to a very rich folklore and literature based on the life and work of Pothuluri Veerabramham, Poet Vemana, Bala Nagamma and Lakshmamma and so on.

Under British Rule

In A.D. 1800, Nizam had given Rayalaseema districts to the British East India Company as Ceded Districts because of his inability to pay the amount due to the Company's subsidiary forces. During A.D. 1800-1807. Thomas Munro, as Principal Collector, had given golden rule to Rayalaseema people by supressing eighty palegars and extended *ryotwari* system. Under the British crown, after A.D. 1857, the worst famine was known as the Dhatu Famine during 1876-1878. It took a toll of 40 per cent of people, who died for want of food. Arthur Cotton and Mackenzy were architects of Kurnool-Cuddapah Canal in A.D. 1872 for Inland water ways (later found uneconomical) and irrigational purposes including drinking water.

Sri Bagh Pact

In 1937, at Madras, at the Sri Bagh residency of Kasinathuni Nageswara Rao, there was a Gentlemen Agreement among Rayalaseema and Coastal Andhra leaders. The objectives of Sri Bagh Pact was to start a Post-Graduate Centre of Andhra University, Waltair (established in 1926) at Anantapur, the surplus water available in Krishna river have to go Rayalaseema and political capital or High Court is to be given to Rayalaseema. Of course, capital was given for very short period of three years 1953-56 and shifted to Hyderabad from November 1, 1956. Potti Sreeramulu, a great patriot, went for fast unto death from October 19, 1952 died on Dec.

15, 1952. N.G. Ranga, Krushikar Party asked Coastal Andhra and Rayalaseema leaders to go for making Tirupati as Capital.

Rain Shadow Area

When comparing other two regions, a distinctive feature of Rayalaseema was low rainfall around 500 m.m., which transformed entire development under backwardness. Seventy-five per cent of cultivated land was under rain-fed. In 1954 Tungabhadra project was started to construct, which gave 20 per cent water and 80 per cent power to Rayalaseema. Unfortunately, much of assured water is being enjoyed by Coastal Andhra and Telangana regions, the uncertain and unreliable surplus water from Srisailam Hydel Project was allotted to the poorest Rayalaseema region. Telugu Ganga was started in 1989, much of water was planned to go for irrigation of Nellore District and Madras for drinking water. In 1992, Galeru-Nagari was conceived. On flood water of Krishna, Srisailam Right Branch Canal, Hundri Niva (lift irrigation), Galeru-Nagari and Telugu Ganga were planned to develop and distribute to Rayalaseema region, which will be a perma-0nent dream. It shows the other two regions suppressed the voice of Rayalaseema people under their brutal force both in Parliament and Assembly. Rayalaseema region may not get assured irrigated water, unless there was a miracle of political will.

Planning Expenditure

State had given top priority for irrigation development in Andhra Pradesh. Irrigation is the only medicine and tonic for disease of chronic droughts. Table 1 provides a bird's eye view of state budget under planning.

Table 1 has given a picture that under planning period 18.96 lakh acres was brought under irrigation in all sources and pre-plan and annual plans the area irrigated was 31.682 lakh acres, in total 50.642 lakh hectares for the year 2003-04. The expenditure column in percentage, further, explains that up to Third Five-year Plan, State spent one-third of its budget for irrigation. Later, except Fifth Five-year Plan, the funds devoted for irrigation was declined. Especially under Telugu Desam Party rule, it reached to bottom level. Of course, again after Congress came to power on May 14, 2004 has given mega or lion's share for irrigation, such as completing 26 Projects with Rs. 46,000 crores, escalation of cost structure became a stumbling block for irrigation. In fact, the First Plan was given irrigated water cost per hectare was Rs. 1060, whereas in Seventh Plan it was Rs. 50,000, i.e., almost raised around 47 times.

Table 1: State Plan Irrigation Created and Expenditure

PLAN	Irrigation potential created (Lakh ha)	Expenditure (in %age)
I Plan years (1951-56)	0.845	22.58
II Plan years (1956- 61)	1.452	34.75
III Plan years (1961-66)	1.408	35.32
IV Plan years (1969 –74)	2.80	22.82
V Plan years (1974-78)	2.67	31.58
VI Plan years (1980 –85)	2.53	26.80
VII Plan years (1985-90)	1.42	24.23
VIII Plan years (1992-97)	0.61	18.44
IX Plan years (1997-2002	2.38	18.84
X Plan years (2002-2004)	1.175	-
Total	**18.96**	-

Source: 1. Government of Andhra Pradesh, *Economic Survey 2004-05,* p. 169

2. *Veekhshanam*, (A Telugu monthly) 2005, Can achieve Irrigation projects - in Effective planning? Nov.15, p.16

There are about 80,000 tanks in the State, of which Telangana has 44 per cent followed by Coastal Andhra 38 per cent and Rayalaseema 18 per cent. Interestingly, the region with the highest dependence on groundwater (Rayalaseema) has the lowest number of tanks. In fragile resource region, groundwater irrigation has become privy to large farmers, denying rights to small and marginal farmers.[5]

Further, integration of tank restoration with watersheds, check dams, water harvesters and pits would not only strengthen the ecological base but also, get the community's sustainability. The changes in the distribution of irrigations across regions have two important repercussions: (1) Well irrigation is concentrated in the fragile resource regions. More important, private people mostly finance well irrigation, while canal and tank irrigation are financed by the state. This aggravated regional inequalities. (2) Development of well irrigation is less favourable to small and marginal farmers when compared to canal tank irrigation due to high capital intensity.[6]

Irrigation Spread

Assured irrigated water is a basic life input for sustainable agricultural development. Naturally, river side, delta areas got opportunity to change their agricultural methods and prospered well. Unfortunately, chronic drought prone areas were still suffering for want of irrigation water. Table 2 explains the area irrigated by different source scenario of Andhra Pradesh.

Table 2 reveals that out of 55.48 hectares of gross area irrigated in the state, 23.6 per cent was the area shown more than once during 2001-02. West Godavari district had the large extent of gross area irrigated in the state with a share of 10.18 per cent of total gross area irrigated followed by East Godavari with 8.06 per cent share.

In Andhra Pradesh, cheapest input is canal irrigation. In Coastal Andhra in kharif crops, more than 50 per cent area was irrigated in 5 districts, out of 9 districts. The other four districts had above 30 per cent canal irrigation. Area of non-food crops in Coastal Andhra were below 10 per cent. It received lion share of 49 per cent of area irrigated.

In Rayalaseema district canal irrigation except in Kurnool District, all are negligible. But much of irrigation was based on groundwater, which was around 60 per cent. Agriculture was shifted to non-food crops, which was uncertain and risky, so that more suicides had taken place in this region. State policies like cheap rice, cheap power, groundwater policies further put this region under more stress and strain. It got only 15 per cent area under irrigation in the state.

The Telangana region, with the exceptions of Khammam and Nalgonda districts, all other district had less than 30 per cent canal irrigation. Eight districts depended on groundwater,

Table 2: Net Area Irrigated by Sources, District-wise-2001-02

(in percentage)

Sl. No	District	Canals	Tanks	Tube-well/ other sources	Total in ha	Area irrigated more than once	Total food crops (in %)	Total non-foods crops (in %)
COAȘTAL ANDHRA								
1	Srikakulam	55.0	34.0	11.0	1,67,036 (100.0)	6.0	96.0	4.0
2	Vizianagaram	31.0	56.0	13.0	1,154,16 (100.0)	22.0	95.0	5.0
3	Visakhapatnam	38.0	24.0	38.0	91,332 (100.0)	41.0	97.0	3.0
4	East Godavari	68.0	8.0	24.0	2,61,965 (100.0)	71.0	95.0	5.0
5	West Godavari	56.0	0.5	43.50	3,35,318 (100.0)	68.0	91.0	9.0
6	Krishna	77	5.0	18.0	2,93,485 (100.0)	36.0	98.0	2.0
7	Guntur	82.0	2.0	16.0	3,68,956 (100.0)	5.0	93.0	7.0
8	Prakasam	36.0	16.0	48.0	2,04,971 (100.0)	4.0	87.0	13.0
9	Nellore	31.0	31.0	38.0	2,38,445	13.0	93.0	7.0
	Total				**20,76,924 (49.0)**			

RAYALASEEMA								
10	Chittoor	1.0	22.0	77.0	1,75,438 (100.0)	28.0	80.0	20.0
11	Cuddapah	12.0	10.0	78.0	1,52,071 (100.0)	19.0	65.0	35.0
12	Anantapur	21.0	11.0	68.0	1,43,366 (100.0)	24.0	67.0	33.0
13	Kurnool	37.0	6.0	57.0	1,65,938	25.0	63.0	37.0
	Total				**6,36,813 (15.0)**			
TELANGANA								
14	Mahabubnagar	10.0	4.0	86.0	163,606 (100.0)	28.0	71.0	29.0
15	Ranga Reddy	4.0	4.0	92.0	71,904 (100.0)	22.0	89.0	11.0
16	Hyderabad	-	-	-	(100.0)	-	-	-
17	Medak	2.0	6.0	92.0	130,209 (100.0)	44.0	97.0	3.0
18	Nizamabad	15.0	11.0	74.0	168,313 (100.0)	59.0	96.0	4.0

(contd.)

Table 2: (concld.)

Sl. No	District	Canals	Tanks	Tube-well/ other sources	Total in ha	Area irrigated more than once	Total food crops (in %)	Total non-foods crops (in %)
19	Adilabad	32.0	28.0	40.0	76,112 (100.0)	23.0	91.0	9.0
20	Karimagar	25.0	11.0	64.0	2,62,858 (100.0)	47.0	88.0	12.0
21	Warangal	1.0	19.0	80.0	3,02,001 (100.0)	18.0	64.0	36.0
22	Khammam	30.0	22.0	48.0	1,55,068 (100.0)	8.0	88.0	12.0
23	Nalgonda	32.0	7.0	51.0	1,94,060	40.0	95.0	5.0
	Total				**1524131 (36.0)**			
	Andhra Pradesh	37.0	13.0	26.0	42,37,868 (100.0)	36.0	87.0	13.0

Sources: GOAP; Statistical Abstract of Andhra Pradesh 2003, pp. 33.

which was highly fluctuated and unpredictable. Mahabub Nagar and Warangal districts went for around 30 per cent non-food crops, which also suffered under suicide shocks. In the state, 36 per cent of irrigated area was found in it

The south-western part of Andhra Pradesh, Rayalaseema was comparatively highly backward both in irrigation and agriculture than Telangana and Coastal Andhra, simultaneously income and employment levels also. In fact, State has to apply location - specific policies, than homogeneous policies to make it sustainable. Equal rights on water distribution for all are a basic ethics. This moral code failed over Rayalaseema region after independence especially Sri Bagh pact, 1937, Bachawat Tribunal Award and State Governments. The two rich regions – Coastal Andhra and Telangana – are working tirelessly denying water rights to Rayalaseema due to weak socio-economic, political and cultural leadership, e.g. Pothireddipadu Head Regulator height issue. It proved that Rayalaseema **begger thy neighbour policy** in Andhra Pradesh irrigation politics. The above facts proved that coastal Andhra and Telangana political leaders are interested to see Rayalaseema as beggar also for irrigated water.

Krishna Water Distribution Dispute: Bachawat Tribunal

In 1960, Maharashtra, Orissa, Karnataka states had raised river water dispute. After prolonged dialogue and formation of States, in March 23, 1963 Centre brought an award that under Krishna 800 TMCs to Andhra Pradesh, 600 TMCs to Karnataka and 400 TMCs to Maharashtra. Again in April 10, 1969, the tribunal changed its verdict, in such a way that Karnataka 700 TMCs, Maharashtra 600 TMCs and Andhra Pradesh 800 TMCs had to be utilised. Surplus water can be used by Andhra Pradesh. This award should have been reviewed after May 31, 2000. Meanwhile, Karanataka State had raised the height of many projects like Almatti and led to chronic water dispute.

Godavari River Water Tribunal Award

During Dec. 19, 1975 - August 7, 1978, State of Andhra Pradesh was interested to construct Ichampalli project.

According to Tribunal, the Andhra Pradesh can avail 1495 TMCs water. Down stream projects like Penuganga, Lendi were considered as projects, whereas Pranahita project will go with Andhra Pradesh Government.

Under joint venture, Tungabhadra Project was started in 1956 and gives water to 86, 617 hectares covers Anantapur, Kadapa and Kurnool Districts. Somasila on Penna in Nellore District was started and covered an area of 56,295 hectares. Yeleru project was launched with Rs. 335 crores, finished the first stage and stabilized ayacut of 44,200 hectares. Polavaram on Godavari, covering an area of 2.9 lakhs hectares, still environmental impact assessment report has not come. Srisailam project, Telugu Ganga, Singur project, Priyadarshni Jurala project, Nizamsagar, Gannavaram Acquiduct, Sunkesula barrage, Pothireddipadu lift, Pulichintala, Alaganur Balancing Reservoir, Galeru-Nagari canal project, Hundri-niva Sujalasravanthi, Bhima lift Irrigation are in different stages.

Issues like the lack of capital, managerial deficiencies, shortage of leadership, failure of efficient political will, bad governance entailed the pace of the projects not to move fastly. By all means, by channeling water resource in right way to field can raise the yield rate up to 50 to 60 per cent higher.[7]

As water levels are falling rapidly, there is a big shift has come up that in future marginal, small farmers may not get irrigated water resources, only medium and large farmers would enjoy. Much of water budget and amounts had been used for diverting water to industrial development, hydel power and drinkable water distribution to Urban areas, than farmers. In fact, in the State, 55 per cent of irrigated water is going to roots of crops and rest is in drainage. Water Users Associations have to play effective role in distribution of water, cropping pattern, pricing of water, water budgeting; which are still infant stage in understanding water democracy. Scientific irrigation schedules must be based on a through understanding of soil-water-Plant-atmosphere relationship.[8]

Irrigation projects and Oustees

In all irrigation projects, three issue are to be taken up carefully – designing project at particular location, construction of project with adequate capital and evacuating people to ensure intact ecology with the storage capacity of project. Vacating villages and tribals, submerging forest land, flora and fauna missing and environmental destruction would be considered seriously by State. Among them the most important issue is vacating people by force became a burning problem. So that many environmentalists like Vandanasiva, Medha Patkar, Sundarlal Bahuguna and opposition party leaders were stressing more on giving packages to Oustees households, who are victims for large scale movement of men and materials from plateaus to plains. Minimum facilities are to be given for displaced people under any project, before construction.

Self-reliance model of Anantapur District irrigation

A study in Anantapur District is briefly highlighted. In a family of 5 members, 2 children were studying Intermediate course. They own an ordinary mud-house and cattle-shed requiring some maintenance every year. The farmer is neither to traditional nor progressive and cultivates "less risky crops" like paddy, Ground-nut and sunflower. The dry land owned by him is not considered. It is arrived that Rs.35,000 per family was required for minimum level of subsistence (MLS). Rs. 400 per person per month was required for food security alone i.e Rs. 24,000 per annum for a family of 5 towards food expenditure alone. The other costs of health, education, house repairs, repairs and maintenance of agri-equipment would make up for Rs. 35,000 MLS. One acre wet under irrigation even with three crops per year is inadequate to meet a family's MLS. The deficit is ranging from Rs. 8,300 to Rs. 19,600. Therefore, it suggests that having one acre under irrigation even with 3 crops per year is inadequate to meet a family's MLS. Whereas 2 acres and 3 acres of irrigated land and with the possibility of 3 crops in a year, the projected surplus is Rs. 17,600 and Rs. 42,400 respectively. So, two acres of wet land would provide some cushion for saving or making some capital investment on agriculture. However, the study indicated that mostly such a surplus went in for treatment of sickness as one or the other in the family fell sick every year. Thirty per cent of the debts in a family are said to have been on account of sickness, Whereas 3 acres of wet, possibility of 3 crops provides a family with comfortable surplus over MLS. The farmer could afford for higher education, higher health needs, functions like marriage, purchase of luxury goods like TV, motor cycle etc. It is rarely possible to have three crops in a year in drought prone areas like Anantapur.

Of course, 2 crops a year situation of 3 acres scenario just crosses the MLS household and has a marginal surplus of Rs. 5,612 and 4 acres scenario provides a surplus of about Rs. 19,000 over the years chronic indebtedness has become an integral part of the rural households in drought prone regions. Excessive indebtedness in recent years had been driving the farmers towards long-term or permanent migration. And some farmers have been resorting to suicides. This phenomenon is not only limited to marginal and small farmers, but also spreading to medium and large farmers. Due to increasing input costs and falling output prices among farming community, the debt trap is covering more farmers.[9]

The rich districts are stabilising their ayacut while backward Rayalaseema is undergoing chronic droughts. The following is an illustration of Polavaram.

Polavaram Project: A Link between Krishna and Godavari

The project is to be built on Godavari, near Polavaram village in West Godavari, is expected to irrigate 7,21,000 acres in the districts of Krishna, West, and East Godavari and Visakapatnam. The project cost is estimated at Rs. 8,188 crores and another Rs. 4,500 crores for resettlement and rehabilitation. The project obtained site and environmental clearance recently and work already has begun on the Right and left canals and the spillway.

Irrigation and Revenue officials tentatively put the figure of displacement at a whopping 1,95,000 people – a majority of them Koya and Kondreddi tribes, making it one of the biggest shifting of indigenous people in the country for an irrigation project. The number of villages to be submerged is put at 280 in all, 209 in Khammam, 42 in East Godavari and 29 in West Godavari District. Twenty more villages in Chhattisgrah and Orissa could be submerged. Such dams perpetrate cultural genocide of tribals. The Government offer of land, resettlement and rehabilitation packages were thin with poor track record from Nagarjunasagar. B.V. Raghavulu, CPI(M) polit-bureau member said that what is the worth of a project that submerges 2,00,000 acres of fertile land, uprooting 2,00,000 Adivasis and creates a new ayacut in an agriculturally well developed region. By dam impact, tribes have started "Vertical migration" back to the hilltops occupying large chunks of forest. The non-Adivasis of the villages to be submerged echo similar sentiments, a farmer raised sugarcane that yields a high 60 tonnes an acre and tobacco eight to 10 quintals. Should we leave all this and go to a new place? People are already feeling the pinch, that is, relatives from other areas look to us, with pity, no new house construction or repairs, no work for a mason. The Project when completed would gobble up 3,500 hectares of forest area some of it typical to the eastern 'Ghats'.[10]

By transferring Godavari Water to Krishna, to make Krishna, Guntur, Khammam Districts to stabilise ayacut. Therefore, it is a hope that Rayalaseema can avail more Krishna river water at Srisailam on to on-going Rayalaseema Projects.

Supplementary Support for Irrigation

Fortunately, State had given preference to short term, low cost, community associated minor irrigation tanks, watersheds, lifts, check dams by using different institutions. They are as follows.

A.P State Irrigation Development Corporation

In 1974, State introduced Andhra Pradesh State Irrigation Development Corporation (APS IDC) to support lift irrigation, Tube-wells, infiltration wells. It all started with good beginning but not worked for longer period, due to non-recovery of over dues and high establishment costs.

Andhra Pradesh State Groundwater Development

It had supported the Integrated Tribal Development Agency also, which was established to help Scheduled Castes and Tribes, Backward caste farmers, like marginal and small farmers by extending financial cooperation, technological support and extension activities to exploit groundwater. It identifies levels of groundwater availability and also suggests grey areas. Scarcity of funds made it to grow slowly.

Panchayatraj Institutions

It had extended helping hand to 80,000 irrigation sources. By this institution around 14.90 lakhs acres were brought under ayacut. It maintains flood control, Tank maintenance. Lack of funds this institution is not effectively functioning in the State.

Cyclone Emergency Reconstruction Project

In May 1990, due to heavy rains and cyclones, many irrigation resources in Coastal districts were destroyed. State went to seek financial help from the World Bank. Though its financial estimate was Rs. 42 crores, but spent only Rs. 10 crores.

Drainage Canal Schemes

Due to bad drainage facilities; delta districts crops were under low yield. Therefore, Krishna, Godavari, Nellore Districts were badly need of drainage canal facility. The total canal was 10,123 km under drainage with World Bank funds. State was interested to do drainage facility by collecting those loans spent through drainage cess, So that it brought two Acts in 1985, 1986 years. It is on snail walk.

Command Area Development Authority

Its objectives are to maintain the level of land, soil health, canal management, warabandi, water management, planning, and supervision. So that with scientific methodology the cultivation will be controlled and expanded for high yield rates. The objectives were defeated and disturbed.

Water Users' Associations (WUAs)

Andhra Pradesh is the first State, which introduced Water Users' Associations through legislation in 1997. The objective is to maximise irrigation potential improving efficiency and stakeholder participation. Under this Act, 10292 WUAs were formed. WUAs elections where conducted in March 2003 for 80 per cent of these minor irrigation systems. It has realised some positive results. Many WUAs Presidents have become money making ventures, than extending irrigation potential.

Conclusion

Unfortunately, Rayalaseema before independence suffered under Sultans, feudal lords, British and presently with State government's uneven policies. Where ever plenty of water was their civilizations flourished. When water shortage is there, the society faces all types of problems like factionalism, growing hunger, immeasurable poverty, jungle of unemployment. Arthur Cotton, is the father of irrigated projects, who introduced Kurnool-Kadapa Canal. Irrigation alone cannot solve agriculture and rural problems. But irrigation can solve many lingering problems and integrates development. Rayalaseema had suffered under chronic droughts and famines. Comparing other two regions with Rayalaseema's irrigation scenario, it is at low ebb. The irrigation spread is around 15 percent, which is highly negligible to overall development. The other two regions - Telangana and Coastal Andhra - were completing existing projects, denied the rights of Rayalaseema like Sri Bagh Pact, Bachawat Award, even after 59 years of independence. The hypothesis is that minimum three acres and two wets irrigations can make a household of five members to sustain. Godavari water is to be transferred from Polavaram to Krishna for Prakasam Barrage, and then Krishna river water can be diverted to Rayalaseema projects from reservoir of Srisailam. Besides long-term projects of Rayalaseema districts, encourage short term projects like watersheds, check dams, water harvesters, sprinklers, drips and awareness campaign will improve the condition. The two elderly brothers should not show step mother policies over continuously suffered youngest brother - Rayalaseema. Let extend helping hand to Rayalaseema's irrigation.

NOTES

1. Daley, K.R. (2003), Integrated Development and Management of Local Resources and Exogenous Water, *National Seminar on Water*, CESS, Hyderabad, July 30-31 p.12.
2. Rao, T. Hamumantha (2003), *Multipurpose Utilisation of Godavari River and the Relevancy of interlinking of Rivers*, CESS, July 30-31, p. 23.
3. Government of A.P., (2005), *Economic Survey 2004-05*, p.61.
4. Ranga Reddy, A. (2003), *The State of Rayalaseema*, Mittal Publications, New Delhi.

5. Ratna Reddy, V. (2003), Irrigation: Department and Reforms, *Economic and Political Weekly*, March 22-29, p.1181.
6. Ratna Reddy, V. (2003), *Irrigation : Development and Reforms, Andhra Pradesh : Economic Reforms and Challenges Ahead*, CESS, Hyderabad.
7. Vidyabhusan (2005), Comprehensive Irrigation projects in effective planning, *Veekshanam* Nov. 15, pp. 16-18.
8. Prihar, S.S. and B.S. Sandhu (1987), *Irrigation of Field Crops*, NCAR, New Delhi, p. 5.
9. Malla Reddy, Y.V. (2003), Irrigation and poverty among farmers - Micro-perspective, CESS on *National Seminar on water.* July, 30-31, 2003 pp. 59-65.
10. Venkateswarlu, K. (2006), Issues: Displaced Development, *The Hindu* (Sunday Magazine), Jan. 8.

11

Regional Disparities in Tank Irrigation: A Micro Analysis of Rayalaseema Distircts in Andhra Pradesh

B. NAGARAJA and C. SAILAJA

In recent years the concept "Equity" has become *mantra* of development strategy. The development economists are arguing that equity is necessary for sustainable development because 'equity' represented by the equal opportunities for all members of the society makes them socially active, politically influential and economically productive (World Bank, 2006). As a result, the equal opportunities exert potentially beneficial effects on poverty reduction. If we interpret this equity concept to 'irrigation poverty' particularly focusing on the poor farmers, who are not having sufficient access to and deprived of adequate irrigational facilities, it is certain that this strategy reduces 'irrigation poverty' in rural areas in general and the marginalized farmers in particular.

That was why the economic analysts are looking forward with optimism that the Chidambaram's budget for the year 2006-07 would be 'sweeter' which ensures equitable development and thinking that real shine to our economy comes from farm sector (Naik, 2006; Mahendradev, 2006; Prabhakaran Nair, 2006). Mr. Chidambaram while indicting the broad contours of the Budget-2006-07 proclaimed that development of agriculture sector, along with measures to boost irrigational facilities is essential to achieve 8% of growth rate in our economy. It was also argued that for sustaining and accelerating the growth momentum, the major emphasis of the budget must be on agriculture and allied sectors. This emphasis emanates from the fact that our Government has been favouring the 311 billionaires and the booming stock market, while completely neglecting the poor farmers, paying a deaf ear to their needs and requirements. And as a result, the growth rate in agriculture has dropped just to 1.5% during the first three years of the Tenth Plan (2002-05). It is also true that even during the "second green revolution" the average percapita income of farm household across India was only Rs.503 in 2003 (Sainath 2005, NSSO 59th round) and 20.21% of farmers are living below the poverty line (Pawar, 2006). The no.of cultivators also declined from 110.7 million in 1991 to 103.63 million in 2001 (*The Hindu*, 2005). Keeping this distress of farmers in view, our Prime Minister asked the experts to aim at an annual growth rate of 4% in agriculture during the remaining years of Tenth Plan by providing crop-specific, region-specific, resource-specific and farm-specific solutions (Parsi, 2005). M.S. Swaminathan also called for "more crop per drop" emphasizing the new water efficient technologies while speaking at International Conference on "Plasticulture and Precision Farming". He also underscored the need for working out the 'economics' of every technology to the advantage of farmers.

Thanks to the Hon. Chief Minister of Andhra Pradesh for having kept his promise given at the inauguration of a national workshop on " Value Addition to Foods: Fruits and Vegetables" at Hyderabad. Rs. 10,041 crores were allotted to irrigation sector in the 2006-07 budget as a part of his promise to Rs.46,000 crore programme to provide irrigation for an additional 65 lakh acres in the next four years. No doubt it is a courageous measure to push the compounded annual growth rate of agriculture sector to 4% and it is a matter of realization that "agricultural renewal" cannot be achieved without take-off point with required attention towards irrigation sector. The Ramachennareddy Commission , which probed into the suicides of the farmers in A.P., highlighted the dangers of neglecting the agriculture sector in A.P. and pointed out that the irrigation budget for the seven financial years during the reign of previous government was only Rs.8287 crores as against Rs. 6374 crore in 2005-06 alone (Kumar, 2005). It is sure that our Chief Minister has been trying to fulfil the incomplete dreams of the farmers, who have committed suicides. Their souls rest in peace after looking at these allocations to irrigation sector and this is a leap forward to stop the occurrences of this type of suicides in A.P. However, the functional efficiency depends mostly on the productive use of these allocations and the call of M.S. Swaminathan "more crop per drop" comes true only when sufficient measures are initiated to reap the benefits from 'irrigation'.

The politicians and the leaders of the people must recognize the fact that India cannot prosper while its agriculture stagnates. Our policy-makers are ignoring the fact that there is no large country in the world, which has attained the status of a developed country , without first developing its agriculture and achieving nearly total literacy among its people. We must learn a lesson from China in the case of agriculture growth and its performance. China achieved sustained agricultural growth which is high and labour-releasing in nature and favourable income distribution through broad based agricultural growth and high levels of human development associated with easy access to credit and inputs. The Hi-Tech supporters in our country have to realize the fact that our agricultural productivity measured in terms of value added per worker in 2000 was only $397, while it was $47566 for US, $38647 in France, $38431 in Belgium and $36702 in Canada (World Bank, 2006).

The summary of the above illustrations and the statistical and empirical evidence throw light on the conviction that poverty will decline only when agriculture sector is the full participant in economic growth, especially that of small and marginal farmers. Given the make up of Indian society, poverty reduction is driven ultimately by raising farm incomes, spent on locally produced goods and services that lead to more village-level employment opportunities. A high growth rate, even more than 4% in agricultural sector is essential within expected economic growth rate of eight per cent. Without it, poverty reduction will be a futile exercise.

The Neglect of Tank Irrigation

Each and every politician today are talking about giving a massive boost to agriculture forgetting the ground realities.

They are talking by according priority to construction of ecologically dangerous major irrigation projects, which consume the major portion of allocations of the budget, ignoring the fact that growth rate in agriculture can also be boosted with existing, appropriate technologies and methods, which are ecologically favourable, investment-saving and farmer-friendly. They are taking into account "new irrigation technologies" forgetting more productive, efficient and well-known systems like Tanks.

Tanks in India and in our States were known for their antiquity and created essentially as a multiple use structures for irrigation, livestock and human uses. Tanks were considered not as mere bodies of stored water but they were treated as a method of conservation of bio-diversity and also a technology for improving environmental quality. They have been performing different special functions in irrigated agriculture – water conservation, soil conservation, flood control and protection of ecology of surrounding area. Tanks represent for extraordinary engineering, managerial and social skills and an extensive system of rainwater harvesting structures. However, after Independence, the Government under successive planning had not given due attention or provided adequate financial support to keep these tanks in a good state. Most of the public investment in irrigation has gone to major and medium canal irrigation and development of groundwater under minor irrigation (Sivasubramanyam, 2005, GOI, 1997). No doubt the area under irrigation increased substantially but tank irrigated areas showed a steady decline during the past 56 years.

Though there seems to be no clear cut evidence to show the most important factors contributing to the decline in the tank irrigation, generally it was said that inadequate water supply to tanks over the years and consequent invasion of well irrigation in the tank command and less profitable paddy cultivation in tank irrigated area are the main reasons for decline in tank irrigated area (Gomatinayagam *et al.*, 2005).

Objectives and Methodology

Keeping the tank irrigation – poverty in view, the present papers aims at analyzing the trends in decline in tank irrigated area at National and at our state level over a period of 50 years. After providing a bird-eye view of decline in tank irrigation at National and State-level, the paper focuses on the regional trends in our state - Andhra Pradesh – with special reference to Coastal Andhra, Rayalaseema and Telengana- by adopting the following two methods:

1. Decrease in the relative importance of tanks *vis-à-vis* other modes of irrigation (Relative Decrease), and
2. Decline in the actual area irrigated by tanks (Absolute Decline)

The present analysis is based on secondary data collected from internet sources, reports of the World Bank and Government of India, Andhra Pradesh and the reports of the Chief Planning Officers for the districts of Rayalaseema districts. The English daily newspapers such as *The Hindu*, *The Business Line* were consulted wherever necessary.

Discussion

First let me provide a micro-analysis of trends in the deterioration of tank irrigation in India and a comparative analysis of relative and absolute decline in tank irrigation. Table 1 presents these details.

Table 1: Comparative Analysis of Decline in Tank Irrigation in India

(Area in Thousand ha)

Period	Sources of Irrigation				All Sources
	Canals	Tank	Ground water	Others	
1950-51	8295	3613	5978	2967	20853
	(39.8)	(17.3)	(28.7)	(14.2)	(100.0)
1960-61	10370	4561	7290	2440	24661
	(42.1)	(18.5)	(30.0)	(9.4)	(100.0)
1970-71	12838	4112	11887	2266	31103
	(41.3)	(13.2)	(38.2)	(7.3)	(100.0)
1980-81	15292	3182	17695	2551	38720
	(39.5)	(8.2)	(45.7)	(6.6)	(100.0)
1990-91	17453	2944	24694	2932	48023
	(36.4)	(6.1)	(51.4)	(6.1)	(100.0)
1999-2000	17995	2706	33632	2905	57238
	(31.4)	(4.7)	(58.8)	(5.1)	(100.0)

Source : www.cwc.org. and GOI, Statistical Abstracts for relevant years.

It is evident from Table 1 that irrigated area under tanks was 17.3% during 1950-51 and canals were the dominant source. Gradually the dominance of canals and tanks has declined and the share of groundwater increased by the end of 1999-2000. Tanks are the only source for which reduction was significant both relatively and absolutely. The area irrigated under tanks constituted about 18.5% during 1960-61 and this proportion has drastically declined to only 4.7% of the total net area irrigated by all sources during 1999-2000. In absolute terms, the area irrigated under tanks was highest at 4561 thousand hectares in 1960-61, which has declined to 2706 thousand hectares indicating a net decline of 1855 thousand hectares (41%) during these 40 years (1960-61 to 1999-2000).

The data amply proves that the groundwater development is the major cause for decline in tank irrigation. According to the 3rd Minor Irrigation Census (2001) there are 5.56 lakh tanks and storages under the surface flow and surface lift schemes as minor irrigation schemes, creating 6.27 million ha. of irrigation potential. The state-wise distribution of tanks shows that West Bengal has the highest no. of tanks (21.2% of the total tanks), followed by Andhra Prdesh (13.6%) and Maharashtra (12.5%). Out of the 5.56 lakh tanks, 4.71 lakh tanks are in use. Remaining 0.85 lakh tanks (15%) are not in use due to different reasons. Due to non-use of these tanks nearly 1 million ha of irrigated potential is lost. Another around 2 million ha of potential is lost due to under-utilisation of tanks in use. Loss of potential due to non-use is more pronounced in Meghalaya, Rajasthan and Andhra Pradesh (30%), whereas loss of potential due to under-utilisation is more than 50% in the cases of Gujarat, Nagaland, Rajasthan, Andaman and Nicobar Islands and Dadra and Nagar Haveli.

Tank Irrigation in Andhra Pradesh

We know well that in a predominantly agricultural economy there can be no economic and social progress unless vagaries of rainfall are encountered and conservation and development schemes for water resources are formulated. The farmers in Andhra Pradesh know this fact well and 'tanks' were constructed for harvesting the rain-water as a counter action to the vagaries of rainfall and hence Andhra Pradesh occupied the second place in our country with 13.6% of tanks in India.

The land-use statistics in Andhra Pradesh reveal net area irrigated by all sources was estimated at 27.47 lakh ha in 1955-56, which has increased to 45.2 lakh ha in 2000-01. However, the statistics reveal that the area under tank irrigation declined both absolutely and relatively. Let me present at first the decline compared to that of our country. Table 2 provides the comparative picture of tank irrigation.

Table 2: The Decline in Tank Irrigation: A.P. and India

Period	Average Net Area Irrigated per year by tanks (lakh ha)		A.P as % of India
	Andhra Pradesh	India	
1951-55	8.85	37.32	23.7
1961-65	12.61	46.67	27.0
1971-75	9.42	37.82	24.9
1981-85	9.32	32.10	29.0
1991-95	7.94	29.79	26.7
1996-2000	7.23	29.70	24.3

Source : Compiled from GOI and GOAP Statistical Abstracts.

The data indicate that in relative terms tank irrigation in A.P. has declined from a highest proportion of 29% (1981-85) to 24.3% (1996-2000). The average net area irrigated by tanks in A.P. during 1961-65 was 12.61 lakh ha. which has declined by 5.38 lakh ha. during 1996-2000, indicating a net decline of 43% in 1996-2000 over 1961-65.

Relative and Absolute Decline in Andhra Pradesh

A casual observation of the data on net area irrigated by different sources reveal that tank irrigation in Andhra Pradesh has declined both relatively and absolutely as shown in Table 3.

Table 3: Trends in Decline of Tank Irrigation in Andhra Pradesh

Year	Source-wise Net Area Irrigated By Tanks (lakh.ha)					All Sources
	Canals	Tanks	Dug wells	Tube wells	Others	
1955-56	12.92	10.68	2.84	—	1.03	27.47
1960-61	13.31	11.51	3.28	—	0.99	29.09
1970-71	15.79	11.12	4.41	0.66	1.13	33.14
1980-81	16.93	9.00	6.29	1.47	0.94	34.63
1990-91	18.68	9.69	10.21	2.83	1.65	43.06
2000-01	16.49	7.27	8.88	10.66	1.97	45.27
2002-03	12.09	4.26	6.90	11.52	1.37	36.14
Increase (+)/ Decrease (-)	- 0.83	-6.42	-4.06	+10.86	+ 0.34	+8.67

Source: GOAP (2002) Agricultural Statistics At a Glance –2002.
GOAP (2003) Statistical Abstract –2003.

A perusal of the data presented in Table 3 reveals that the dominance of tank irrigation has declined during the 48 years under study. In 1960-61 the irrigated area under tanks constituted 40% of the total net area irrigated by all sources and this proportion has declined to 11.8% during 2002-03. In absolute terms the net area irrigated by tanks has declined by 6.42 lakh ha during 48 years of period as it has declined from 11.51 lakh hectares in 1960-61 to only 4.26 lakh hectares in 2002-03. On the contrary, the area irrigated by dug wells and tube wells has increased by 51% in 2002-03 compared to 1955-56.

The Regional Spread and Decline

Since the main focus of the present paper is on the analysis of regional decline in tank irrigation, an attempt is made in the discussion to look into regional spread and disparities of tank irrigation in Andhra Pradesh. The absolute and relative decline in tank irrigation is presented in the following discussion. Table 4 presents the regional spread of tanks.

Table 4: Region-wise Distribution of Tanks in Andhra Pradesh: 2003-04

Category of Tanks	No. of Tanks in			
	Coastal Andhra	Rayala Seema	Telengana	Andhra Pradesh
1. Small Tanks (<100 acres)	24650	9499	25540	59689 (87.4)
2. Large Tanks (>100-4942 acres)	3383	1036	4176	8595 (12.6)
3. Very Large Tanks (>4942 acres)	2	0	2	4 (Neg.)
All Tanks	28035 (41.1)	10535 (15.4)	29718 (43.5)	68288 (100.0)

Source: Dr. K. Dasaratharamaiah, Prof. M. Jayaraj, M. Reddi Ramu (2005), *Tank Irrigation in Andhra Pradesh: An Overview*, Paper presented to the National Seminar on " The Political Economy of Drought and Deterioration of Tank Irrigation in Rayalaseema", organised by the Deptt. of Economics, PVKN Government College, Chittoor held during October, 27-28, 2005.

A look at regional distribution of tanks shows that 87% of the total tanks are small tanks with an ayacut of less than 100 acres and only 13% are large tanks. When we look into the regional distribution of tanks, of the total tanks in Rayalaseema region, 90% are small tanks (9499/10535) and these tanks constitute 88% and 86% in Coastal Andhra and Telengana regions respectively.

Of the total tanks in A.P., Telengana has the highest no. of tanks (43.5%) followed by Coastal Andhra (41.1%) and Rayalaseema (15.4%).

Regional Decline in Tank Irrigation

An analysis is carried out to present the regional trends in declining tank irrigated area in our state so as to identify the region, in which the decline is comparatively high. In 1966-67 in which the area under tank irrigation was highest is taken as bench-marking year and this situation is compared with that of 2002-03 for appraising the regional trends in tank irrigation-poverty. Table 5 presents the regional imbalances in tank irrigation and its decline.

Table 5: Region-wise Decline in Tank Irrigated Area

(Area in lakh ha)

Region	1966-67			2002-03			Decline in Tank irrigated area in 2002-03 over 1966-67	
	Tanks	Other sources	All sources	Tanks	Other sources	All sources	Area	%
Coastal	5.98 (47.5)	11.64	17.62	2.38 (55.9)	15.75	18.13	3.60	60.2
Rayalaseema	1.72 (13.7)	3.11	4.83	0.35 (8.2)	4.98	5.33	1.37	80.0
Telengana	4.88 (38.8)	3.37	8.25	1.53 (35.9)	11.14	12.67	3.35	68.7
A.P.	12.58 (100.0)	18.12	30.70	4.26 (100.0)	31.87	36.13	8.32	66.1

Source: Computed Based on the Statistical Abstracts of Andhra Pradesh.

A comparative analysis of area irrigated by tanks shows that between 1966-67 and 2002-03, area under tank irrigation decreased significantly. The net decline in 2002-03 works out to 66.1% over 1966-67. The decline was highest at 80% in the case of Rayalaseema region, followed by Telengana region (68.7%) and Coastal Andhra (60.2%). Though the tank irrigated area declined by 3.6 lakh ha in Coastal Andhra, its proportion in the State has increased from 47.5% to 55.9% showing the highest tank irrigated area in our State. The decline was serious in Rayalaseema region as the tanks constituted 13.7% of the total net area irrigated in 1966-67 and the same has declined to 8.2%, indicating an absolute decline of 1.37 lakh ha. In 2002-03. Telengana has also prone to absolute tank irrigation-poverty as the irrigated area under tanks has declined from 4.88 lakh ha. to 1.53 lakh ha.

The data also show that of the total net area irrigated in the respective regions, the area under tanks has declined from 34% to 13.1%, from 36.0% to 6.6% and from 59% to 12.1%

in the case of Coastal Andhra; Rayalaseema and Telengana regions between 1966-67 and 2002-03 respectively. In absolute terms, tank irrigated area was serious in Rayalaseema region and in relative terms the decline was highest in the case of Telengana.

The data also present that during 1966-67, tank irrigated area constituted 41% in the net area irrigated by all sources in Andhra Pradesh and this proportion has declined to 11.8% during 2002-03. The absolute decline was 8.32 lakh hectares, which accounted for a decline of 66.1% in 2002-03 over 1966-67.

The Case of Rayalaseema Districts

An attempt is also made to have an idea of trends in the decline of tank irrigated area in Rayalaseema districts, as it was found that decline in tank irrigated area was serious in the region (refer Table 5). Hence, an observation is made by focusing on the decline taking 1956-57 and 2002-03 as reference period.

Relative Decline

Table 6 presents the relative decline in tank irrigation compared to other sources of irrigation.

It is evident from the Table 6 that the relative importance of tanks compared to that of other sources has drastically declined during the last 46 years. Tanks were the dominant source of irrigation representing 46.7% of the net area irrigated by all sources during 1956-57. This dominance has dipped into 6.6% during 2002-03 indicating a decline of 1.5 lakh ha of irrigated area. This accounts for a net decline of 81% in 2002-03 over 1956-57. Tube wells and other wells dominated the irrigation scene in Rayalaseema over these 46 years associated with a decline in the dominance of tanks, canals and other sources.

Absolute Decline

Tank irrigation in Rayalaseema region not only declined in relative terms, but in absolute terms also. An analysis of decline in tank irrigated area proves this fact. To be more meaningful, the analysis is carried out to know the intensity of decline in the disctricts of Rayalaseema region. Table 7 present these details.

Table 6: Relative Decline of Tank Irrigation in Rayalaseema Region

Source of Irrigation	Net Area irrigated (in ha)		Decline(-)/increase(+) in 2002-03 over 1956-57	
	1956-57	220-03	Area	%
Canals	82,875 (21.1)	64,900 (12.2)	–18,075	– 21.8
Tanks	1,84,022 (46.7)	35,147 (6.6)	–1,48,875	–80.9
Tube Wells	—	2,97,662 (55.9)	+ 2,97,662	+ 100.0
Other Wells	1,07,835 (27.4)	1,23,946 (23.2)	+ 16,111	+ 14.9
Others	19,108 (4.8)	11,162 (2.1)	–7,946	– 41.6
All Sources	3.93,940 (100.0)	5,32,817 (100.0)	+ 1,38,877	+ 35.3

Source : GOAP, Statistical Abstracts for the relevant years.

Table 7: Absolute Decline of Tank Irrigated Area in Rayalaseema Region

Source of Irrigation	Net Area irrigated (in ha)			Decline(-) in 2002-03 over 1956-57	
	1956-57	220-03	2002-03	Area	%
Chittoor	87,401 (7.4)	67,542 (6.1)	20,332 (4.8)	67069	77
Kadapa	30,732 (2.6)	26,895 (2.5)	1,158 (0.3)	29,574	96
Kurnool	21,371 (1.8)	14,139 (1.3)	11,510 (2.7)	9,861	46
Anantapur	44,518 (3.8)	45,433 (4.1)	2,147 (0.50)	42,371	95
Rayalaseema	1,84,022 (15.6)	1.54,009 (14.0)	35,147 (8.3)	1,48,885	81
A.P.	1,18,168 (100.0)	1,09,980 (100.0)	4,25,677 (100.0)	7,56,419	64

Source: GOAP: Statistical Abstracts for the relevant years.

Table 7 shows that tank irrigated area declined by 1.49 lakh ha. in Rayalaseema region during 1956-57 to 2002-03, indicating a decline of 81%. The decline is highest at 96% in Kadapa district followed by Anantapur district (95%), Chittoor (77%) and Kurnool district (46%). Rayalaseema region constituted 15.6% of the tank irrigated area in A.P. during 1956-57 and this proportion declined to 8.3% during 2002-03.

A district-wise observation in irrigated area under tanks reveals that among the four districts, Chittoor dominated with 47.5% lakh ha. of the total tank irrigated area (87,401 ha) in the region followed by Anantapur (24.2%), Kadapa (16.7%) and Kurnool (11.6%) districts in 1956-67. During 2002-03, Chittoor occupied first rank with 57.9% of the total tank irrigated area among four districts in the region followed by Kurnool (32.7%), Anantapur (6.1%) and Kadapa (3.3%) districts. Viewed from the State-level shares, Chittoor had 7.4% of the tank irrigated area of A.P. in 1956-57 and its share has declined to 4.8% in 2002-03. Like-wise the shares of Kadapa and Anantapur have also declined drastically.

The analysis of the data presented in Table 7 shows that management of tank irrigation is of high priority in Kadapa, Anantapur and Chittoor districts in Rayalaseema region.

Conclusion

We must recognize that "Development" is more of an 'operational' concept than a 'philosophical' one. It is a strategy of planned social change in a direction which is considered desirable by the members of the society. We might have joined the 'elite 10k Club' along with US, Japan and Hongkong and consider the stock-market as an index of growth. But we must bear in mind that in our country, 70% of the people are dependent on agriculture and are contributing only 22% to the total national income and 250 million youngsters between the age group of 18-35 years are waiting hopefully for a guarantee of employment to have a decent life.

Hence, it is essential, as one of the Report of the Asian Development Bank has observed, growth is to be pro-poor and "when it is labour absorbing and accompanied by policies and programmes that mitigate inequalities and facilitate income and employment generation for the poor, particularly women and other traditionally excluded groups, then only the plan allocations are considered productive and efficient.

To sum up, keeping in view the "Budget Wish List – 2006-07" and the findings of the *Economic Survey, 2005-06*, "the great part of the concern regarding distribution of income can be addressed by focusing on agriculture and the dynamics of poverty, inequality and unemployment also can be addressed well by strengthening the agricultural sector with the economic and productive use of irrigation - particularly tank irrigation. The renovation and development of tanks and efficient tank irrigation use - management systems certainly provides an answer to the employment guarantee and as a tool to conserve the environmental quality with a special attention to the soil conservation and small and marginal farmers of our agrarian economy.

REFERENCES

Gomatinayagam, P., Dr. R. Sakthivadivel, Er.A.B.S. Raj. Er. D. Sundaresan and Dr. J.D. Sophia (2005), Proceedings of the National Seminar on *The Political Economy of Drought and Deterioration of Tank Irrigation in Rayalaseema*, Deptt. of Economics, PVKN Government College, Chittoor, October 27-28, 2005, pp.29-47.

Government of India (1997) *Report of the Working Group of the Ninth Plan.*

http:/www. planning commission.nic.in/plns/planrel/fiveyr/9th/vol.2/ v2c4-2htm.

John, M. Alexander (2005) "Economic Growth and the Millennium Goals", *The Hindu*, October 6, p.10.

Kumar, Nagesh, S (2005) "Focus on the Farm Sector", *The Hindu*, Dec. 22, p.11

Mahendradev, S. (2006) "Ensuring Equitable Development through Reforms", *The Hindu*, Jan.21, p.10.

Naik, S.D. (20060 "Budget Must Focus on Growth with Equity", *The Business Lines*, Feb15, p.10.

Parasi, Gargi (2005) "Country Poised for Higher Growth", *The Hindu*, Oct. 28, p.13

Pawar, Sarad (2005) Minister for Agriculture told in the Rajyasabha in a written reply to a query on farmers living below poverty line.

Prabhakaran Nair, K.P. (2006) "Real Shine Must Come From Farm Sector" *The Business Lines*, Feb.8, p.10.

Sinath, P. (2005) "Falling farm incomes, growing inequalities" *The Hindu,* Nov.18. p.10.

Sivasubramanyam, K. (2005) "Decline of Tank irrigation in Tamilnadu: Causes and Consequences", Proceedings of the National Seminar on *The Political Economy of Drought and Deterioration of Tank Irrigation in Rayalaseema*, Deptt. of Economics, PVKN Government College, Chittoor, October 27-28, 2005, pp.29-47.

Special Correspondent (2005) *The Hindu,* Nov. 28, p. 9.

World Bank (2006) *World Development Report – 2006,* pp. 97 and 296.

12

Groundwater Market Dynamics in the Villages of Andhra Pradesh

K. ADISESHU and K. MADHU BABU

Irrigation is the crucial input in agricultural development. In Andhra Pradesh the present annual growth rate in agriculture is around 2 per cent only. The state government in its draft agricultural policy, envisaged an average annual growth rate of 6 per cent in its agricultural sector. To achieve this growth, it is essential to harness the available surface and groundwater resources and to encourage usage of water conserving irrigation systems, in a planned and focused manner. Besides surface irrigation, groundwater irrigation has been the key force for the agricultural development in the state. In the context of limited scope for development of surface water potential, more focus and trust was given for increasing irrigation potential through groundwater development. According to the 3rd Minor Irrigation Census[1] there are 20.36 lakhs Minor Irrigation sources in Andhra Pradesh during the year 2000-01 as against 16.64 lakhs sources in 1993-94 census showing an increase of 22.32 per cent. The irrigation potential created by these Minor Irrigation sources is 52.52 lakh hectares and the gross area irrigated by them is 33.80 lakh hectares during 2000-01. The gap between them.is 18.72 lakh hectares which is around 37 per cent. Out of 20.36 lakh sources, 17.47 lakh sources were in use showing 86 per cent of the total sources as against 14.22 lakh sources out of 16.64 lakhs showing 85 per cent to the total sources during 2nd Minor Irrigation census. Of the 20.36 lakhs Minor Irrigation sources, groundwater sources i.e. dug-wells, shallow tube-wells and deep tube-wells consist 94.76 per cent which create a potential of

33.27 lakh hectares, of which 22.94 lakh hectares (68.95%) were actually irrigated. Moreover, among the dug-wells, about 90 percent are maintained by electric motors and oil engines. But still the groundwater sources are inadequate. On an average 6 to 7 small farmers are sharing one well for irrigating their lands. Similarly 3 to 4 medium and 1 to 2 percent from large farmers group are sharing a single source. Therefore, there is wide scope for developing groundwater irrigation by extracting the untapped potential and reduce the risk on a large part of agriculture, which is subjected to vagaries of monsoon in the state.

In recent years, due to failure of tanks and also due to untimely and inadequate rain fall, the farmers have to solely depend on groundwater sources. Almost all districts in Andhra Pradesh have reported the decrease of groundwater table due to failure of tanks and decreased quantum of percolated water from surface flows. In the expansion of groundwater irrigation, private investments play a crucial role and mostly the large and medium farmers can afford to take up such investments. Thus small and marginal farmers have relatively less access to the groundwater, which is a common property resource. If there is a well-developed marker for the groundwater the small and marginal farmers can have better access for this resource. It may also have an expansionary effect on cropped area, yields, employment and agricultural incomes, through adoption of technology and change in crop pattern.

As groundwater is a common property resource, Water Extracting Mechanisms (WEM) are mostly privately owned and over extraction of groundwater cause externalities due to environmental degradation, development of groundwater markets may pose the issues of equity and environmental problems. To analyze these problems an understanding of the aspects like who are the major participants in these markets, how these markets are operating and how these markets are affecting crop pattern, yields and incomes of players us inevitable.

This paper is based on the study "Role of Water Markets in groundwater Management in Andhra Pradesh" conducted by the Agro-Economic Research Centre, Waltair in 2004 using the primary data collected from a sample of farmers. For selecting the sample farmers, a multi stage stratified Random Sampling design is used. At the first stage, two districts (one developed and the other less developed), where the groundwater market operation are widely going on, are selected in consultation with the officials of the groundwater department and the department of Agriculture. The selected districts are Chittoor (developed) and Visakhapatnam (less developed). At the second stage, using the same criteria two mandals, Srikalahasthi from Chittoor district and Madugula from Visakhapatnam district are selected randomly. At the third stage, three villages from each selected mandal are selected. All the farmers in the selected villages are listed out and they are classified into two groups as owners of Water Extracting Device and non-owners of water extracting device. Basing on the land holding, the farmers in each group are classified into three categories viz., small farmers (<2 hectares), Medium farmers (2 to 4 hectares) and large farmers (above 4 hectares). A minimum of 20 owner farmers and 20 non-owner farmers are randomly selected preferably from each of the size classes comprising 50 per cent owners and 50 per cent non-owners of groundwater structures/devices having a total of 120 in each of the selected district. Thus a total of 240 farmers from the size of sample for the present study. From these farmers data collected by canvassing a pre-designed schedule taking 2001-02 as the reference year. Moreover, attempts are made to track down the details of marketing channels, practices etc., from the different stake holders i.e. knowledgeable persons of the selected villages, traders, farm leaders etc., in the field of groundwater management.

This paper aims to present the groundwater market dynamics i.e. (1) the crop wise number of irrigations required and the number of irrigations actually provided by the farmers to the important crops like sugarcane, paddy and groundnut (2) the conditions imposed by the owners of water extracting devices on non-owners to release water and (3) the extent of water rates demanded by the owner farmers.

Results and Discussion

Groundwater Market in the Villages of Srikalahasthi Mandal

The selected villages of Srikalahasti Mandal are irrigated by bore wells and energized dug-wells. In these villages, the groundwater can be exploited at a depth of 50 ft to 60 ft, in some areas where the lands are nearer to the largest perennial source Thondamanadu tank. In the lands, which are further from the tank, the groundwater can be exploited at a depth of 150ft to 200 ft. Even in the bore wells nearer to the "Thondamanadu" tank, the water-table has declined due to over exploitations and also due to erratic nature of rain-fall. The selected farmers in these villages have mainly grown three crops viz., sugarcane and paddy in kharif and ground in rabi season.

Sugarcane is grown as an year long crop. The farmers usually provide irrigation to the crop once in 10 days. The farmers in these villages harvest this crop by eleven months. Thus an average, they have to provide 33 irrigations during the crop season. But due to decline in the water tables the farmers having the water extracting devices are getting about 30.1 irrigations in total period of the crop season. Each irrigation is given for a continuous period of 10 hrs per hectare. Thus, on the whole the farmers provide irrigation about 301 hours per hectare in a crop season while their requirement being 330 hrs. On the other hand the non-owners of water extracting devices (or buyers) are able to provide irrigation about 283 hrs per hectare while their requirement being about 330 hrs.

The owners of water extracting devices pay the electrical costs as per the horse power of the motor. If a farmer is having a motor of 5 HP, he has to pay Rs.175 per month and the costs are Rs.120 per month in case of farmers having 3HP motors. These rates are fixed by the state Electricity Board. Among the sample farmers, on an average the electrical charges incurred in a crop season are reported to be Rs. 804 per hectare. Across the groups, the costs ranged from Rs. 318 in case of large farmers to Rs. 1675 in case of small farmers. The reason to have reported higher costs in case of small farmers may be attributed to the number of 5 HP motors used by the farmers (The other maintenance costs shown in the table are the costs incurred for the maintenance of motor).

The non-owners of water extracting devices purchase water from the owners and pay the charges demanded by the owners. There will not be any fixed rate. The rate varies according to the changes in the crop conditions and also the distance of fields from the water source. The owners charge at a rate of Rs. 10 to Rs. 15 per hour to the lands nearer to the water extracting source. This rate of water per hour increased as per the changes in the crop condition. In cases of emergency conditions of the crop, the sellers charge Rs. 20 to 25 per hour. There are evidences from the farmers purchased water for Rs. 40 per hour. On an average the non-owner farmers paid the water charges about Rs. 4998 per hectare of sugarcane crop. Across the groups, the water charges per hectare paid by the farmers varied from Rs.4191 in case of large farmers to Rs. 5558 in case of medium farmers. The water charge per hour, among non-owner farmers, varied from Rs. 14.87 in case of large farmers to Rs. 19.70 in case of medium farmers while the average charges per hour being Rs. 17.68. The water charges per hour reported to have paid by the small and large farmers are less than the average charge per hour. This indicates that the small and large farmers are having lands nearer to the water source. The other costs shown in the table are the conveyance costs of water from the source to the cultivator fields. The particulars of per hectare irrigation charges incurred by the owner and non-owner farmers in respect of sugarcane crop are presented in Table 1.

The second major crop that is grown by the farmers is paddy. The total crop season of paddy is about four months. Usually, the farmers in these villages provide irrigation to the crop once in a week. Therefore, on an average the farmers have to provide 16 irrigations during the crop season. But due to decline in the water table, the farmers having water-extracting devices are getting about 12.7 irrigations in the total period of the crop season. Each irrigation is given for a continuous period of 12.5 per hectare. Thus on the whole,

Table 1: Irrigation Particulars

District: Chittoor, Mandall: Srikalahasti, Category: Owners, Crop: Sugarcane

Irrigation Source : Borewells

Size Group	Area under the crop (ha.)	No. of Irrigations required during crop season	No. of Irrigations available during crop season	No. of hours required for each irrigation per hectare	Elect./Fuel cost of each season (Rs.) per ha	Other maintenance cost (if any) per hectare
SF	19.12	33	30.5	10	1675	689
MF	34.60	33	29.2	10	784	272
LF	32.80	33	30.8	10	318	274
OA	86 52	33	30.1	10	804	365

Category: Non-owners

Size Group	Area under the crop (ha.)	No. of Irrigations required during crop season	No. of Irrigations available during crop season	No. of hours required for each irrigation per ha	Watercharge perhour (Rs.)	Watercharge paid in a season (Rs) per ha	Other maintenance cost (if any) per hectare
SF	6.20	33	28.7	10	16.74	4806	237
MF	29.20	33	28.2	10	19.70	5558	574
LF	18.80	33	28.2	10	14.87	4191	356
OA	54.20	33	28.3	10	17.68	4998	460

the farmers provide irrigation about 158.75 hours per hectare in a crop season while their requirement being about 200 hours. On the other hand, the non-owners of water extracting devices are able to provide irrigation about 115 hours per hectare, while their requirement being about 200 hours.

The owners of water extracting devices pay the electrical costs as per the horse-power of the motor. Among the sample farmers, on an average the electrical charges incurred in a crop season are reported to be Rs. 976 per hectare. Across the groups the per hectare costs varied from Rs. 583 in case of medium farmers to Rs. 1284 in the case of small farmers. Similarly the other maintenance costs ranged from Rs.325 per hectare in case of large farmers to Rs. 834 in case of small farmers.

The non-cwners of water extracting devices, purchase water from the owners by paying the charges demanded by the owners. The buyers have to incur more charges depending upon the distance of their fields from the water source. During the reference year, the non-owner farmers growing paddy incurred an average charge of Rs.17.25 per hour. The per hectare water charges paid by the non-owner farmers are reported to be Rs.1994. Across the groups, the per hectare charge varied from Rs. 1935 in case of medium farmers to Rs.2016 in case of small farmers. But the other costs of maintenance are reported to be higher in case of medium farmers than in the case of small farmers. Due to decline in the water table, the quantum of water extracted is very less. As such, the farmers utilize the water extracting device for more number of hours, which caused for the payment of excess amounts to the owners. The details of the per hectare irrigation charges incurred by the owner and non-owner farmers are presented in Table 2.

In these villages, the farmers grow groundnut during rabi season. The total duration of the crop is about four months. The farmers, usually, provide is irrigation to this crop only twice in a month. Therefore, on an average the farmers have to provide 8 irrigations during the crop season. But due to decline in the groundwater potential the owner farmers are getting about 6.9 irrigations in the total period of the crop

Table 2: Irrigation Particulars

District: Chittoor, Mandal: Srikalahasti, Category: Owners, Crop: Paddy

Irrigation Source: Borewells

Size Group	Area under the crop (ha.)	No. of Irrigations required during crop season	No. of Irrigations available during crop season	No. of hours required for each irrigation per hectare	Elect./Fuel cost of each season (Rs.) per ha	Other maintenance cost (if any) per hectare
SF	18.12	16	12.6	12.5	1284	834
MF	11.40	16	12.5	12.5	583	404
LF	4.00	16	13.5	12.5	700	325
OA	33.52	16	12.7	12.5	976	627

Category: Non-owners

Size Group	Area under the crop (ha.)	No. of Irrigations required during crop season	No. of Irrigations available during crop season	No. of hours required for each irrigation per ha	Watercharge perhour (Rs.)	Watercharge paid in a season (Rs) per ha	Other maintenance cost (if any) per hectare
SF	16.70	16	9.4	12.5	17.23	2016	310
MF	6.40	16	8.9	12.5	17.32	1935	598
LF	-	-	-	-	-	-	-
OA	23.10	16	9.2	12.5	17.25	1994	390

season. Each irrigation is given for a continuous period of 12.5 hours. Thus, on the whole, the farmers provide irrigation about 86.25 hours per hectare in a crop season while their requirement being about 100 hours. On the other hand, the non-owners of water extracting devices are able to provide irrigation about 66.25 hours per hectare while their requirement being about 100 hours.

On an average, the owner farmers paid the electrical charges about Rs.1038 per hectare. Across the groups, the per hectare electrical charges varied between Rs.303 in case of large farmers to Rs.1601 in case of small farmers. The other costs of maintenance also varied from Rs.192 in case of large farmers to Rs.420 in case of small farmers. The non-owner farmers, on an average paid the electrical charges about Rs. 1076 per hectare for the purchase of water at the rate of Rs.16.11 per hour. The per hour water charge ranged from Rs.15 in case of large farmers to Rs.18.91 in case of medium farmers.

Thus the per hectare water charges paid by the non-owners varied from Rs.938 in case of large farmers to Rs.1359 in case of medium farmers. The other costs of maintenance varied from Rs.160 per hectare in case of large farmers to Rs.345 in case of small farmers. The reason to have reported higher payments in case of small and medium farmers is that their lands are located far away from the water source. The details of per hectare irrigation charges paid by the owner and non-owner farmers growing groundnut under bore wells are presented in Table 3.

In spite of huge amounts of investment towards irrigation, the farmers in these villages could not obtain much yields and incomes as they usually expect (Table 4).

In spite of huge investment towards irrigation in case of sugarcane crop, the non-owners could not obtain as much yields as obtained by the owners. Accordingly, the non-owners have obtained lower incomes than the owners. The reason to have obtained lower yields in case of non-owners, may be attributed to inadequate quantum of water reached to the crop. In case of paddy crop, through the non-owners farmers obtained more yields than owners; they could not obtain much incomes as

Table 3: Irrigation Particulars

District: Chittoor, Mandal: Srikalahasti, Category: Owners, Crop: Groundnut

Irrigation Source: Borewells

Size Group	Area under the crop (ha.)	No. of Irrigations required during crop season	No. of Irrigations available during crop season	No. of hours required for each irrigation per hectare	Elect./Fuel cost of each season (Rs.) per ha	Other maintenance cost (if any) per hectare
SF	9.40	8	7.0	12.5	1601	420
MF	3.60	8	6.4	12.5	632	306
LF	5.20	8	7.0	12.5	303	192
OA	18.20	8	6.9	12.5	1038	332

Category: Non-owners

Size Group	Area under the crop (ha.)	No. of Irrigations required during crop season	No. of Irrigations available during crop season	No. of hours required for each irrigation per ha	Watercharge perhour (Rs.)	Watercharge paid in a season (Rs) per ha	Other maintenance cost (if any) per hectare
SF	7.48	8	5.3	12.5	15.75	1053	345
MF	1.60	8	5.8	12.5	18.91	1359	231
LF	2.00	8	5.0	12.5	15.00	938	160
OA	11.08	8	5.3	12.5	16.11	1076	295

Table 4: Costs and Incomes - Per hectare

District: Chittoor
Mandal: Srikalahasti

Crop/category	Electrical costs including other costs of maintenance (Rs.)	Total costs (Rs.)	Value of Output (Rs.)	Net Income (Rs.)
Sugarcane				
Owed	1169 (5.56)	21029	72053	51024
Nowed	5458 (17.88)	20521	70507	39987
Paddy				
Owed	1603 (15.51)	10336	24705	14369
Nowed	2384 (20.80)	11459	25284	13824
Groundnut				
Owed	1370 (8.42)	16279	36044	19765
Nowed	1371 (8.48)	16169	32374	16205

Owed: Owners Of Water Extracting Device

Nowed: Non-owners of Water Extracting Device

Figures in parentheses are the percentages to total costs.

the owners obtained per hectare. The reason to have reported lower incomes by non-owners is high rates of water charges due to long distantly located cultivator fields. Though much difference is not found the respect of electrical charges towards irrigation, the non-owner farmers, in case of groundnut crop could not obtain as much yields as obtained by the owners. Accordingly the incomes are also comparatively lower than the owners.

Groundwater Market in the Villages of Madugula Mandal

The selected villages of Madugula mandal are irrigated by bore wells and energized dug-wells. Previously these villages were irrigated by "Palagadda vagu" and Padderu Reservoir". The groundwater can be exploited at a depth of 50ft to 60ft in the soils which are nearer to these and in the soils which are further to these sources the groundwater can be extracted at a depth of 100 ft to 150ft. But, since the mandal frequency faces severe droughts, the surface flow has declined. As a result, the groundwater potential has also decreased due to decreased quantum of percolated water from the surface flow. The farmers in these villages have mainly grown two crops sugarcane and paddy. No farmer has reported to have grown any crop during rabi season.

In these villages, the sugarcane crop is grown about 9 months, due to inadequate irrigation facilities. The farmers provide irrigation to the crop twice in a month. Thus, on an average the farmers provide 18 irrigations during the crop season. But due to decline in the water table, the farmers having the water extracting devices are getting about 14 irrigations in the total period of the crop season. Each irrigation is given for a continuous period of 15 hours per hectare. Thus, on the whole the farmers provide irrigation about 210 hours per hectare in a crop season while their requirement being 270 hours. On the other hand, the non-owner farmers of water extracting devices are able to provide irrigation 201 hours per hectare, while their requirement being about 270 hours.

Among the sample farmers, on an average the electrical charges incurred in a crop season are reported to be Rs.1118 per hectare. Across the groups, the costs ranged from Rs.536 in case of large farmers to Rs.1790 in case of small farmers.

The reason to have reported higher costs by small farmers may be attributed to the number of 5HP motors use by the farmers. The other costs of maintenance ranged from Rs.259 in case of medium farmers to Rs.842 in case of small farmers. Higher maintenance costs reported by small farmers is due to frequent repairs of motors.

The non-owner farmers purchase water by paying the per hour charges demanded by the sellers. The per hour charge of water varies in accordance with the charges in crop conditions and also the distance of fields from the water source. Among the sample farmers, on an average the water charges paid by the farmers are about Rs.3997 per hectare of sugarcane crop. Across the groups the water charges paid by the farmers varied from Rs.3733 in case of large farmers to Rs.4306 in case of small farmers. The per hour water charge ranged from Rs.19.05 in case of medium farmers to Rs.20.84 in case of small farmers while the average charge being Rs.19.94. The water charge per hour reported to have paid by the medium farmers is less than the other two groups. The reason may be attributed to the average per hour. This indicates that the lands of medium farmers are nearer to the water source. The other maintenance costs reported to have paid by the small farmers are higher than the hired conveyance charges from the water source to the cultivator fields. The details of per hectare irrigation charges incurred by the owner and non-owner farmers in respect of sugarcane crop grown under bore wells are presented in Table 5.

In case of paddy crop, the farmers in these villages usually provide irrigation to the crop thrice in a month. Therefore on an average the farmers have to provide 12 irrigations during the crop season. But due to decline in the water table, the farmers having the extracting devices are getting about 7.9 irrigations in the total period of the crop. Each irrigation is given for a continuous period of 20 hours. Thus, on the whole, the farmer provide irrigation about 158 hours per hectare in a crop season while their requirement being about 24o hours. On the other hand the non-owner farmers are able to provide irrigation about 156 hours per hectare while their requirement being about 240 hours.

Table 5: Irrigation Particulars

District: Visakhapatnam, Mandal: Madugula, Category: Owners, Crop: Sugarcane

Irrigation Source: Borewells

Size Group	Area under the crop (ha.)	No. of Irrigations required during crop season	No. of Irrigations available during crop season	No. of hours required for each irrigation per hectare	Elect./Fuel cost of each season (Rs.) per ha	Other maintenance cost (if any) per hectare
SF	20.20	18	14	15	1790	842
MF	21.20	18	14	15	1015	259
LF	19.60	18	14	15	536	408
OA	61.00	18	14	15	1118	500

Category: Non-owners

Size Group	Area under the crop (ha.)	No. of Irrigations required during crop season	No. of Irrigations available during crop season	No. of hours required for each irrigation per ha	Watercharge perhour (Rs.)	Watercharge paid in a season (Rs) per ha	Other maintenance cost (if any) per hectare
SF	15.56	18	13.8	15	20.84	4306	225
MF	16.34	17	13.9	15	19.05	3980	153
LF	17.20	18	12.4	15	20.00	3733	58
OA	49.10	18	13.4	15	19.94	3997	143

Among the owner farmers, on an average the electrical charges incurred in a crop season are reported to be Rs.1068 per hectare. Across the groups the per hectare costs varied from Rs.280 in case of large farmers to Rs.1817 in case of small farmers. Similarly the other maintenance costs ranged from Rs.272 in case of medium farmers to Rs.1038 in case of small farmers. The reason to have reported higher maintenance costs by small farmers is due to frequent repairs of motors.

The non-owner farmers growing paddy incurred an average charge of Rs.20.82 per hour. The per hour charge ranged from Rs. 18.80 in case of small farmers to Rs.21.88 in case of medium farmers. The reason to have reported higher rate of per hour charge by medium farmers indicates that their lands are further from the water source. The per hectare water charges paid by the non-owner farmers are reported to be Rs.3254. Across the groups, the per hectare charges varied from Rs.2898 in case of small farmers to Rs.3447 in case of medium farmers. The details of per hectare irrigation charges incurred by the owner and non-owner farmers in respect of paddy crop are presented in Table 6.

Though the non-owner farmers achieved comparatively more yields than the owners, they could not derive as much income as the owners. The reason may be not only due to excessive costs incurred by them, but also due to preparation of jaggary slabs, which as comparatively low rate of sale value than the cane value sold at factories. Hence, the non-owner farmers received lower income per hectare than the owned. In case of paddy crop, inspite of huge amount incurred towards irrigation charges, the non-owners could not obtain as much yields as obtained by the owners. Accordingly the per hectare incomes are also lower than the owners. Though the non-owners farmers could provide more number of irrigations as provided by the owners, the quantum of water reached to the crop is inadequate. Moreover, during the reference year, due to inadequate and untimely rainfall during crucial periods of the crop, almost all owner and non-owner farmers faced the problem of crop failure. As a result, they could obtain meagre incomes. The details of costs and incomes of the owner and non-owner farmers are presented in the Table 7.

Table 6: Irrigation Particulars

District: Visakhapatnam, Mandal: Madugula, Category: Owners, Crop: Paddy

Irrigation Source: Borewells

Size Group	Area under the crop (ha.)	No. of Irrigations required during crop season	No. of Irrigations available during crop season	No. of hours required for each irrigation per hectare	Elect./Fuel cost of each season (Rs.) per ha	Other maintenance cost (if any) per hectare
SF	18.40	13	8.6	20	1817	1038
MF	18.00	12	7.9	20	739	272
LF	10.00	12	6.9	20	280	-
OA	46.40	12	7.9	20	1068	517

Category: Non-owners

Size Group	Area under the crop (ha.)	No. of Irrigations required during crop season	No. of Irrigations available during crop season	No. of hours required for each irrigation per ha	Watercharge perhour (Rs.)	Watercharge paid in a season (Rs) per ha	Other maintenance cost (if any) per hectare
SF	8.20	11	7.7	20	18.80	2898	98
MF	17.72	12	7.9	20	21.88	3447	65
LF	3.20	12	7.8	20	20.00	3100	-
OA	29.12	12	7.8	20	20.82	3254	67

Table 7: Costs and Incomes – Per hectare

District: Visakhapatnam

Mandal: Madugula

Crop/category	Electrical costs including other costs of maintenance (Rs.)	Total costs (Rs.)	Value of Output (Rs.)	Net income (Rs.)
Sugarcane				
OWED	1618	19623	33717	14094
NOWED	4140	27117	34501	7384
Paddy				
OWED	1585	10744	20211	9468
NOWED	3321	14131	19327	5196

OWED: Owners of Water Extracting Device

NOWED: Non-owners of Water Extracting Device.

Constraints in the Utilization of Groundwater

1. Most of the tanks are in the state of disrepair. Some tanks have completely become dry due to inadequate rainfall. As a result, the quantum of percolated water released from the outlets of the tanks has decreased. Hence, the groundwater table has declined to a considerable extent.
2. Majority of the small farmers are not capable enough to afford to install a water extracting device of their own. Hence they have to depend on the owners of water extracting devices for irrigating their lands.
3. The owners of water extracting devices charge exorbitant rates to release water per hour.
4. Due to untimely power cuts, the farmers are unable to fully irrigate their lands. As a result, they are obtaining lower yields.
5. The water extracting devices are getting damaged due to frequent power cuts, which cause to incur heavy expenditure towards the repairs of the motors. Some times the burden of the repairs has to be borne by the buyers of the water.

Suggestions for improvement:

1. The watershed development programmes should be implemented by the government, to improve the groundwater potential
2. The tank bunds must be repaired and strengthened, to improve the storage capacity of the tanks.
3. The bore wells with water extracting devices must be provided to small and marginal farmers on subsidized basis so that their dependence on owners can be avoided.
4. Continuous power supply, at least in the crucial periods of the crop conditions must be provided.

NOTES

1. "3rd Minor Irrigation Census, 2000-01 of Andhra Pradesh", Directorate of Economics and Statistics, Government of Andhra Pradesh, Hyderabad.
2. "Role of Water Markets in Groundwater Management in Andhra pradesh & Orissa", Agro-Economic Research Centre, Andhra University, Waltair. May-2004.

13

Tank Irrigation Management at the Peril: Emerging Issues and Challenges

G. SREEDHAR

Introduction

Tanks served the needs of local communities for drinking water (both for human beings and livestock), irrigation and washing of clothes in various parts of India since times immemorial. It becomes evident from economic history that tank irrigation played a critical role in the development of agriculture in drought prone regions. On the eve of the British rule, the total number of tanks in the country was put at not less than three lakhs, irrigating about four million hectares even by conservative estimates (Sengupta 1991: 70). At the time of Independence, the net area irrigated by tanks was about 3.5 million hectares. The land use statistics shows that the area under tank irrigation reached an ail-time high of 4.78 million hectares in 1962-63 which declined to 3.07 million hectares by 1985-86 (GOI 1992: 62)[1]. The average area irrigated by tanks during the five year period ending with 1990-91 stood at 3.12 million hectares (NIRD 1994).

The decline of tank irrigation could be traced to the latter half of the 19th century due to colonial land revenue policies and bureaucratization of irrigation administration. The government allocations for maintenance of tanks were reduced by half and the ownership of tanks was handed over to Public Works Department, leading to the disintegration of traditional people's participatory water management institutions. The ownership of hills and forests around the tanks also passed from the villagers to the government, resulting in large scale deforestation and soil erosion, and the consequent silting-up of the feeder channels. Even though the deterioration of tank irrigation had started during the British rule, it was intensified due to various policies of the government after independence, which emphasised the major and medium irrigation projects' and neglected the upkeep and repair of traditional sources of irrigation including tanks. Thus, the deterioration of tank irrigation could be attributed to weakening of traditional institutions, neglect of upkeep and repair of damages to structures and silting-up of storages and channels (Vaidyanathan, 1999: 96).

The government policy of providing cheap loans and electricity to the farmers for irrigation purpose augmented the digging of private wells at an undesired pace, often circumventing the legislation pertaining to the regulation and use of the groundwater resources. The green revolution also gave a fillip to well irrigation. The diffusion of private wells extended to tank command areas also, due to uncertain and inadequate availability of tank water, which turned out to be detrimental to the collective management of tanks. As a result, the share of tank irrigation in the net irrigated area of the country fell from 16.51 per cent in 1952-53 to 5.18 per cent in 1999-2000. This decline in the share of tank irrigation appears to be closely associated with a rise in the share of groundwater irrigation, which increased from 30.17 per cent to 55.36 per cent during this period (Palanisami, 2005).

Even though the tank irrigation declined at the national level, its importance is still felt in varying proportions and dimensions across the different states of the country.[2] In arid tracts of Rajasthan, social institutions" and norms sustained tanks for many centuries. In Jaisalmer district which receives the lowest rainfall of 164 mm in the country, it is surprising to note that all but one of 462 inhabited villages have their own water management arrangement based on local resources (Mishra 1993: 60-61). The significance of tank irrigation for the drought prone regions becomes evident from the limited scope for developing canal irrigation on the one hand and increasingly expensive well irrigation due to receding water table levels on the other. Huge investment costs, long gestation period, heavy operation and maintenance costs and ecological problems associated with the major and medium irrigation projects also underline the need for utilising the existing tanks since it appears to be a cost-effective strategy for optimum utilisation of rain water for sustainable agricultural development in the semi-arid tracts of the country. The success achieved by Japan and China,[3] which planned their modernisation programmes on traditional methods in the field of irrigation suggests the need to give due importance to the development of tank irrigation in our country.

Thus, it becomes clear that tanks need to be restored and put to use, especially in drought prone regions, which invariably calls for mobilising a massive financial support from the international aid agencies and the active involvement of the farmers. This situation, along with the increasing realisation of the need to use water resources in an efficient manner, led to the launching of efforts in different parts of the country during the early 1990's to undertake pilot projects forming water users associations (WUAs) as informal agencies so as to involve the farmers in the management of a command area of a tank or a minor canal or a distributary, with the ultimate aim of improving the water use efficiency. Several states such as Gujarat, Maharashtra, Tamil Nadu, Karnataka, Orissa, Uttar Pradesh, Rajasthan and Andhra Pradesh were involved in the efforts to promote participatory irrigation management (PIM). Later, several states enacted legislations, following the Big-Bang approach adopted by Mexico, which involved simultaneous and uniform adoption of PIM throughout one region or state, usually based upon legislation and government orders. Andhra Pradesh became the first state in the country to pass the A.P. Farmers' Management of Irrigation Systems (APFM1S) Act, 1997. Similar legislations were enacted by other states also,[4] while the process is underway in Maharashtra and Gujarat.

The Andhra Pradesh model provided for the constitution of WUAs at the minor level, Distributary Committees (DCs) at the distributary level and Project Committee at the project level and Apex Committee at the state level. Each WUA was divided into four to ten territorial constituencies (TCs), depending upon the extent of command area. One WUA was formed for each tank under the control of the Irrigation Department (ID)[5]. Elections were conducted to 10292 WUAs in June 1997 and to 174 DCs in November 1997, while the project and apex committees were not formed. Out of the total number of WUAs, those formed for the minor irrigation sources (mostly tanks) numbered 8128 (79%), while those constituted for the major and medium irrigation sources stood at 1729 (16.8%) and 435 (4.2%) respectively. The tenure of office of these bodies was originally fixed at three years, but later it was extended up to five years. These bodies functioned up to 2002, but afterwards were placed under special officers of the cadre of Deputy Executive Engineer to undertake routine tasks, because elections were delayed.

The APFMIS Act was amended in October 2003, incorporating some modifications in the election process, number of TC members and the tenure of office. While elections at all levels were direct earlier, now only TC members would be elected directly and at other levels indirect elections would be held, i.e., the TC members would elect the president and vice-president of a WUA, the WUA presidents would elect the DC president and vice-president, and so on. The number of TC members to be elected from each WUA varied from 6 to 12.

Even the tenure of office of the TC numbers was modified in such a manner that one-third of those elected for the first time would have two years term, one-third four years term and another one-third six years term. Later on, all the elected members would have six years term uniformly. These changes were made with a view to ensure the continuity of the functioning of WUAs. Elections were held to these bodies in April 2005.

In Andhra Pradesh, minor rehabilitation works were undertaken as a part of the Andhra Pradesh Economic Reconstruction Project (APERP) for the restoration of tanks through the WUAs. Works worth up to Rs.12 lakhs were entrusted directly to the WUAs for execution, while those costing above Rs.12 lakhs were executed by calling for the tenders and entrusting the work to the contractors. The ID entered into agreements with the WUAs for this purpose and payments were made to WUA presidents through cheques for the execution of works undertaken. The Government of Andhra Pradesh also issued a GO Ms. No. 115 Revenue (LR-3) Dept. dated 13-2-2001 specifying the allocation of water charges among the different agencies involved in PIM. In the case of minor irrigation tanks, the water charges were fixed at Rs.100 per acre out of which Rs.90 would be allocated to the concerned WUA and Rs. 10 to the Gram Panchayat. However, water charges were collected only when the tank water was let out for wet crops. Thus, efforts have been initiated in a big way to renovate the tanks and place them in the hands of WUAs for collective management. Against this backdrop, it becomes pertinent to examine the following issues, which have a bearing on tank irrigation management, including the role of WUAs.

- What are the current trends in tank irrigation and whether these reflect the impact of works undertaken for the minor rehabilitation of tanks through WUAs on the water inflows in terms of a rise in tank irrigated area?
- What is the present status of tanks in terms of the condition of important physical structures, viz., bunds, sluices, surplus weirs and field channels?
- Whether there are changes in the land ownership patterns across the tank command areas over a period of time and whether these are conducive to collective management of tanks?
- What is the extent of well irrigation in the tank command areas and whether it has had any impact on the collective management of tanks?
- What is the present arrangement for the distribution of tank water and whether it takes into account the principle of equity?
- What are the changes in the cropping pattern in the tank command areas and the livelihood opportunities of the farmers due to reduced water supplies and expansion of well irrigation over a period of time?

The present paper attempts to address these issues in the context of Anantapur district of Andhra Pradesh, which occupies a prominent place in the state in respect of tank irrigation for centuries. The study is based on the secondary data collected from various sources such as statistical abstracts. Irrigation Department, interactions with the concerned officials and other relevant published literature.

Current Trends in Tank Irrigation

In Anantapur district, the average net area irrigated by tanks per annum was considerably high at 96888 acres during the decade ending with 1951, which declined to 73439 acres during the decade ending with 1981. The downslide of tank irrigation continued in the subsequent decades also; the average net irrigated area by tanks per annum stood at 47535 acres and 25249 acres respectively during the decades ending with 1991 and 2001.

During the last four years (2001-02 to. 2004-05), the average net area irrigated by tanks per annum worked out to 9378 acres only. The trends in tank irrigation from 1997-98 to 2004-05 are shown in Table 1, from which it is clear that there are fluctuations in the tank irrigated area from year to year, but there has been a rapid decline on the whole.

Table 1: Source-wise Net Area Irrigated in Anantapur District from 1997-98 to 2004-05 (Area in Acres)

	Canals	Tanks	Wells	Others	Total	Net Sown Area
1997-98	74185	25853	236725	3924	340687	2303766
1998-99	82848	30074	248680	2669	364271	2466439
1999-00	82212	13692	331583	11327	438814	2590194
2000-01	79558	14414	327298	11844	433114	2597756
2001-02	75463	25094	325966	11214	437737	2578155
2002-03	50580	5392	327256	5184	388412	2489521
2003-04	55898	4245	288774	1502	350419	2379890
2004-05	65515	2780	279083	2896	350274	2647058

Table 2 shows the MI tanks taken up for repair under APERP (Minor Rehabilitation) from 1998-99 to 2004-05, after the formation of the WUAs. It could be seen that 218 tanks (71.5%) out of the total of 305 tanks were taken up for repair during the above period. In the case of 43 per cent of tanks, the amount spent ranged between Rs.2 and 5 lakhs. The expenditure incurred was of the order of Rs.1 and 2 lakhs only in the case of 28 per cent tanks. Thus, in the case of a majority of tanks (76%), the expenditure incurred per tank was less than Rs. 5 lakhs. There were only 20 per cent tanks in whose case the expenditure incurred stood between Rs.5 and 10 lakhs, while it exceeded Rs.10 lakhs in respect of the remaining five per cent tanks. The information collected from the ID showed that the total expenditure incurred towards the minor rehabilitation of tanks in the district from 1998-99 to 2004-05 was of the order of Rs.9.45 crores.

Table 2: MI Tanks taken up for repair under APERP (MR) from 1998-99 to 2004-05

Expenditure incurred (Rs. Lakhs)	No. of tanks in Anantapur Division	No. of Tanks in Penukonda Division	Total	Percentage
Up to 1.0	3	8	11	5.05
1.01 to 2.0	19	41	60	27.52
2.01 to 5.0	12	82	94	43.12
5.01 to 10.0	11	32	43	19.72
Above 10.0	3	7	10	4.59
Total	48	170	218	100.0

Source: Compiled from the information available with the Irrigation Department.

It is learnt that the government has since sanctioned the phasc-1 of a pilot project for rehabilitation of tanks, at a cost of Rs.l 3.76 crores aimed at rehabilitating 37 tanks in two years, which should be completed by 2006-07. The share of Government of India and the Government of Andhra Pradesh in the project is 75 per cent and 25 per cent respectively. But, it is surprising to note that no works were undertaken so far even though the first year is coming to an end, obviously because of the absence of clear guidelines on modalities to take up the works through the newly formed WUAs. During the recent visit of the Principal Secretary (Irrigation), it has been decided to form a Task Force comprising the irrigation experts and NGOs to chalk out the rehabilitation project in consultation with the farmers of the concerned tanks. The ID officials also prepared Phase-II of the pilot project at an estimated cost of Rs.46.4 crorcs for rehabilitating 253 tanks in the district, which is awaiting the approval of the government.

Thus, it becomes clear that the efforts made so far towards the minor rehabilitation works pertaining to tanks in Anantapur district touched only the tip of the iceberg in the sense that problem of decline of tank irrigation is so deep rooted and damages inflicted on tanks were quite considerable that the meagre amount allocated for their minor rehabilitation and the way it was spent could not restore the tanks on a full-fledged basis. The current trends in tank irrigation in Anantapur district clearly indicate that the tank rehabilitation efforts have not been reflected in a rise in the tank irrigated area. In fact, the decline of tank irrigation continued unabated.

Present Status of Tanks in Anantapur District

The present status of 305 tanks under the control of the ID and for which WUAs are functioning in Anantapur District, in terms of the condition of physical structures, is shown in Table 3.

Table 3: Present Status of Tanks in Anantapur District (Per cent)

S. No.	Present Condition	Bunds	Sluices	Surplus Weirs	Field Channels
1.	Good	34.8	42.7	44.0	16.9
2.	Required Repairs	64.2	54.6	55.0	76.2
3.	No Information	1.0	2.7	1.0	6.9
	Total (N- 305)	100	100	100	100

Source: Compiled from the tank memoirs prepared for individual tanks by the Irrigation Department, Anantapur.

It could be seen from Table 3 that a majority of tanks required repairs in respect of bunds, sluices, surplus weirs and field channels. Over three-fourths of tanks require the repair of field channels, while the bunds are weak and need to be strengthened in the case of nearly two-thirds of the tanks. Over half of the tanks require the repair of sluices and surplus weirs. Thus, the present condition of tanks in respect of four important physical structures appears to be bad, which clearly reflects the utter neglect to which these sources of irrigation were subjected to by the government. In the case of many tanks, silting-up or encroachment of feeder channels could be noticed, resulting in no supply of water or negligible and irregular inflows at times. Most of these tanks become full hardly once in five or six years and in some cases once in ten years. In most of the tanks, tank bed cultivation was also taken up. In fact, when the district experienced severe drought for four consecutive years during the current decade and many farmers had to sell away their cattle and milch animals due to severe scarcity of fodder, the government encouraged the cultivation of fodder on tank beds in most cases. As a result of cumulative effect of all these factors, most of the tanks were left in a state of disuse and in the process became dysfunctional.

Land Ownership Patterns in Tank Command Areas

It is important to examine the land ownership patterns in the tank command areas in terms of caste and landholding size and how the ownership changed hands over a period of time, which are critical in determining the collective management of tanks. This is an essential aspect to be taken into account before planning any tank rehabilitation project. A detailed study of three rainfed tanks in the district revealed that the upper castes and the backward castes held more or less equal share in the tank command areas, with the scheduled" castes left with hardly about two per cent. The upper castes accounted for a higher share in the head and middle reaches as compared to the backward castes. In terms of landholding size, the big and medium farmers accounted for about 72 per cent of the tank command areas, while the small and marginal farmers accounted for the rest. It was also noted that the medium and big farmers had a higher share of land in the head reaches when compared to the small and marginal farmers. An analysis of land transfers that had taken place from 1963-64 to 1993-94 revealed that the only about one-third of the farmers were involved in land transfers and the extent of land transacted was also limited. Of the land transacted, 41 per cent was among the intermediate castes[6] themselves and another 47 per cent was transferred from intermediate castes to dominant cultivating castes[7] or form among the dominant cultivating castes themselves (Sreedhar, 1997: 71-91). Thus, it appears that land transfers had not altered the land ownership patterns in a major way, and are skewed in favour of the socially and economically powerful sections in the tank command areas, particularly in the head reaches.

Extent of Well Irrigation in Tank Command Areas

Since well irrigation in the tank command areas is bound to influence the collective management of tanks by the farmers, it is important to examine this aspect before planning tank rehabilitation projects. It was found in a detailed study of three rainfed tanks in Anantapur district that the extent of net cultivated area accounted for only about 70 per cent of the tank command areas and over three-fourths of the cultivated area was served by well irrigation. It was also noted that relatively well-endowed farmers alone could go for well irrigation. On the whole, over 70 per cent of the farmers were involved in digging of 464 wells out of which about half were in working condition. About one-third of the farmers were involved in selling water to their neighbours. The average area served by each well ranged between one and three acres. It was also found that most of the wells were dug after 1985, roughly around the time when the state government first provided cheap electricity to the farmers (*Ibid*: 94-98).

Besides the government incentives of cheap loans and electricity for irrigation and uncertainty with regard to the availability of tank water, another important factor that contributed for the growth of well irrigation in the tank command areas is the general practice of not letting out tank water for cultivation purpose until the tank becomes full to the extent of three-fourths of its capacity. If the tank becomes full to the extent of less than three-fourths of its capacity, the water is not let out through sluices. The decision-making in this matter vests with the revenue officials in consultation with the village elders including representatives of the farmers.

As such, many farmers had gone for well irrigation because tanks would not become full or near full in most of the years and if they possess wells, there would be water in the well due to percolation effect that facilitates cultivation.

Regarding the impact of the spread of well irrigation on the collective management of tanks, there is a general tendency among the farmers with wells not to evince much interest. It is also common for those farmers without wells not to show keen interest in collective management because water would not be available to them as it would not be let out through sluices any way in most of the years'. Thus, all the farmers would lose interest in collective management. It would adversely affect the living conditions of relatively poor farmers who could not afford to go for well irrigation and who continue to depend on tanks. As such, well irrigation is bound to pose problems for proper management of tank irrigation.

Arrangements for the Distribution of Water

It is important to examine the existing arrangements for the distribution of water in the tank command areas while planning tank rehabilitation projects. The lower level functionaries of the ID such as the Work Inspector, Laskar or Majdoor generally do not interfere with the distribution of water below the outlet. Therefore, farmers used to maintain Neerkattis, who would undertake the distribution of water among the farmers traditionally on hereditary basis. Usually one Neerkatti would be appointed for each sluice or to a particular crop area. They would be paid in kind at the rate of 50 kg paddy per acre. But, now with the irregular availability of water in the tank and with the spread of well irrigation, Neerkattis are appointed only when there is adequate flow of water into the tank. They are usually appointed by the village officials in consultation with the village elders. They are paid at the rate of 25 kg paddy per acre or Rs.800 per month for the required period. Regarding the satisfaction of farmers with regard to present arrangement, a majority of them at the middle and tail reaches were not satisfied because they get insufficient water, that too not when water is really required for the standing crop. They complain that if only the distributaries and the field channels were maintained properly they would have got their due share of water. But, it was noticed that these were not at all maintained properly in most of the tanks. Another important issue of relevance here is the equity in the distribution of water. With the expansion of well irrigation, the farmers with wells would become indirect beneficiaries because even if there is little water in the tank, for instance, even to the extent of one-fifth or one-fourth of its capacity, there would be water in their wells with which they can pursue their cultivation. In such a case, the farmers without wells would not get their equitable share in the tank water. Thus, the basic principle of equity that sustained tank irrigation for centuries is at stake.

Changes in the Cropping & Occupational Pattern

The inadequate availability of water forced many a farmer to change their cropping pattern in the tank command areas. It was noted that crop diversification took place in the rainfed tanks in Anantapur district, indicating a shift from paddy and ragi to high value cash crops like sunflower, groundnut, mulberry, sugarcane, etc. Thus, the response of the farmers to the adverse situation could be termed as positive, of course with the aid of well irrigation in the tank command areas. It was also found that occupational diversification took place in the farmers' households due to uncertain tank water; the percentage of workers engaged in services, non-agricultural labour, business and artisan works increased over a period of time. Such a rise in the dependence on non-agricultural activities was more pronounced in the case of fanners without wells than those with wells. Even the share of non-agricultural sources of income increased considerably in these households. Thus, the uncertainty with regard to tank water led to crop and occupational diversification and resulted in greater dependence on non-agricultural sources of income among the farmers' households, particularly those belonging to poorer sections. Such a trend is not conducive to the collective management of tank irrigation.

Conclusion

From the above discussion, it becomes clear that tank irrigation management is at peril in the drought prone regions.

First, the current trends of tank irrigation in terms of the effective tank irrigated area are not encouraging. The WUAs appear to be not very effective in promoting PIM in Andhra Pradesh, especially in the tank command areas, as indicated by dismal performance of tanks during the last eight years. The present condition of tanks does not seem to reflect the amount spent under minor rehabilitation schemes undertaken through WUAs. It appears that the damages inflicted upon the tanks due to their utter neglect over the past century must be so severe that the amount spent so far has not yielded the desired result. It is also likely that the user groups have become user friendly as has been widely criticised and whatever the money allotted has not been spent prudently for the specific purpose. Such issues need to be probed in greater detail to get to the truth. Nevertheless, it appears that the tank rehabilitation projects were not designed in a comprehensive manner in consultation with the farmers concerned so as to enlist their active participation and to put the tanks back on the rails.

Second, before designing tank rehabilitation projects, it is important to examine the various issues that are likely to have a bearing on the collective management of tanks. The existing land ownership patterns are skewed in favour of economically and socially powerful sections and their cooperation is essential for the success of any arrangement for collective management. Hence, it is important to hold a series of deliberations with all the farmers in order to convince them about the need for sustainable use of water and at the same time give due respect to the principle of equity. Organising exposure visits to successful tank rehabilitation projects in Maharashtra, Tamil Nadu and Rajasthan may be of some use in this context. Involving the NGOs in tank rehabilitation projects has proved to be not only cost-effective but also successful in enlisting the active participation of the farmers so as the sustain tank irrigation in future.

The expansion of well irrigation in the tank command areas is another major concern in the present context as it would equally dissuade the farmers with wells and those without wells from participating in collective management of tanks. Closely linked with this problem is the practice of not letting out the water until the tank becomes full to the extent of at least three-fourths of its capacity. To overcome such challenges, it is necessary to revive traditional methods of irrigation management adopted successfully by farmers themselves in certain places. For instance, in some parts of Karnataka, a system known as Damasi is being practiced in which the farmers agree to irrigate only a proportion of the command area in times of insufficient water (Ramaswamy 1985). Similarly, in certain parts of Sri Lanka, there is a traditional custom called *Bethma* in which water supplies that are not adequate to the full command area are allocated to a part of the area and all land owners are given proportional land share in the irrigated part (Leach, 1961). Another practice that is prevalent in some tanks of Anantapur district is sluice rotation in the sense that if farmers under one sluice are allocated water during one season or year, the farmers under another sluice would be allocated water during the subsequent season or year. There is yet another practice prevalent in some tanks of Anantapur district where all the irrigators agree to irrigate only a portion of their land in proportion to the availability of water, and all of them adopt a uniform cropping pattern. There are bound to be several problems in striking a right solution in accordance with the equity principle, which may be different for each tank, but constant persuasion is likely to yield the desired result.

While designing and implementing tank rehabilitation projects, it is important that these projects should be made an integral component of the poverty reduction programmes of the government because studies[8] proved that the decline in collective management of tanks would adversely affect the poorer sections. It is also important that the tank rehabilitation projects are closely linked to the watershed development programme so as to make them more effective. Another important challenge that is critical to tank irrigation is the stricter implementation of existing rules regarding well irrigation. Yet another challenge is careful planning for crop diversification, including the promotion of fodder crops, which becomes crucial for occupational diversification so as to promote sustainable livelihoods for those dependent upon the tanks. Unless these measures are adopted on a comprehensive basis, tank irrigation management continues to be at stake.

NOTES

1. Major and Medium irrigation projects (each with a command area of more than 10000 hectares and 2000-10000 hectares respectively) accounted for nearly two-thirds of the irrigation budgets in the post-independence period.
2. Tanks are practically the only sources of irrigation in the Himalayan states of Himachal Pradesh, Sikkim, Assam, Arunachal Pradesh, Nagaland, Mjoram, Meghalaya, Tripura and Manipur. In states like Jammu and Kashmir and Kerala, they account for over half the net irrigated area. In Bihar. Karnataka, Tamil Nadu and West Bengal, they account for over a quarter of net irrigated areas of those slates. In Madhya Pradesh and Andhra Pradesh, they constitute over 20% of net irrigated area. In UP, tanks irrigate over 400,000 hectares, most of which lies in the hilly northern districts, where other irrigation sources are scant. In Rajasthan too, these sources account for most of the irrigation facilities available in region around Aravalli ranges (Sengupla 1993: 14-17). Rajasthan has 4600 minor irrigation tanks irrigating about 630.000 hectares. Most of these projects involve building of small dams to create reservoir or a tank. More than 50% of them were built before independence, but share of irrigation from these sources is only 189,000 ha. (Gulati 1999: 2-10 to 2-11) During 1996-97, some 40,825 minor irrigation works irrigated 930,000 hectares in Karnataka (Ibid 2-15)
3. Both China and Japan have had a long and sustained tradition of water conservancy development through local effort. The projects require beneficiaries to contribute labour and materials for construction even when the government takes up the projects. Large projects account for only a fraction of total effort that has gone into the development of irrigation. In China, during the mid fifties, surface irrigation accounted for over 80% of the irrigated area, over 90% of it consisting of local systems like farm ponds, weirs, small ditches and aqueducts. Similarly. Japanese irrigation systems are large in number and their average size is small. There is hardly any system serving more than 20,000 hectares (Vaidyanathan, 1999: 12-14).

4. These include Bihar Irrigation Act, 1997. Karntataka Irrigation and Certain other Laws (Amendment) Act 2000, Rajasthan Farmers' Management of Irrigation Systems Act 2000, Tamil Nadu Farmers' Management of Irrigation Systems Act 2000, Madhya Pradesh Farmers' Management of Irrigation Systems Act 2002, and Orissa Pani Panchayat Bill, 2002.
5. In Andhra Pradesh, all tanks with a command area of 100 acres and above were placed under the control of Irrigation Department, while those tanks with a command area of less than 100 acres were placed under the control of the Panchayati Raj Department. WUAs were formed only for those tanks under the control of the Irrigation Department.
6. Intermediate castes include Golla, Kuruba, Pamasali, Boya, Dudekula, Rangaraju, Mangali, Bestha, Uppara and Muslims.
7. Dominant cultivating castes include Reddy, Kamma and Balija.
8. For details, see Kei Kajisa *et al.*, 2004.

REFERENCES

Government of India (1992). Eighth Five *Year Plan,1992-97.* New Delhi

Gulati, Ashok, Ruth, Meinzen-Dick, Raju. K.V. (1999), F*rom Top Down to Bottoms Up: Institutional Reforms 'in Indian Canal Irrigation,* Delhi: Institute of Economic Growth.

Kei Kajisa, K. Palanisami and Takeshi Sakurai (2004), "Declines in Collective Management of Tank Irrigation and their Impact on Income Distribution and Poverty in Tamil Nudu, India". Policy Research Institute, Ministry of Agriculture, Forestry and Fisheries, Japan.

Leach, Edmund (1961). *Pul Eliva: A Village in Ceylon,* Cambridge, U.K.: Cambridge University Press.

NIRD (1994). *Rural Development Statistics.* Hyderabad.

Mishra, Anupam (1993). *Aaj bhi Khare Hain Talaab (Hindi),* New Delhi: Gandhi Peace Foundation.

Palanisami, K (2005), "Sustainable Management of Tank Irrigation Systems in India". Internet.

Ramaswamy, V. *et al* (1985), "Damasi: A Concept of Equity and Productivity in Irrigation", *Wamana,* Vol. 5. No. 3, July, pp. 1 and 15-22.

Sengupta, Nirmal (1991), *Managing Common Property: Irrigation in India and Philippines.* New Delhi: Sage Publications.

Sengupta, Nirmal (1993) *User-Friendly Irrigation Designs',* New Delhi: Sage Publications.

Sreedhar, G. (1997). *Tank Irrigation in Semi-Arid Zones,* Bangalore: Sunrise Publications.

Vaidyanathan, A. (1999). *Water Resources Management: Institutions and Irrigation Development in India.* New Delhi: Oxford University Press.

14

Strategies for Participatory Irrigation Management

M. SANKARA REDDI, M. CHANDRAYYA, M. SUNDARA RAO and M. RAMESH

Introduction

Today, the world over, examples of successful community based natural resource management can be seen but, with very few exceptions, these initiatives have remained "islands of development" and have only affected a fraction of the communities that could benefit from such success.

In India, these successes will need to be repeated thousands of times. Clearly to facilitate such a transformation, some scaling-up will have to be attempted. This paper critically examines the successes and will suggest how to scale the better elements for effective National or State policy. Today's governments have become sensitive to the issues of equity, efficiency and have understood largely the importance of involving people in the development process. If the magic elements learnt form successful community based initiatives can be introduced into the mainstream policy making process, then we have moved not two but four steps ahead in winning the battle for giving sustainable rural livelihood opportunities for the millions. Over the past decade there has been an attempt to apply lessons from these small-scale "development experiments" to a larger area. This includes programmes formulated by the government. The paper argues that with political will to alleviate poverty based on appropriate Indian Network on Participatory Irrigation Management. India values rather than populist ideology, and with a robust policy initiative backed by legal sanctions, benefits can reach more people in a short time. Latest estimates show that 36 per cent of India's population lives below the poverty line. Poor survival chances, landlessness, malnutrition, environmental pollution and social exclusion arising out of caste and gender discrimination characterize the lives of these people. Increased scarcity and degradation of land and water resources makes it difficult for people to meet their daily subsistence needs. Livelihoods dependent on land-based resources are adversely affected. Most of the time, the effect on women is particularly severe because women are the primary collectors and users of natural resources in most parts of rural India. Regeneration of natural resources through effective conservation and management practices is crucial to achieving the goal of food and livelihood security.

Agricultural progress and regeneration cannot take place without water. In order to overcome the severe water crisis, both for domestic use and irrigation, at present and in the foreseeable future, water harvesting and management is most important. In spite of large-scale irrigation systems developed in India, there are many problems in maximizing the full benefits of these installed irrigation systems. Unless people accept responsibility and ownership of the interventions, water management initiatives cannot become sustainable. Farmers who depend on irrigation water for their livelihood have the strongest incentive to manage that water carefully. One of the ways in which this issue can be addressed is through the introduction of Participatory Irrigation Management.

The paper argues that Participatory Irrigation Management cannot succeed without a political will and the readiness of the irrigation bureaucracy to change. In additon, while critics may argue that there are qualitative losses in scaling up, this paper argues that once reforms assume the shape of a people's movement, or at least a farmer's movement successes may be institutionalized at broader social scales while the quality of programme benefits is maintained. Finally, a variety of factors create incentives for farmers to manage and maintain their system and land and affect investment in increased agriculture production. The present paper will examine the Irrigation Sector Reforms underway in India with reference to the remarkable example Andhra Pradesh.

Background

A quick overview of the growth of the Irrigation sector in India after independence will help set the context for the current state of affairs. The total geographical area of India is 329 million hectares. The total cultivable area of the country at present is around 142 million hectares and the gross cultivated area around 185 million hectares. At the time of independence (1947) the irrigation potential in India was 22 million hectares but by the end of 2000 it had grown to an estimated 90 million hectares. India now has the second largest irrigated area in the world second only to China. Under the leadership of Mr. Jawaharlal Nehru, the first Prime Minister of India, a great deal of emphasis was placed on centralised economic planning and on construction of large irrigation projects both for hydro power and for increasing the food grain production. In the 1960's, coupled with construction of the irrigation projects, there was a focus on the use of high yielding varieties of seeds, chemical fertilisers etc. which ushered in the Green Revolution in India. The production of food grains increased from 50 million tons in 1951 to nearly 200 million tons at present.

Today the environmental, social and second-generation problems associated with Green Revolution are well documented. Given the significant role of irrigation in bringing about the Green Revolution in India it should not be surprising that the irrigation sector is problematic as well. It is important to note here that in the Welfare State approach adopted by the various political parties in India this kind of over governmental zeal and enthusiasm to provide everything to the masses was inevitable. The belief was that government intervention and control over the economy and the assets of the growth engine was to ensure economic welfare of the people but today the government is rethinking its strategy.

Government owned and managed large irrigation systems had become so centralised and one sided that farmers have been almost completely excluded from the system. The system was set into a downward spiral of disuse and neglect and, ultimately, broke down in many places. Faced with strong criticism, policy makers were introduced to concepts such as people's participation, bottom up approach, decentralisation and devolution. A 1995 government document reports that the irrigation sector in India is beset with problems related to investment priorities, poor management, and corruption, deteriorating physical infrastructure, lack of adequate financing, social equity and no incentives to use water optimally. Today governments have become sensitive to the issues of equity and efficiency and have come to understand, largely, the importance of involving people in the development process. Participatory Irrigation Management is a concept that is not new to India. In fact, farmermanaged irrigation systems are recorded as far back as the third century B.C. Kings would generally provide the material for building the dams and canals and then the people would be responsible for managing and maintaining the systems and resolving conflicts.

Today, participatory irrigation management (PIM) refers to the involvement of irrigation users in all aspects and at all levels of irrigation management. "All aspects" includes the initial planning and design of new irrigation projects or improvements, as well as the construction, supervision, financing, decision-making, operation, maintenance, monitoring, and evaluation of the system. "All levels" refers to the full physical limits of the irrigation system, up to the policy level. In any management function, including the setting of policies, can and should have a participatory dimension to it.

Conceptual Framework

Increased farmer participation in irrigation is part of a worldwide trend of devolution in natural resources management. In many countries the move to transfer responsibilities of managing the irrigation system from government agencies to farmer organisations is gaining momentum. Mexico, Philippines, Colombia and Turkey are some of the well-known examples where there has been a major effort for transfer of irrigation systems through Participatory Irrigation Management processes. Mexico has served as a model for other countries considering irrigation management transfer programme. The end of 1996, the government had transferred 87 per cent of the area under medium and large irrigation districts in the country to users' associations. Turkey has succeeded in transferring nearly one million hectares, or 61 per cent of the publicly managed irrigation in the country, to local government units or special purpose irrigation associations created at the local level. Irrigation Management transfer in Colombia was unusual in that farmers initiated it rather than by a government initiative. Since the first two schemes were transferred in 1976, 16 out of the 24 medium and large schemes in the country, covering about two-thirds of the 750,000 hectares under such irrigation, have been transferred to local associations to manage.

Transferring irrigation responsibilities has been seen as a way of reducing pressures on thinly stretched government finances, while improving irrigated agricultural production and ensuring the long-term sustainability of irrigation systems. Irrigation management transfer remains a vague concept. The world-wide, transfer has assumed some of the following forms:

- Introducing irrigation service fees.
- Fostering competition in service delivery.
- Contracting with the private sector to provide irrigation services.
- Vending irrigation services to those who pay a fee.
- Franchising the right to provide irrigation services to private organisations.
- Subsidising a local organisation to provide irrigation services.
- Joint investments by agency and users.
- Making the management agency financially autonomous.
- Joint management by agency and users.
- Devolution of responsibility or control to users.
- Shedding of government functions.
- Privatisation of assets.

There are close parallels between the concepts of irrigation manenegment transfer and decntralization. Decentralization encompasses a broad range of forms as well. Researchers described it as the "transfer of planning, and decision making or administrative authority from the central government to field organization, local government or non-government organization". Though this definition does not reflect the importance of shifting the locus of power from the state to the public or, in the case of irrigation, the user groups. Fisher (2000) refers to this latter form of decentralization as "devolution". Ostrom, Schroeder, and Wynne have pointed out that temporary decentralisation and local organisations established, as part of construction or rehabilitation projects often did not have a significant long-term impact because the basic institutional framework was not changed.

The paper argues that in the Andhra Pradesh Irrigation Reform process since there has been a conscious effort to introduce institutional changes in the overall irrigation sector, there has been a decentralisation of decision-maker's powers at the WUA level.

Irrigation Management Transfer in India: A Case Study

The issue of Irrigation Management Transfer in the context of India implies the transfer of irrigation management responsibility from state government agencies, mainly the irrigation departments, to Water User Associations (WUA) or other farmer organisations. The Indian constitution identifies those subjects that are the responsibility of the central government and those that are the responsibility of each of the 29 states. Water, including irrigation, is within the state's jurisdiction, although the central government does allocate financial resources to every state and so through a few centrally sponsored schemes can influence state policies. The states operated medium and major surface irrigation systems accounting for 36 per cent of the net irrigated area in India. The remainder of the irrigated area includes area irrigated by private groundwater irrigation (49 %), traditional tank irrigation schemes (7%), and other sources of irrigation (8%).

Over the last two decades various initiatives have sought -troduce participatory forms of irrigation management. But many of these efforts have been half-hearted. A few WUAs have formed below the minor outlets in some of the major canal systems and the sporadic efforts of NGOs remained localised. In the 1990s financial pressure on various state governments and pressure to improve the performance of irrigated agriculture, and to ensure the sustainability of the irrigation systems, led many states to acknowledge that reforms are inevitable. Today, virtually all states in India are considering adoption of irrigation management transfer policies. The results of the Irrigation Reforms in Andhra Pradesh and conditionality attached with World Bank loan agreements are also hastening the process in a few states. Though there is danger that they merely remain reforms on paper. Andhra Pradesh is the first state in India to introduce overall institutional reforms in the irrigation sector at the state level. This was achieved the an historic legal act, the Andhra Pradesh Farmers Management of Irrigation Systems Act 11 of 1997 which sought to involve farmers in irrigation management and ultimately achieve irrigation management transfer to farmers across the entire state.

Pioneering Irrigation Reforms in Andhra Pradesh

Andhra Pradesh is the fifth largest State in India with a population of about 75 million and a geographical area of 27.68 million ha. Of the state's geographical area, 47 per cent (12.9 million ha) is under cultivation and the net sown area is about 11.04 million ha (4.88 million ha irrigated). It is primarily an agrarian state with about 70 per cent of its population dependent on agriculture. The economy is essentially agriculture-based. The majority of the farmers have small landholdings, averaging less than 2 ha. The agricultural sector generates about 36 per cent of the state's gross domestic product and employs some 70 per cent of the population. Irrigated agriculture constitutes 40 per cent of the state's cropped area and contributes over 60 per cent of the state's total agricultural production. Ninety five per cent of rice, the main crop grown in AP and the state'sprincipal staple food, is produced on irrigated lands. A wide variety of other irrigated crops are also grown, including cereals, pulses, oilseeds and non-food crops. Irrigated agriculture contributes to about 18 per cent of oil seed production, 55 per cent of other food crops like chillies, vegetables and fruits, 15 per cent of non food crops such as tobacco, cotton and sugarcane, and about 36 per cent of other minor crops. The state's three major rivers, namely Godavari, Krishna and Pennar drain 70 per cent of the state's land area. The water potential of Andhra Pradesh is estimated to be 2746 TMC. The major rivers are seasonal with more than 90 per cent of the total flows occurring between June and December depending on the rainfall that varies from year to year. The ultimate irrigation potential from all sources is estimated to be 9.50 mha. This includes 7.30 mha from surface water and 2.20 mha from groundwater.

Water User Associations

In 1984, the government of Andhra Pradesh passed the Andhra Pradesh Irrigation and Command Area Development Act, 1984, which authorized the creation of Command Area Development Authorities and Pipe Committees. These Pipe Committees were to be responsible for the internal distribution of water below the minor outlet and the maintenance of the micro system network. The committees, however, proved to be unsustainable and powerless. The water supply at the minor outlet was not reliable because of a lack of coordination between the Irrigation and Command Area Development authorities. The Pipe Committees were too small to have any say in the maintenance of the main system. They had neither clear-cut rights and responsibilities nor any means to raise resources. They lasted as long as they had the support of the Command Area Development Department and became non-functional once this support was withdrawn.

In 1995 the Government issued another Government Order (G.O. no 101 of 19 July 1995) calling for the promotion of farmer's participation in the management of irrigation. The order established Water Users' Associations (WUAs) at the minor level of the irrigation system. These associations were to be autonomous democratic bodies and were given full responsibility for the maintenance and operation of the irrigation network within the area of their operation. The Department of Irrigation (DOI) was directed to give increasing [illegible]nsibility of managing irrigation systems to WUAs and to assure the availability of reliable water at the head of the minor. Further, the Department of Irrigation was to undertake rehabilitation and modernisation of the internal water distribution system wherever WUAs were formed. The WUA were at liberty to regulate distribution of water-to-water users on volumetric or any other basis and to levy and collect penalties if any, fixed by it for violation of the water distribution schemes finalised for the irrigation system under its administrative supervision. Though, the DOI was instructed to facilitate fixation and collection of operation and maintenance charges from water users. Further, WUAs that improving efficiency and saved water were at liberty to sell the surplus.

A pilot programme was started on a small scale with a command area of about 500 ha under Sriramsagar Project. Between 1995 and 1997, this programme was expanded to cover a command area of about 20,000 ha under six different distributaries in the Sriramsagar Project. Farmers in the command area were helped to form the WUA, take up minimum feasible maintenance works for ensuring free flow of water up to the tail reaches in the system, organise water distribution in the entire system, resolve disputes, if any, internally and adopt their own crop planning. The net result of this experiment was increased awareness amongst the farmers. Irrigated area increased from a pre-project level of about 50 per cent to around 80 per cent using the same quantity of water as was supplied in the earlier years and without any substantial investment in system repairs. Beyond this, it was learned that the WUAs need proper legal status to be easily recognisable by the irrigation authorities and the relationship and lines of accountability between the WUAs and the irrigation department needed to be spelt out in clear terms so that proper water budget could be developed.

At roughly the same time, in 1996, the Government of AP issued a report that noted a number of significant problems in the irrigation sector. In addition to low cropping intensities, low farm yields yields and under financing of operations and maintenance, a serious decline in net irrigated area was observed. Only 2.3 million ha of the 4 million ha of potential irrigated area created was actually under irrigation (a gap of

52% between potential created and actual irrigated area). Further, the paper cited inefficiencies in the water distribution system including significant wastage of diverted water and inequitable distribution of water within schemes, especially between head and tail ends. The report suggested that farmer empowerment and management should form the heart of the reforms and that the process should be bold and comprehensive rather than incremental.

The irrigation reforms in AP would not have been possible unless there was a political will to change and introduce radical steps to revert the crisis in the irrigation sector. This political will came in the form of the dynamic Chief Minister Mr. Chandrababu Naidu of Andhra Pradesh, and some of the pro-poor reforms introduced by his party. He used the slogan "Janmabhoomi" (land of birth) to inspire communities and government to work together in new ways to improve their economic and social well-being. Two central themes emerged: grassroots participation in decision-making and programme implementation and cultural changes in the way government works.

A few committed officials from the Irrigation Department based, learning from the pilot action research project and their PIM experiences from other parts of India and international experiences formulated an idea and presented it to the Chief Minister. The idea got a go ahead and after several months of consultations involving the state legislature, various government agencies, political parties, farmer groups, and the media, the Andhra Pradesh Farmers Management of Irrigation Systems Act, 1997 was passed by the Legislative Assembly. *The Andhra Pradesh Farmers Management of Irrigation Systems Act (1997),* The Andhra Pradesh Farmers Irrigation Act (Act 11 of 1997) was enacted in April 1997 by the Andhra Pradesh government to involve farmers in irrigation management and ultimately transfer irrigation management from state agencies to farmers. The act called for the formation of water users associations across all types of irrigation systems in the state, the implementation of large-scale training on the issues related to irrigation reform programme both for farmers and staff of the irrigation department, and introduced significant financial reforms to influence quality performance of users organisations. The Act applies to the whole of the state of Andhra Pradesh except the scheduled areas, and the properties vested within the gram *Panchayats* (elected village councils). Though some provisions in the act afford the government considerable flexibility in applying the act (DICAD, GOAP 1997), an important provision in act the makes irrigation department staff accountable to the WUAs and require irrigation department staff to implement the decisions of the WUAs.

The WUAs are authorized to resolve conflicts internally. The act enables the WUAs to allocate funds for the improve irrigation the irrigation systems based on resources raised or from out of the grants given by the government as a percentage of water charges collected from the WUAs. The associations are also guaranteed access to critical information and permitted to prepare operational and maintenance plans. Following recommendations from the pilot project, farmers are afforded more freedom in cropping patterns.

Steps in Farmer Organizations

The term farmer's organisation is used as a generic term in the act and includes a water user association at the primary level a distributory committee at the distributory level a project committee at the project level and an apex committee level at the government level to resolve any disputes relating to the farmers organization. Elections have been conducted for 10,292 Water User Associations in the state and about 174 distributory committees. It has also been proposed that the Project Committee be elected as well.

A chairman or member of the managing committee can be recalled after a period of one year by giving a written notice signed by not less than one-third of the total number of voting members of the farmers organisation.

A water users area is divided into territorial constituencies for giving equitable representation to all areas in an irrigation command; namely, the head, middle and tail end reaches. Groups of outlets are clubbed into a territorial constituency. The number of territorial constituencies varies depending upon the type of the irrigation system and the extent of the command.

In the Andhra Pradesh, irrigation reform process occurs at the tertiary or secondary level where there has been devolution of power; but, at the primary level there is no transfer of power as of now. Also it not "decentralisation" in its truest sense, but more administrative devolution of powers for management. In large-scale government owned irrigation systems the ownership or primary responsibility of the physical assets (at least) will remain with the government system. The government retains overall ownership and control over the water resource, reservoirs, and main canals. Maintenance and (perhaps) operation of lower level canals are turned over to Water Users Associations.

According to Raymond Peter (Peter 2000) one of the architects of the PIM reform process in Andhra Pradesh, PIM in A.P. evolved in 8 stages: Stage one Generating Political support at the highest level. This is essential to provide the required motivation. Stage two Creating favorable environments. Stage three Developing legal frameworks. Stage four Formation of farmer's organization – WUAs and Distributory Committees. Stage five Implementation of the programme with clarity of roles of the farmer's organization, irrigation department and other government agencies. Stage six capacity building of WUA, Irrigation department and other government agencies. Stage seven Ensuring transparency, accountability in the working of Farmer organizations and social audit Stage eight Monitoring and mid course corrections.

Impacts After Three Years of Reform

After only three to four years, it is still to early to comment on the success or failure of the reform programme, but it is a good time to evaluate the achievements of the reform process and suggest possible mid course corrections.

Increase in Net Irrigated Area

The reform process was hastened by a decline in the net irrigated area in the state. In the late 1980s the net irrigated area reached a plateau and it fell from 2.9 million ha in 1990 to 2.3 million ha in 1994. Out of the 4.8 million ha of potential irrigated area created, only 48% are actually being irrigated.

The data from the Sriramsagar Project indicates an increase in reported irrigated area after the hand over to the

WUAs in June 1997; in some locales the gross irrigated area more than doubled in the kharif and rabi seasons. Remarkably this increase in irrigated land area was achieved using two thirds as much water as in 1996.

This increase may be attributed, at least in part, to improvements in the delivery system (i.e. the cleaning of canals). Also water utilization was monitored in an effort to minimise water losses. When analysing the increase in irrigated area, it should be remembered that, farmers are more willing to report irrigated area of the WUA than to the revenue department officials because under-reporting of irrigated area meant lesser water tax. After turnover, the WUA is reporting the exact irrigated area resulting in better tax recovery. Even if one discounts this increase in reported area, there has been a general net increase in the irrigated area.

Increase in Water Tax

Increasing water tax has always been a sensitive issue in Indian politics. The tax, really a token charge, has not changed for years in many states; and still, recovery of the water tax from the farmers is difficult. In a bold step, irrigation water charges were raised three fold on April 1997. Farmer leaders and various political parties across the state debated the price hike. Finally, after it was explained that the increased water tax would in some way filter back to the WUAs for maintenance of the irrigation system, the increase was accepted. Oblitas (1999) attributes this eventual approval to a "combination of a widespread consultation and public outreach process preceding the increase, and the presentation of the increase not as a single measure but as a part of a package of measures which were seen by the rural communities and the political parties as, overall, beneficial to the farmers".

Good Quality Operation and Maintenance

In 1998, during the first phase of the $28.1 million rehabilitation and maintenance works, more than 70% of the works were accomplished by the farmer organisations. The works were planned by as farmers walked through the command area along with officials of the irrigation department and together they decided which areas were highest priorities. This represents a dramatic change from the time when farmers were forced to rely on unscrupulous contractors. The WUAs have executed the same works for a lesser cost than charged by the earlier contractorsand actual funds for O and M has increased for the first time.

Environmental Benefits

It's still too early to comment on the environmental impacts of the reform process. According to field observations, but one of the farmers in the Godavari Delta area reported that levels of salinity in the soil and water had declined after the reform programmeme due to improvements in water distribution. More water has been reaching the tail end areas and was used for flushing the salts from the soils. Also, due to a greater availability of canal water, farmers in tail ends have stopped or decreased their use of bore well water (which has high levels of salinity). Discussions by the author with some WUAs presidents from the delta region also highlighted the fact that, after channels were cleaned and drainage improved, the incidence of water logging has reduced. Such findings, if they could be documented and attributed to the reform, could be information of potential global significance.

Emergence of a New Leadership (WUA Presidents)

According to Shri Kishen Reddy, Chairman of Distributary Committtee 16 in the Tadikal, Sriramsagar Project, "a new leadership was developing because of the reform process which is young and dynamic and concerned with the welfare of the farmers". This is a very positive, and unanticipated, outcome of the reform process. In the Indian political scene this is like a breath of fresh air. Though some critics disagree and suggest that rural elite and politically powerful have hijacked the programme, the author is of the view that in a politically conscious and active democracy in India this is bound to happen. This is rural reality. what must be seen that at the end of the day is a new leadership that delivers the goods and participates in the reform programme in the right spirit. Also, if the WUA is strengthened, the exploitative tendency, of the rural elite, (if it exists), will also decreases.

Analyses Political Will for Reforms

As stated in the conceptual framework, the paper argues that political will is the prerequisite for bringing about irrigation reforms. Lack of political will is the only reason that the PIM programme has not been implemented on a large scale in any of the other states in India. Maharashtra and Gujarat, two states that were pioneers in introducing the concept of PIM in India have to date done little more than setting good examples. They have not demonstrated political commitment or enacted any enabling policy for scaling Irrigation Management Transfer to the state level.

Political will is very significant in the democratic institutions prevalent in India. The political party in power can only bring about wide reaching policy change. No political party wanted to initiate irrigation sector reforms, as this would required tackling unpopular issues such as increasing water tax and restructuring the balance of power of existing irrigation bureaucracy. Increasing water tax is politically unpalatable because farmers are "poor" and evenmore distasteful because the poor constitute a major voting block bank for politicians. In the long run, this dynamic between elected officials and electorate may be the bane of any good agricultural policy evolving in India.

The reforms in A.P. have shown that if bold positive steps are taken and farmers feel that the government is sincere and accountable, then, even harsh measures like increasing water tax can be successful. The farmers are most interested in the delivery of goods (water), at assured times and in the right quantity. If farmers see this happening then they are willing to pay.

Still, political will for a one-time introduction of reforms is insufficient. Reforms have to be sustained and so require continuous follow up and coaxing. This is the major difference between A.P. and Madhya Pradesh where irrigation reforms were recently launched. In A.P. there has been continuous follow up from the level of chief minister to ministers and senior bureaucrats. Continuity has been maintained through innovative programmes like "Dial Your Chief Minister", publication of a monthly news magazine and holding state level conferences of the WUA presidents. In M.P. after the introduction of the Act there has been no political follow up. The result is that politicians are seen as lax, the bureaucracy proceeding with business as usual perceives reforms as no more than a political gimmick and the entire spirit of the reform is killed. The argument thus presented is that constant political will acts like a watchdog over the fat-cat tendencies bureaucracy. In short political will puts pressure on the bureaucracy to perform.

The emergence of new political leadership (WUAs/DC presidents) is also a positive sign that a new generation of leadership and will put pressure on the system to perform. Many of the presidents in the future will enter the contest for mainstream political positions, which could be beneficial for the sustainability of irrigation reforms.

Enabling Legal Environment

One of the distinguishing features of irrigation reform in A.P. is a clearly stated legal act defining the various processes, roles and responsibilities of the WUAs and the irrigation department. The WUAs are formed as legal entities. Powers are devolved to the WUA and backed by legal rights and obligations.

As mentioned earlier, the Act mainly gives the WUAs water rights and control of the system. It provides functional and administrative autonomy so that the WUA can make decisions. Most importantly, the Act makes the Irrigation department accountable to the WUA. The Act also defines the contracts between the irrigation department and the WUA, helps to clarify roles and responsibilities and provides a forum for communication between the two. The Act makes it compulsory for all farmers to be members of the WUA. In most other cases or states, membership is voluntary. One of the major weaknesses in the WUAs promoted by NGOs in other states of India is that they have not been legally recognised by the irrigation department so no rights or powers are transferred to the WUAs. This defeats the entire purpose for forming the WUAs.

Some have debated whether irrigation reform should be legislated a separate Act (as was the case in A.P.) or if "proper" changes in existing state irrigation acts can bring about the same desired effect? Evidence from literature shows that merely tinkering with the existing acts has not helped much and, unless there is a clear cut legal provision giving rights and devolving powers to the WUAs, mere cosmetic changes favour business as usual. The A.P. experience highlights the role of a legal act applicable to the entire state, and all irrigation (surface) systems. It is important to note here that the Administrative bureaucracy, at least at the lower levels of power, understand only a legal language.

Irrigation Department as Agents of Change

Large-scale irrigation systems have given rise to large and centralized bureaucracies. Over the years the attitude of the irrigation department has become that of providers and thus brought about certain arrogance in the department while dealing with farmers, who are looked upon as recipients of the generosity heaped onto them by the department. The irrigation bureaucracy is resistant to any change, like many other administrative departments. Fear of losing power and privileges is one of the major reasons for resistance to change. Also, some may fear that if the works component is transferred to the WUA then chances of rent seeking are lost. So, along with a political will, there also has to be an administrative will for change and reforms. The administrative will does not mean a few committed and highly motivated individuals at the highest echelons of power trying to force change but, rather, administrative will is a gradual attitudinal and behavioral change among all the ranks in the department. This task is easier said than done. It is most important that the assistant engineer responsible at the WUA level believes in the reform process and believes that he is an employee of the WUA and not the reverse. The officer of the irrigation department is nominated as the "competent authority" at the WUA level. The officer coordinates with the WUAs and gives technical guidance in the preparation of estimates and maintenance of hydraulic particulars and structures. In A.P., changes in attitude and behaviour, especially amongst the technical bureaucracy were brought about by a series of training and awareness programmes. These measures were strengthened by the will and zeal of higher-level officials, which has had a positive impact on lower level staff.

What A.P. has shown is that unless the Irrigation Department is made the agent of change, reforms will not succeed. Constructive farmer participation often hinges on the ability to move beyond an adversarial or paternalistic relationship between bureaucracy and farmers to a partnership. This is not easy because farmers often distrust the irrigation agency. Developing a service orientation among agency staff and a collaborative attitude between agencies and farmers has been essential for successful joint management and irrigation transfer programmes in the Philippines, Sri Lanka, United States, Mexico and other countries.

Field interactions with the WUAs showed that there was a perceivable change amongst the irrigation staff and that the majority of the WUAs were happy with the support of the departmental staff, and had developed an excellent rapport with the engineers. Discussions with engineers revealed that many of the lower level staff of the department was unaware of the rapid changes taking place. Only senior officials attended training programmes. So, awareness and orientation programmes for the lower level staff are needed if reforms are to succeed and progress in the right spirit of partnership.

Engineers suggested that all levels of staff should be continuously trained in attitudinal and behavioural change and that farmers and engineers should participate equally in the reform process. Also, it was noted that political interference in the role of engineers should be minimized. Further, engineers expressed that an environment that facilitates smooth transition while at the same time ensuring the feeling of security amongst officials should be created. Finally, they recommended that committed personnel be hired to promote and guide the programme at the lower level.

Mobilization of Financial Resources to Sustain Reforms

Limited financial resources have been a key factor in motivating governments to introduce irrigation reform. With thinly stretched financial resources and a majority of the budget committed to administrative requirements (salaries etc.) governments have little resources for operations and maintenance and are ready for PIM. Herein lies the catch.

Farmers do not want to assume full responsibility for deteriorated or defunct systems and then farmers fear that the government will not provide any support after the transfer and that they will have to pay increased water taxes. The issue is that financial resources will need to be committed to the reform process to cover basic O and M of the system before transfer or in conjunction with the transfer process. In the case of A.P., key reformers in the irrigation department argue that minimum rehabilitation before transfer is a myth and they achieved this without doing minimum reforms. In the view of the author this is another myth being created. When the Act was passed and WUAs formed no minimum rehabilitation of the system was done. But a couple of financial incentives were promised like there was a financial sop if the election to the WUAs presidentship was unanimous. The WUA gets a grant of Rs. 50,000 if elections are not contested. With assistance from the World Bank, Rs. 118.1 crores ($28.1) was provided in 1998 for minimum rehabilitation works (an investment of approximately Rs. 100/acre). Previously the government allocated Rs. 40 per acre for O and M, but approximately Rs.35 of this was used for Irrigation department staff salaries and fixed overhead costs, leaving barely Rs 5 per acre for actual maintenance work. The Rs. 100 per acre allocation for minimum rehabilitation from WB funds was to be used only for actual maintenance works, exclusive of department salaries. From January 1998 to March 1999, 22,887 works were undertaken, of which 70% were implemented by WUAs or DCs.

At present the water tax is collected by the Revenue Department and goes into the treasury of the state government. It is proposed that, in the near future, the water tax would be collected by the WUA and the money collected would flow back to the WUA in the manner described in the table below. The WUA would use this money for O and M purposes as well as administrative expenses etc. In A.P., financial resources were provided to WUA and DCs for minimum rehabilitation works. So farmers did not have to spend anything for rehabilitation of the system.

Proposed Irrigation Revenue Sharing Pattern Across the Schemes

Level	Major	Medium	Minor
WUA	50 %	60 %	90 %
DC	20 %	30 %	-
PC	20 %	-	-
Local government	10 %	10 %	10 %

Source: DICAD, GOAP 1997.

The point here is that financial funds for minimum rehabilitation of the system prior to or during reforms must be made available if if reforms are to succeed. The Government of Andhra Pradesh funded the reform programme with support from the World Bank. Though the government defends that even without World Bank aid they would have gone ahead with the reforms, critiques disagree. The initial piloting of WUAs on the Sriramsagar scheme was assisted, including use of retroactive financing, under the Andhra Pradesh Third Irrigation Project, World Bank project approved in May 1997. The statewide reform programme is being financed under the Irrigation Component of the Andhra Pradesh Economic Restructuring Project (APERP), approved in June 1998 and with retroactive financing available from August1997. The Irrigation component of the APERP provides support, totalling $142 million to the GOAP's irrigation sector reform programme.

How then might other States want to introduce reforms in the absence of World Bank funding? Some options include:

- The government transfers all the O and M funds from the department to the WUAs
- The minimum rehabilitation programme is scaled up in phases a portion of water tax goes back to the WUA for O and M. Once this cycle is in order, sustainability of the programme can be ensured.
- Rights to WUAs to raise their own money.
- Collecting increased water tax over and above the government rates.

- Promoting and motivating farmer contributions to the programme.
- Using existing State and Central government schemes meant for these kinds of activities.

There are likely enough financial resources within the government; but because of high rent seeking tendencies over the last two decades, excessive leakage and sub standard work, have contributed to fiscal problems. An accountable WUA, in collaboration with the government and a proper Monitoring and Evaluation strategy should stem this rot.

Devolution of Powers to WUA and Other Issues

The foundation of the irrigation reform process is the Water User' Association. The election process to establish the WUAs was democratic, fair and participatory. Field observations and discussions with farmers and WUA presidents suggest that, because of the WUAs, farmers feel they have an equal say in management of their affairs, for the first time. Furthermore, the quality of the structures and maintenance has improved and crop production has increased. Many of these issues have already been highlighted in other sections of the paper. Here, it is important to identify the powers that have actually been devolved to the WUA. At the primary level power to maintain the system, resolve conflict and keep records has been devolved. The irrigation department recognizes its accountability to the WUA. But the WUA presidents and farmers are of the view that unless the Project Committee is formed and farmers have a right in the management of the main system, reforms will be incomplete. Still, new problems with the WUAs surfacedand need immediate attention. For instance, WUAs have acted as petty contractors. The entire reform process at least in its first phase has been construction oriented with the majority of the works being done through the In many cases the President, being a dominant person, acted as contractor and took on the work himself.

Siphoning of Funds in the Process or Doing Sub-standard Works

As the officials have to pass the bills of the sanctioned works, the compliance with the President has increased their rent seeking behaviour. In other cases, government officials have acted as petty contractors and, in compliance with the presidents, executed the works to curb this practice. More awareness campaigns need to be launched regarding the rights and salient features of the programme. Secondly participatory monitoring and evaluation processes have to be set in place and pressure for accountability on the part of both the irrigation department and the farmer organizations needs to be increased.

Collection of Water Tax by WUAs

In the near future it is expected that the WUAs will collect water tax from the farmers. While this is a logical step in the reform process, some WUA presidents are apprehensive that they will not have sufficient work force to collect the water tax. One of the DC presidents said that, at present, more than 16 revenue officials are needed to collect water tax in his jurisdiction. The government may have to devise a strategy for sharing government employees with the WUA, at least until the capacity increases and the WUAs become financially self-sufficient.

Federation

One of the salient features of the APFMIS Act is that it stipulates the formation of a Federation of WUAs. Formation of the Federation is one of the best instruments for building social capital. It allows the issues of the WUA at the lower most end of the system to be raised. It is also a good mechanism for conflict resolution in a multi-structured multi-stakeholder highly complex system. To date, the Distributary Committees have been formed, but the Project Committee and the Apex Committee have not been formed. The delay in elections for the Project Committee has become an issue among the WUAs.

The Presidents feel that they now want a say in the management of the project at the main system level. The government, however, is not convinced to allow the farmer representative (WUAs) such a major say at the Project Level. They fear that the Project Committee will be too powerful and may be difficult for the administration to handle. The author is of the view that elections for the PCs should be held as soon as possible and that the Apex Committee should be constituted. This will complete the entire structure and one could say powers have been devolved at all levels. The non-formation of the committees at this level has led farmers to question the sincerity of the government in putting the reforms in place. Linkages with other line departments and institutions The WUA should become the focal point for all further agricultural development activities. Agricultural credit, extension and seed supply should be carried out through WUAs. As mentioned earlier, this also gives the WUAs an opportunity to earn revenue and, in the end, become financially viable. Departments like Cooperatives and Horticulture, for instance, should also cooperate with the WUAs. Vibrant and robust WUAs might move expand from their role in managing the irrigation system to other aspects of agriculture production and marketing. For this, the WUAs may even hire professional staff once they become financially independent. This will also help agriculture to move from subsistence level, as it currently is in most places, to an economically profitable enterprise.

Capacity Building

Though there have been serious efforts at training and capacity building by the government from the beginning of the reform process, there is still a need for strengthening this activity. Training has to be a continuous process to build up the skills and capacities of both the irrigation department personnel and WUA so that these organizations are equipped to adapt to new situations that might arise during the reform process. The government has produced many manuals on how to operationalise various parts of the Act. The author is of the view that this is not sufficient. In the field, even after four years, many farmers still do not that the Act exists and those who have heard about it don't know much about the details. Secondly WUA functionaries need to be trained in office management, accounting and similar tasks that are new to them. At the irrigation department level attitude and behavioural change training programmes need to be conducted for the middle and lower level officials. They need to more exposure to the new concepts and to better understand their roles and responsibilities in the new reform environment. This is not happening at present.

WALAMTARI, the Government Water and Land Management Institute faculty need to further training in the finer aspects of the reform process. Some of the faculty has gone through orientation programmes, but this is not sufficient. Good quality "Training of Trainer's" programme will have to be conducted if the trainer's themselves are truly expected to spread the message. NGOs can play a major role, in the entire capacity building part of the programme, but sadly they have been excluded from the A.P. reform programme and the Act does not refer to a role for NGOs. Given the Andhra Pradesh Irrigation reforms, were based to a large extent, the pilot projects implemented by NGOs, it is surprising that they have not been included in the up scaled programme. The author is of the view that NGOs can play an active role not only in the capacity building of the irrigation department as well as the WUAs but also in identifying weaknesses and problem solving in the field. The Irrigation Department should involve a few of the experienced NGOs in conducting action research, monitoring and evaluation exercises and conducting training programmes to strengthen and add value to the entire programme.

Accountability

The reforms in A.P. empowered by the enabling legal provision have brought more accountability into the functioning of the irrigation department. Prior to the Act, the department officials thought about themselves as providers and had no accountability towards the farmers. Today the department officials play a facilitator's role to the WUAs. In fact, some junior level officials of the of the irrigation department have been transferred from the irrigation departments to the Farmer Organizations.

In the case of the WUAs, the Presidents and office bearers are accountable to their Members. The Act has the provision for Recall, wherein if the members of the WUAs are dissatisfied with the functioning of the President they can recall him from that position with a third majority of the members calling for the Recall. This clause in the ACT is a revolutionary step in the devolution process of management powers to the WUAs. In the past in other sectors, once a person is elected, he stays there for 5 years or the duration of office and has no compulsion to prove himself or perform, because he is guaranteed office for his full term. More than 70 Presidents have been recalled to date. This has put social pressure on other Presidents to perform because of the social stigma attached to Recall. The author is of the view that these elements of the Act have ensured downward accountability in the reform process, a vital element for the success of devolution.

Conclusion

One of the key issues in any policy formulation is institutionalizing people centered processes and scaling up participatory approaches in large, public bureaucracies for irrigation management. Perry (in Merrey, 1996) suggested there are three determinants of "proper" irrigation management: defined water rights, infrastructure capable of providing the service embodied in the water rights and, assigned responsibilities for all aspects o system operation. Water rights, infrastructure, and responsibilities interact and are interdependent. The Andhra Pradesh irrigation reforms have shown that a political will and an enabling legal environment establishes an institutional framework that is conducive for the implementation of the factors mentioned by Perry. The irrigation department and WUA are the two sides of a coin. What is important to note here is that reforms are meant for the benefit of the farmer? Policy makers have to keep in mind that if reforms are to succeed, then the farmer must be convinced that the reforms are for his benefit and that his participation in the programme is in his interest. At the end of the day the farmer is willing to pay for services (water) if he is assured of timely and delivery at the right time.

Top Down Vs Bottom Up Approach?

From the analysis of the paper the author would like to argue that we have created a myth when we say bottom up approach or top down approach. The author would like to argue that there is no top without a bottom or no bottom without a top. What is needed is linkage between the two. Some researchers (Parthasarthy, 2000) suggest that the approach in Andhra Pradesh is top down while the approach in Gujarat in bottom up. The author would argue that this is all a play of words and rhetoric. In Gujarat there are not more than a couple of hundred WUAs, of which almost all are defunct today. So what is bottom up approach here? The issue is that if a National or State Policy that has all the ingredients that NGOs thought should be there (like rights to local communities, involvement in decision making, equity and efficiency issues etc.) then would you still call this policy or approach a top down approach? The answer to this would be no. In a political democracy like India this is one of the best methods that can work, and this method is "good governance". The reforms in Andhra Pradesh have a lot more to achieve and it's too early to even say whether they are successful or failed, but what's important is that they have shown the way. Terms like successes and failures are many a times misleading, and can become tools in the hands of both the proponents and critiques. What is important from a rational perspective is to see what one can learn and to ask if this learning translates into a feedback mechanisms for managing the programme better and achieving the goals it set out to achieve.

15

Irrigation Development and Agriculture Growth in Andhra Pradesh

K. KISHORE BABU and A. BALA KRISHNA

Water is indispensably a demanding necessity in agriculture and is often referred to the fifth factor in producing accomplished agriculture output. Irrigation may be defined as to relish the soil with source of water through the effort and endeavor of human agency to accomplish the growth of crop.

In modern times the importance of irrigation has been immediately increased and more reforms have been introduced for the effective utilisation of water for irrigation. In the developing world the production of food crops is obligatory and is to be extensively increased to meet the needs of growing population. If the irrigation facilities are being provided in an optimum manner, the yield of crops will be increased to good extent. It stimulates the farmers and affords them economically and encourages them to carry on agricultural activities with greater satisfaction.

In the developing countries, the allocation for agriculture in their plans has been increased to improve the production so as to meet the demand for increasing population.

Although irrigation work in India can be traced back to the pre-historical period, substantial development took place during 20th century. Andhra Pradesh being a progressive state in the country, it has achieved development of irrigation to maximum extent possible. The first five year plan of India was essentially an agricultural plan. Of the total outlay

(Rs. 1960 crores), an amount of 310 crores (15.82%) has been allocated for the development of irrigation.

Table 1: Sector Distribution of Plan Expenditure in India and Andhra Pradesh

(Rs. in Crores)

Plan	Period	India			Andhra Pradesh		
		Total outlay	Irrigation & flood outlay	%with total outlay	Total outlay	Irrigation & flood outlay	%with total outlay
1	1951-56	1960	310	15.82	376.24	13.21	3.51
2	1956-61	4600	420	9.13	380	48.06	12.65
3	1961-66	8573	665	7.76	576	82.09	14.25
Annual	1966-69	6641	471	7.09	429.81	41.96	9.76
4	1969-74	15779	1354	8.59	1242.30	162.04	13.04
5	1974-79	39426	3877	9.83	2516.18	298.61	11.87
Annual	1979-80	12177	1288	10.58	2079	329	15.82
6	1980-85	109292	10930	10.00	7368	786.85	10.68
7	1985-90	218730	16590	7.58	11107.29	941.58	8.48
Annual	1990-92	123120	8206	6.67	5459.15	460.64	8.44
8	1992-97	434100	32525	7.49	21071	1691.68	8.03
9	1997-2002	875000	57735	6.6	25248	2629	10.41

Source: Working on Ninth and Tenth Five Year Plans.

It indicates that the Government of India realizes the need for the irrigation development and as such this sector receives the highest share of the budget outlay. Afterwards the share for irrigation development was reduced in subsequent plans. In the Sixth Plan 10 per cent of the Plan out lay was allocated to irrigation development. In Andhra Pradesh the Government allocated due share with increasing amount in first plan to fourth plan. Later the share of irrigation development was decreased in the Sixth, Seventh and Annual and Eighth Plans. In the Ninth Plan 10.41 per cent of the out lay was allocated to the development of irrigation sector.

Irrigation Potential Development under Five Year Plans

In the pre-plan period the irrigation potential created in India was 226 lakh hectares. While for Andhra Pradesh it figured 12.90 lakh hectares (Table 2). And it reached 14.06 lakh hectares by the end of First Five-year Plan. The share of Andhra Pradesh in the total irrigation potential created in the first five-year plan, with just 5.70 per cent showed a considerable increase of 6.64 per cent at the end of Eighth Plan and further reduced to 3.70 per cent at the end of Ninth Plan.

Table 2: Irrigation Potential Development under Five-year Plans (lakh ha)

Plan Particulars	Andhra Pradesh			India
	Major & Medium	Minor	Total	
Pre-Plan period	9.70	2.20	12.90	226.0
1 (1951-56)	12.19	1.86	14.06	262.6
5 (1974-78)	24.72	2.58	27.30	520.2
7 (1985-90)	31.52	15.00	46.52	765.3
8 (1992-1997)	32.96	23.64	56.60	852.89
9 (1997-2002)	35.35	4.03	39.38	1066.1

Source: Report of working group of Eighth& Ninth Five year plan on Major Medium and Minor irrigation.

Status of NCA, GCA, NIA AND GIA

The state of Andhra Pradesh having just 29.09 lakh hectares of land as net irrigated area in 1960, but a decade later, it reached to 33.13 lakh hectares by 1970. It indicated an increase of 13.89 per cent (Table 3). As the time passed on an increasing trend was observed in the development of net irrigated area in Andhra Pradesh. It grew to a high of 45.27 lakh ha in 2000-01. The increase was 55.65 per cent. Similar to this, the trend in gross irrigated area of the state obviously was a rising one over the period of 41 years. It recorded an ascendant of 70.39 per cent in 2000-01 over 1960. And also the gross cropped area of the state was increased from 133.47 lakh hectares to 135.45 lakh hectares. The percentage of increase is from 12.96 to 14.07 per cent during the last 41 years. And finally the net cropped area in the state

Table 3: Decadal Changes in NCA,GCA, NIA and GIA in India and Andhra Pradesh

Particulars	1960		1970		1980		1990		2000	
	Andhra	India	AP	India	AP	India	AP	India	AP	India
NCA	107.84	1332	117.35	1043	107.38	1400	110.22	1430	111.15	1438
*	-	-	8.81	-21.7	-0.42	5.11	2.21	7.36	6.79	7.22
GCA	118.2	1528	133.47	1658	122.82	1726	131.93	1857	135.45	1895
*	-	-	12.96	8.52	3.94	12.99	11.64	21.6	14.07	24.07
NIA	29.09	247	33.31	311	34.63	326.3	43.05	427	45.27	46.2
*	-	-	13.89	26.12	19.04	32.35	47.99	73.3	55.65	89.46
GIA	34.72	280	42.22	381.9	43.42	387.2	53.69	478	59.16	551.4
*	-	-	21.66	36.49	25.05	38.38	54.64	70.8	70.39	198.93

* Percentage change over 1960-61 to 2000-01.

Source: Directorate of Economics & Statistics, Government of Andhra Pradesh Hyderabad (1955-56 to 2000-01),Compendium of Area and land use Statistics of Andhra Pradesh.

increased from 107.84 lakh hectares to 111.15 lakh hectares. The percentage of increase is from -8.10 to 3.1 per cent during the past 41 years.

Irrigated Area under Major Crops

The cereal crops viz. paddy and pulses, commercial crops viz. sugarcane, cotton and onions amongst the vegetable have the maximum acreages in the state. The area irrigated under paddy seems rising from 1970-71 to 2000-01 (Table 4). The increase in the total pulses irrigated are indicates continuous rising over the period 1970 -71 to 2000 -01 sugarcane is one of he most important cash crops in Andhra Pradesh. Abnormal growth can be seen in area under sugarcane crop during the same period. The growth rate of area under sugarcane in Andhra Pradesh was more than that of all India level during the same period 1970-71 to 2000-01.The percentage of area irrigated under the commercial crops like cotton increased more in the state of Andhra Pradesh than that of all India level during the last two decades 1980-81to 2000-01.In Andhra Pradesh the irrigated area under onion crop had increased for two decades from 1960-61to 1980-81 and during the period 1980-81to 2000-01 it decreased.

Source of Irrigation in Andhra Pradesh

The net irrigated area increased from 2909 thousand hectares in 1960-61 to 4528 thousand hectares in 2000-01 with 55.65 per cent growth over 41 years time period in the state of Andhra Pradesh (Table 5). During the same period the area irrigated under wells increased more than that of other irrigation sources. As against this the gross cropped area increased by 14.63 per cent to 30.65 per cent during the period 1960-61to 2000-01 which had a positive change by 28.05 per cent.

Conclusion

Andhra Pradesh being a progressive state in the country has taken very active step for the development of irrigation potential. Yet it has not achieved the necessary levels of development. So the major objective of irrigation development should be aimed at sustainable agricultural development. The strategies of irrigation development taken into consideration

Table 4: Progress in Irrigated Area under Major Crops (000 Ha)

Crops	1960-61		1970-71		1980-81		1990-91		2000-01	
	A.P	India	A.P	India	A.P	India	A.P	India	AP	India
Rice	27.52	12560	33.21	11435	33.78	16341	38.30	19424	40.40	22746
	-	-	20.67	14.93	22.84	30.1	38.35	54.65	46.91	81.1
Sugar	87.441	1677	117.78	1897	170.81	2168	224.74	3207	3.60	3595
*	-	-	35.63	13.12	95.40	29.68	158.62	91.23	313.79	114.37
Cotton	0.02	967	0.14	1316	0.22	2135	0.82	2448	1.92	3344
*	-	-	600	36.09	1000	120.78	4000	153.15	9500	245.81
Onions	0.10	Na	0.16	Na	0.47	250	0.18	300	0.27	480
*	-	-	60	-	370	-	80	20	170	92
Pulses	0.26	1885	0.01	1983.5	0.015	1958.9	0.19	2589.3	0.21	3025.14
*	—	—	-96.15	5.24	-94.23	3.93	-26.92	37.38	-19.23	60.5

* Percentage change over 1960-61 to 2000-01.

Source: Directorate of Economics &Statistics Government of Andhra Pradesh, Hyderabad (1955-56 to 2000-01); Compendium of Area and land-use Statistics of Andhra Pradesh.

a sever drought condition in the state for the last one-decade. In the light of these experiences a cautious approach is necessary in respect of new irrigation projects.

Table 5: Area Irrigated by Various Sources in Andhra Pradesh

Year	Area Irrigated		Net Irrigated Area	Gross Irrigated Area	Inten. of Irrig. Cropping	GCA	% of GIA/GCA
	Wells	Other sources					
1960-61	327	98.8	2909	3472	19.35	11816	29.38
1970-71	509	112.6	3313	4223	27.46	13347	31.64
1980-80	776	93.2	3462	4341	25.39	12282	35.34
1990-91	1303	166	4305	5370	24.74	13192	41.02
2000-01	1954	197	4528	5916	30.65	13545	43.68
*	497.56	99.39	55.65	70.39	58.40	14.63	

* Percentage change over 1960-61 to 2000-01.

Source: Directorate of Economics &Statistics Government of Andhra Pradesh Hyderabad (1955-56 to 2000-01) and Compendium of Area and land use Statistics of Andhra Pradesh

Therefore for efficient water utilization, priority should be given to modernization of existing irrigation system before taking up the new projects. Conservation of groundwater resource and their proper utilisation through watershed development programme needs priority in the policy. Efficient water management through strengthening of Water Users Association is need of the day. Thus irrigation system should be constructed and managed in such a way that they are socially equal, economically efficient and environmentally sustainable. Any efforts in this direction make the irrigation sector in the state more vibrant efficient and sustainable. Then only we can achieve targets and levels of growth in agricultural sector.

REFERENCES

Compendium of Area and land use Statistics of Andhra Pradesh.

Dhawan (1982), "Impact of Irrigation", *Indian Journal of Agriculture Economics.*

Directorate of Economics & Statistics, Government of Andhra Pradesh Hyderabad (1955-56 to 2000-01).

Navadkar, D.S., Birari K.S. and D.V. Kasar (2003), "Irrigation Development: A Boon for Sustainable Agriculture Development in Maharashtra". *Agricultural Situation in India*, pp. 141 to 145

Sivasubramaniyan, K. (2000), *Impact of Irrigation on Cropping Intensity, Cropping Pattern and Productivity under Tank Commands*, Vol.XLII, No.4 December 2000. pp. 325-349

Vaidyanathan, A. (1987), Irrigation and Agriculture Growth, Presidential Address, Annual Conference, Indian Society of Agriculture Economics, September 23, 1987.

Index

C

D

E

F

G

J

❑❑❑